Almost Home

Almost Home

*A Brazilian American's Reflections
on Faith, Culture, and Immigration*

H. B. Cavalcanti

THE UNIVERSITY OF WISCONSIN PRESS

The University of Wisconsin Press
1930 Monroe Street, 3rd Floor
Madison, Wisconsin 53711-2059
uwpress.wisc.edu

3 Henrietta Street
London WC2E 8LU, England
eurospanbookstore.com

Printed in the United States of America

Library of Congress Cataloging-in-Publication Data

Cavalcanti, H. B., 1956–
    Almost home : a Brazilian American's reflections on faith, culture, and
    immigration /H. B. Cavalcanti.
        p.   cm.
    Includes bibliographical references and index.
    ISBN 978-0-299-28894-5 (pbk.: alk. paper)
    ISBN 978-0-299-28893-8 (e-book)
    1. Cavalcanti, H. B., 1956–   2. Brazilian Americans—Biography.
3. Immigrants—United States—Biography.   4. Sociologists—United States—
Biography.   5. United States—Emigration and immigration—Social aspects.
I. Title.
E184.B68C38   2012
301.092—dc23
[B]
2012009960

To
J. ROCKWELL SMITH,
of Lexington, Kentucky, who brought the South
to my Brazilian hometown . . .

Contents

Illustrations

Preface

While research on immigration tells us much about relocating to a host country, transitioning into a foreign culture, and forging a brand new identity, much remains to be explored in migration studies, especially for those who continuously bridge two separate countries over their entire lifetime. American sociology has explored in depth the usual assimilation pattern for immigrants. In fact, its early linear model assumed it would take three generations for an immigrant family to be fully integrated into the American "melting pot." Current models see it more as a *segmented* process, one where immigrants do not have to surrender their previous identity.

Today we know that people leave their homelands without forfeiting their mother culture. They knew it back then as well—when the early immigration studies were conducted. But the assumption was that integration would lead to a fading of the original culture. This book is concerned with revisiting that process, perhaps adding a personal dimension to it. Those of us who grow up between two different worlds spend a lifetime making sense of the wondrous and disorienting experience. Take missionary kids, for instance—they suffer from a sense of nostalgia that is hard to explain from lacking people in their lives who fully understand their two different "homes" and identities. Children of American businessmen, military officers, or academics, who spend a good deal of their parents' careers abroad, face similar fates.

Bicultural folks like us are haunted by the same malady. As a Brazilian I miss the Land of the Southern Cross as much as I miss the Home of the Brave when I am visiting family in South America. We are all equally at home in two worlds, part of ourselves always there, part here. At times we can pray in both languages; at others in only one. Sometimes the song that soothes our blues comes in Portuguese, Spanish, French, sometimes in English only. We cobble a life together from many pieces of different cultures. But somehow, inside of us, it all fits.

Though we have learned a lot about immigration to the United States, we have yet to fully explore these aspects of an immigrant's life, the struggles and comforts of folks who bridge two separate worlds throughout their lives. After studying immigration for more than a decade, I have found few studies that focus on this particular aspect of immigration, especially when both worlds keep tugging at us for our exclusive loyalty. We are not transnationals, who flit between two worlds for business reasons. We are people who *grew up* with both worlds and whose lives only make sense seen *from the prism of both*.

No easy explanation is found for those of us who (a) grow up bilingual, (b) are exposed to significant life experiences in both cultures, and (c) keep lasting friendships in different parts of the world. As we grow older, our double identities become the *connecting nodes* between our two worlds, the thing that makes our lives meaningful. Our friends in different countries may not know each other; and if they did, they would not be able to communicate in the same language. But in us, they are part of a single journey; in us they create a whole picture of it.

And that is the key underlying motif of this book. While equally capable of decoding the norms and cultural patterns of two separate worlds, it takes longer for us to realize that those two worlds *co-exist only inside of us, and inside of people like us*. Most of the time, we are simply using the appropriate cultural script for one of the worlds. But in fact, we hold the two worlds within (as if our souls were the only place where the two realities ever met) to create the strange and unique home we inhabit. When people like us bump into each other, we sit for long spells listening to our stories, to what it takes to keep such bifurcated lives in balance.

This book is a personal reflection on such a life. It provides a window into many immigration studies, but for the most part its bits and pieces reveal parts of my own bifurcated experience. Hopefully, in reading it you'll find traces of what it is like to live in two cultural worlds, with the double historical influences that come to define a *cultural hybrid*. My life is linked in indelible ways to a certain period of time in Brazil and in the United States. By focusing on some of its aspects, the book highlights a journey that intrigues as much as it exasperates. In my case, the cultural transmission flows from the United States to my homeland and back—my family converted to southern U.S. Protestantism before I ever discovered English or the American South.

So it took me a while to figure out how immersed I've been in both worlds from the start. My hope, in offering a sample of unique moments in this journey, is that it will resonate with others who share a similar path, and with those curious about us *hybrids*. The personal details in my growing up may not fully square with other hybrids' experiences. That's okay. They still know what I am talking about. They too can discern the amount of work it takes to make hybrid life work. So, kudos to those who have spent a lifetime practicing the art of being hybrid— you are not alone.

And I believe that there are enough similarities in my experience and theirs to make my case worth studying, worth exploring. My reflections show the ebb and flow of cultural mix, how countries in a globalized era cannot create their own isolated, sanitized stories. Out of their cultural comingling we are created. At any rate, given our globalized age, perhaps my story will add to that of others, to a better understanding of the multifaceted versions of migration in the twenty-first century. As travel and communications continue to expand, and people continue to cross borders on a regular basis, I imagine my experience will represent simply the early stages of a much larger phenomenon.

Almost Home

1

A Southern Beginning

The first thing which attracted [us] . . . to the South America field was the fact that after the reverses of the war a number our countrymen had founded new homes among the Brazilian people. It was thought by ourselves and others that the social and commercial relations of these settlers with the natives of the country would greatly facilitate our communication with the latter, and afford a rare opportunity of teaching the adherents of an apostate church the evangelical truths of our own.

   J. Nash Morton and E. E. Lane, letter from Brazil, 1868

People assume that immigrants learn about the American ways once they get here. But many of us come to the United States already well-versed in certain aspects of its culture. For instance, I have been immersed in southern culture for as long as I can remember. Whether in prose, poetry, or song, my life was organized around old notions of southern chivalry and faith. Stephen Foster's songs filled my childhood, long before I fathomed the full measure of their import.[1] For four generations, on my mother's and father's sides, we were Southern Presbyterian to the core—in hymns, creeds, or orthodoxy, and in the way my ancestors labored to eke out a living under the everlasting watch of a rigid Protestant ethic. We even inherited the southern ambivalence toward human suffering caused by racial atrocities. And in town or country, we dreamed of that everlasting home that so haunted southern writers since antebellum days.

   My adult life has been spent in the South as well. Graduate education and academic career both unfolded in southern cities. My graduate degrees were awarded by two southern institutions, the Southern Baptist Theological Seminary in Louisville, Kentucky, and Vanderbilt

University in Nashville, Tennessee. My son was born in Nashville. Southern universities have also been home to my professional life— first the University of Richmond, then James Madison University. After residing in Richmond, the capital of the Confederacy, I relocated to the Shenandoah Valley, site of many shrines to the lost cause of the Confederacy.[2] I teach classes on southern religion, my research is conducted in southern archives, and my early activism took place in progressive southern organizations.

None of this would be surprising, had I not been born and raised in Recife, northern Brazil, by very Brazilian parents. In fact, my early exposure to American culture was *dubbed* in Portuguese by American missionaries. Oh, it was still couched in the cadences of a southern faith but preserved in my mother's tongue. My ancestors left Europe for Brazil around the 1530s, long before southern missionaries had reached our shores. We spread through the hinterlands of Pernambuco and neighboring states, as we made a home for ourselves in the New World. Some of us rose to power in the nascent empire and later republic. And to this day we may be slightly overrepresented in civil, military, and business circles in Brazil.

But most of us led humbler lives. My grandmothers were seamstresses, one grandfather a mechanic, the other a chauffeur. Their parents were the ones who found southern religion in the last quarter of the nineteenth century, a time of change for Brazilians and southerners alike. That was the time when a good number of southern families relocated to Brazil in the aftermath of Lee's surrender at Appomattox. Slavery was still legal in my country of birth, and our emperor was eager to attract European and North American settlers to Brazil's hinterlands. Southern settlers brought along to Brazil their ministers, to help preserve the faith. Once they learned Portuguese, it was only a matter of time before they reached out to the locals.

That is how southern religion reached my great-grandparents, as the first Presbyterian missionaries alighted in our part of the country. My ancestors' conversion resulted in a wholesale adoption of an alien culture, one that alienated them from family and kinship networks. And it would take me a lifetime to realize how deep those American southern roots ran—not until I had been living in the United States for a decade or so. When you are raised a certain way, it is just "the way the world is." There is no cultural distance, no sense of perspective, no need to question one's life. Growing up, my American roots were simply the way a few Brazilians practiced their transplanted faith.

In hindsight, there was far more to the bargain than simply religion. Along with the faith, we purchased from sojourning missionaries an inherited ethos, one that rejected wholesale our very own culture.[3] Everything Catholic and Brazilian was seen as less developed and less modern. We were taught to avoid all manner of "licentious Brazilian behavior" and to rid ourselves of the most mundane forms of Brazilian leisure. Converts were not allowed to drink, smoke, or gamble. Protestant churches disciplined followers who did not live up to those standards. So, we grew up trying to be less Brazilian, to ignore the ever-present, all-surrounding Iberian Catholic culture, with its citywide celebrations and rambunctious street festivals that so delighted neighbors and friends.

The South Moves South

How did this mess all begin? In what could be a plot for many a work of southern fiction, Southern life reached Brazil through a series of historical accidents. A sleepy Portuguese colony at the beginning of the nineteenth century, Brazil was literally shut off from the rest of the world, lacking the energy and drive of its North American counterpart some 4,200 miles away. In 1808, under the threat of Napoleon's army, the Portuguese court had to hastily relocate to Rio de Janeiro. Until then, Dom João VI, the Portuguese king, had kept a tight grip on his colony *d'além mares* (across seas). There was no free press in colonial Brazil (unlike the wild pamphleteering in Boston and Philadelphia), no industry of any sort, and no reputed national schools to train local elites.

Dom João VI's arrival changed everything. The court's relocation drastically transformed the colony. Step by step, Brazil would become the center of the Portuguese empire. By January, the king had opened Brazilian ports to all "friendly nations." In April, he revoked the 1775 ban on manufacturing on Brazilian lands. By December 1815, with approval from the Congress of Vienna, Dom João elevated Brazil from the status of colony to one of kingdom (Brazil was the only self-sufficient European kingdom in the New World). Between 1808 and 1820 the king methodically re-created in the tropics a fully functioning European state, one with all the attending ministries needed to handle foreign and domestic affairs.

Bringing Portugal's largest colony to the level of a fully operational, modern European nation state required that Dom João VI upgrade its entire colonial infrastructure. To that end, he centralized fiscal and judicial structures, founded the Bank of Brazil, professionalized the armed forces, and developed a governmental bureaucracy that reached deep into Brazil's most remote regions. He encouraged primary education, and imported enough artists and scholars to found five professional schools—a national fine arts college, a school for the army and another for the navy, and two medical schools. By then, national newspapers were circulating somewhat freely, and printed materials from Europe had found a steady clientele in Brazilian lands.[4]

But it was trade that inadvertently opened Brazil's doors to Protestantism. In 1810, the king signed a treaty with England that included freedom of worship for British subjects in Portuguese lands. Since the Portuguese king was the supreme Defender of the Catholic faith in his entire realm, he had to obfuscate on the matter: the British were allowed to worship, but privately. They were allowed to hold their own funeral rites, but in private cemeteries. They could have Protestant congregations, but no sanctuaries with visible outward religious identifying signs. Thus Protestantism began to flourish below the equator, based on subterfuge and evasion.

Nevertheless, the first Protestant house of worship was founded in Rio de Janeiro in 1819, by British Anglicans. Once Brazil gained independence from Portugal, our first constitution (1824) granted Protestants the freedom to reach out and make converts. By then Protestant work had already spread through Brazil's southern provinces. The need to populate a vast empire had pushed Dom João's son and grandson (Brazil's first and second emperors) to recruit settlers among Europeans and North Americans. And the Europeans responded by the millions. What James S. Olson and Heather Olson Beal said of immigrants to American shores could certainly be said of those Europeans who chose to resettle in Brazil: "Many immigrants are often restless people, willing to abandon their families, temporarily or permanently. . . . They tend to be less tradition bound and cautious than compatriots left behind. . . . Most immigrants are risk takers, with optimism imbuing their worldview. They seize opportunities when lesser hearts forgo them. Chances are worth taking because the potential success justifies the risk. Cautious people stay home, unwilling to venture out."[5]

Starting in the 1820s, for almost a century, some 4.5 to 5 million European immigrants arrived on our shores. By midcentury, German Lutheran immigrants had settled the southern provinces of Rio Grande do Sul, Paraná, and Santa Catarina. Similarly, Congregationalists and

Presbyterians had reached southeastern Brazil and our nation's capital, at that time Rio de Janeiro. A Scottish physician, Dr. Robert Kalley, was the founder of Brazil's first Congregational church in Rio de Janeiro. The Reverend Ashbel Green Simonton left his home in Pennsylvania to bring Northern Presbyterianism to Brazil's capital in 1859.[6]

But American southerners took a little longer to respond to the emperor's entreaties. In truth, they had considered Brazil as a possible mission field as early as 1835, when Bishop James Andrew from Tennessee sent Rev. Fountain Pitts on a mission surveying trip of Brazil and Argentina. A few other Methodist Episcopal missionaries followed Pitts's footsteps in 1838, but by 1842 the effort had petered out. Brazil would be noticed again in 1857, as the Reverends James Fletcher and Daniel Kidder coauthored a travel book describing their adventures in the country.[7] Fletcher even worked hard to set up regular steamship lines between Brazil and the United States, a project that eventually came to fruition in 1865.

It was those steamship lines that brought Southern Presbyterians to my hometown.[8] They also gave a good number of southern families an opportunity to relocate in my homeland right after the Civil War. Starting in 1865, between 4,000 to 20,000 southern souls made their way to Brazil, looking for a fresh start.[9] They would set up at least four Confederate colonies in the country, including one at the heart of the Amazon jungle![10] For many it would be a short stay, fewer than five years. But from the Amazon to São Paulo (a distance akin to that of the Great Lakes to the shores of the Gulf of Mexico in Louisiana), former Confederate generals, officers, doctors, dentists, engineers, school teachers, and farmers started anew in a country a bit larger and just as fertile as their homeland.

As southern farms were established in Brazil, and American villages built (some that still have Confederate cemeteries to this day), the newcomers introduced Brazilians to a whole array of modern things—from new agricultural methods to improved household devices to modern education.[11] Southern settlers introduced the first trolleys, plows, and wagons. They brought modern amenities such as modern brick houses, stoves, kitchen utensils, coffee pounders, kerosene lamps, sewing machines, the buckboards, new land-surveying techniques, and four brand new crops: upland cotton, rattlesnake watermelon, grapes, and pecans.[12] The single exception was their old-time religion.

In fact, it was the newcomers' never-ending requests for missionaries from the United States that eventually drove southern churches to send ministers to Brazil. Settlers from Georgia, Louisiana, Mississippi, the Carolinas, and Texas pushed their denominations and home states to extend religious support to the Brazilian settlements. The few ministers who had originally come with them were far too few to reach settlements so spread out in a country of continental proportions. Moreover, many returned home, felled by tropical illnesses. Replenishments were needed to continue the work. As late as 1879, Pastor E. H. Quillin was still urging southern clergy and lay people to come to the rescue: "Some entire Baptist churches, including pastor, deacons and clerk [should] emigrate and settle in these favored lands, and establish a large Baptist community . . . they would do a work that could never be forgotten, and by industry and economy under providence, would firmly lay the foundation of an earthly fortune that would shade their declining years and go down to posterity."[13]

Southern churches responded by shipping out the graduates of their best theological schools to the Land of the Southern Cross. Baptist preachers came from the Southern Baptist Theological Seminary in Louisville, while Presbyterians graduated from Union Theological Seminary in Richmond. Those who went to southern Brazil would spend time at the language school in Campinas, state of São Paulo, before proceeding to their mission fields. Once they learned Portuguese, it was only a matter of time before the missionaries reached out to locals. And those of us who converted grew up between these two similar, yet quite disparate, cultures.

Plantation Cultures

The American South is to the United States what the Northeast of Brazil is to my home country. Both regions are quite similar in history, economic development, and local culture. Both were the first in their respective countries to be populated by Europeans. While Jamestown was settled in 1607, Recife—my hometown—was founded in 1537. If the Virginia colony faced the unknowns of New World land, crop, and game for the sake of gold, Portuguese sailors came to our shores seeking Brazil wood, the source of an expensive dye for their nobility's luxurious textiles. Both came to the New World for riches; both brought long-term changes to their respective continents.

From the time of our first colonial *povoamentos* (settlements) until now, the Northeast of Brazil has developed a unique regional culture, a

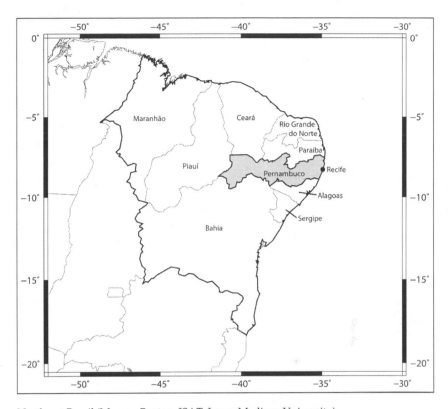

Northeast Brazil (Morgan Benton, ISAT, James Madison University)

rich mixture of Portuguese, African, and Native Brazilian ways. Our mix is perhaps more syncretic. But the American South was created by a similar patchwork of British, African, and Native American traits, stretched over similar wide regions. Our plantation system, so aptly described by Gilberto Freyre in *The Masters and the Slaves*, organized economic life in the Northeast the way southern plantations formed the basis for local economies in the southern United States. What the Yale historian Stuart Schwartz said of Brazilian plantations could very well be said of southern ones:

> This society inherited classical and medieval concepts of organization and hierarchy. But it added to them systems of rank that grew from the differentiation of occupation, race, color and status—distinctions resulting from the American reality. It was a society of multiple hierarchies of honor and esteem, of multiple categories of labor, of complex divisions of color, and of varied means of mobility and change; but it was also a society

with a profound tendency to reduce complexities to dualisms of contrast—master/slave, noble/commoner, Catholic/gentile—and to reconcile the multiple rankings to one another so that rank, class, color, and civil status tended to converge in each individual.[14]

To someone familiar with both worlds, the similarities are uncanny. In both Jamestown and Recife, white Europeans clashed with native civilizations they were ill-prepared to trade with or comprehend. Nothing in the European worldview prepared sailors for the new peoples they would discover by moving West across the Atlantic. Both the British and the Portuguese equally assumed the natives would make good converts and willingly withstand the European need to plunder their lands. And in both places the land was tamed at the brutal cost of African slave labor. Here and there, landed European gentry set the terms for dealings with the Old World in similar ways. Again, what Stuart said of the Brazilian landed gentry could very well have been said of the southern gentry too:

Nobility was, in a sense, defined by what a person did not do. Working with one's own hands, shopkeeping, artisan crafting, and other "mean" occupations were the domain of the commoners. Nobles were expected to live without recourse to such activities. Nobles sought instead to live from rents or offices and to maintain an aristocratic way of life, which usually meant a large household of retainers, relatives, and servants.[15]

Eventually, as the Brazil wood trade dried up, the Northeastern economy replaced it with sugar cane, produced in large land holdings for the benefit of European markets. The southern economy in the U.S., by its turn, was founded on cotton and tobacco (and to a lesser extent rice in South Carolina and sugar in Louisiana) grown in large plantations for the same consumers. Ships that left the New World loaded with agricultural riches garnered much-needed European capital to purchase African slaves on their way back. That ignoble trade triangle would not be broken until the late nineteenth century, almost four hundred years from the time both regions were settled.

Needless to say, both forms of European settlement generated long-term social inequalities, leaving deep scars in both regions. Disease, war, and forced relocation decimated local native populations. The legacy of slavery and racism continuously haunt both areas to this day. And just as Brazil's Northeastern political dynasties relied upon the injustices of the plantation system to prosper, so did southern elites in North America. Neither region surrendered its chattel voluntarily. Both regions declined by its abolition, unable to sustain more creative forms of economic development. Eventually, they ended up as the least developed areas of their respective countries.

As late as the mid-twentieth century, the Brazilian Northeast and the American South had the lowest levels of education, health care, social services, urbanization, and industrialization. Modernization—whether measured in laws and customs, a secular lifestyle, the creation of large urban centers, or the rationalization of industrial production—arrived late for both. And the agrarian foundations of the two regions generated other forms of social injustice as well. The Northeastern *lavrador*, usually of mixed racial stock, who scratched out his living on a small plot of land while working hard for an absentee landlord, found his parallel in the southern sharecropper, often from nineteenth-century Ulster, who toiled sun up to sun down to pay for his indentured service. Both types fled the Old World under the false promise of affluence and prosperity on the other side of the Atlantic, only to find themselves in servitude upon arrival in the New World.

Those injustices would eventually lead to the radicalization of the working classes in both countries. In Brazil, by the mid-twentieth century, Francisco Julião was organizing the communist Peasant Leagues (Ligas Camponêsas) to fight against the landed gentry, at the height of the Cold War.[16] In the South, the Southern Tenant Farmers' Union was bringing the socialist gospel to white and black sharecroppers across fields and farms of the region.[17] Both movements dreamed of a better world, a fairer society, and yet both failed to create that different social order. But the struggle generated comparable stories of educational leaders deeply engaged in social change on both sides of the hemisphere. In Brazil we find Paulo Freire organizing the *lavradores* to fight for their rights through literacy campaigns (so aptly described in his book, *Pedagogy of the Oppressed*). In the South, Myles Horton founded the Highlander Folk School in Tennessee to train union organizers in the 1930s and '40s, and civil rights leaders in the 1950s and '60s (he too described his efforts in a moving autobiography, *The Long Haul*).

The similarities stretch further into the development of strong regional cultures. Both the South of the United States and the Northeast of Brazil have rich local cultures, quite different from the broader mores of their respective nations. Take music for instance—the rural sounds of the

Northeast's *baião, forró, xaxado, côco* find their counterparts in the southern country rhythms of bluegrass, honky-tonk, and Appalachian folk music. Both the American southern and Brazilian Northeastern country music genres—so far apart geographically—hark back to the same roots, to the European fairs and minstrel ballads of the Middle Ages and the Renaissance. The American genres were heavily influenced by the sounds of the British Isles, while the Brazilian ones were impacted by the syncretic rhythms of the Iberian Peninsula.

Similarly, in literature, Northeastern writers give us a vivid glimpse of the region, of its foibles, vanities, and wild customs. People like João Cabral de Melo Neto, Jorge Amado, Rachel de Queiroz, Graciliano Ramos, and Raimundo Correia offer vivid pictures of a deep, settled way of life by tapping into local roots that are capably woven in regional tales. Their southern counterparts, writers such as William Faulkner, Eudora Welty, Flannery O'Connor, Zora Neale Hurston, Sterling Allen Brown, Tim Gautreaux, Erskine Caldwell, Lee Smith, and Wendell Berry, also expose us to the depths and undercurrents of their own region.

What I find ironic in all of this is that it takes someone equally comfortable in both worlds to appreciate those many parallels. Both regions were the stage for the first European effort to transplant a patrimonial, land-based form of civilization across the Atlantic. Both operated under monarchical rule at first, driven by two powerful seafaring trading nations. Both were deeply influenced by other traditions brought to the New World in the form of African faiths, Muslim rites, and the oral histories of their enslaved peoples. Both benefited from the rich lore and know-how of native cultures. And both developed *mestizo* versions of their respective European cultures—fiercely proud, sternly independent, and highly resilient.

Yet, most Northeasterners in Brazil would not know anything about southern culture, just as southerners would be completely unaware that there is a similar land, far south of their borders, whose patterns of settlement are quite like their own. If you asked a Brazilian Northeasterner to explain life in the U.S. South, she would be completely baffled by the question. She would lack the most basic framework to describe the history, culture, and ways of everyday life in the region. I imagine, in all fairness, that the same could be said about the southerners' knowledge of Brazil's plantation world. However, for someone like me—caught between the two worlds all my life—the parallels are quite obvious.

Creating Cultural Hybrids

What does it take to be both southern (American) and Brazilian? When did the two cultures cross paths? How was it possible that such an island of southern culture could have developed on such a tropical land? We have already covered its beginning—the arrival of Confederates on Brazilian shores, their early settlements, and eager recruitment of religious ministers to preserve a very southern way of life far below the Equator. But the story picks up pace when they make their first local converts, when the culture they brought from abroad begins to find resonance amid the natives. In my case, that is the beginning of a *hybrid* life, one set for me by my great-grandparents.

In fact, cleaning up old documents last spring, I bumped into papers from one of my mother's distant cousins. In an essay revisiting his childhood, he had included a 1938 photograph of the family's old Presbyterian congregation, the Igreja Presbiteriana do Zumbi. Zumbi was a working-class neighborhood in the outskirts of the greater Recife. Even then, Recife was the economic hub for the Northeast region. As a

Zumbi Presbyterian Church, 1938 (Cavalcanti family records)

port city, Recife was the main terminal for the regional sugar trade, so its connections to the many plantations of the area were well known. Families from the hinterlands would migrate to the city's edges, seduced by the promises of an "easier" urban life.

I'm quite sure my maternal grandfather is in that photo, though I cannot recognize him. In the picture, his entire Sunday School class sits at the feet of their elders, gazing earnestly at the camera, Grandpa included. My mother could probably pick him out in that crowd, but by the time I came along grandpa was already an old man, so I never saw pictures of his youth days. Try as I might, it is hard for me to find traces of him in these fresh young faces. They all look so earnest, respectful, as Protestant converts should be. They had a lot to prove. Renouncing the Brazilian cultural ways meant living up to high Protestant standards. And there he sits, his entire extended family surrounding him as part of that religious community.

In the photo, the Zumbi congregation poses together in front of its modest sanctuary. The building could easily be mistaken as another domicile in the neighborhood, another humble shack amid thousands of working-class shacks in the area. But for those who knew, the small, discrete signs that marked it as a Protestant refuge betrayed a lot of collective effort, energy, and pride. Those enterprising folks were working hard to build a transplanted faith, to create a tropical version of Calvinism—one shipped from Scotland to North America during colonial days and now finding its way to the Northeast of Brazil.

What is striking for me in that picture is the seriousness of their faces, children and all. Taciturn, those early Presbyterians gaze into the camera with a deep sense of composure, of dignity, and what I—as an "insider"—perceive also as slight sadness. They had traded their own culture—lock, stock, and barrel—for a whole new way of life. The American way of life was alien to everything they had known. Certainly being Protestant in the 1930s did not win them many friends in the larger community. But they were also working hard to make ends meet in the "big city." So, one wonders whether the sadness had more to do with their working-class condition, the seriousness of their inherited faith, or both.

Life in the big city in the 1930s must not have been easy. The trade imbalances created by the American Great Depression had squandered any promises of a brighter life for many of these internal migrants. The price of sugar and coffee, Brazil's largest trade commodities, had hit bottom in the world markets. The country was under military rule, and there was sporadic famine and social unrest, so their undeniable stoicism is easy to understand; this stoicism also reflects a certain Presbyterian mood I know only too well. We find similar religious self-control and reticence in the working-class outskirts of Protestant Edinburgh and Glasgow. It seems that the world of the predestined is always seriously circumscribed, no matter the region of the globe.

Looking at it from the comforts of my Virginia home, I gaze at these faces and wonder about the price they paid for following a measured and guarded American faith. Brazilian culture is nothing if not exuberant! Wild colors, loud sounds, delicious spicy food, sensuous dances, and unbridled revelry have always defined urban living in my country since colonial days (as France's president, Charles de Gaulle, is reputed to have said, "Brazil is not a serious country"). There is an all-pervading joie de vivre in Brazilian culture that is deeply reflected in the general mood of its people. Brazilian Carnival is the loudest party in the world. Despite poverty, urban blight, high levels of unemployment, and other hardships they may face, Brazilians are a resilient and happy people.

That must have made the price of conversion only dearer for members of the Zumbi congregation. Conversion gave them a sobering heart. It also cut them off from their roots and kinfolk. Everything about Brazil's Catholic culture was defined by agents of American Protestantism as strange, sinful, regressive, and superstitious.[18] They had brought us a cutting-edge faith and ideology. We grew up looking down upon our own culture, with that whiff of Presbyterian superiority that was proper for the elect. Such an attitude must have further alienated converts from their unconverted kinfolk. That happened to my own paternal great-grandfather, who was kicked out of his affluent family for joining the Presbyterians. He spent the rest of his life making a meager living as a town clerk.

His daughter, my grandmother, never forgave the extended family for his ignominy. To her dying days she would retell the story with a mix of sorrow and anger in her voice. His example shows that conversion also extinguished all form of patronage or official support afforded by your family's political networks. Once cast out for their new faith, people lost jobs, friendships, and the esteem of their peers. Their children would be educated in missionary schools, segregated from the rest of their culture, else they might fall prey to old ways. And they would have to start again, seeking to make a living among Protestant networks. Those would become their foster family of sorts, providing the much-needed support their own families refused to bestow upon them.

Conversion also led to political repression. In 1930 a bloodless coup placed a military officer, Getúlio Vargas, in power. As Brazil's ultimate *caudillo* (much like Perón in Argentina) Vargas used the mantle of nationalism to tighten his regime's grip on the country. The 1934 constitution gave him presidential powers akin to Mussolini's. His fascist initiatives boosted industrial production but at the serious cost of union rights and civil liberties. Under the threat of incoming elections, Vargas staged a second coup in 1937, launching the Estado Novo (the New State). That allowed him to abolish political parties, to impose media censorship, to create a centralized police force, and to imprison all political dissidents.[19] Were it not for U.S. pressure during World War II for Brazil to democratize, his reign might have been prolonged a tad longer.

Under Vargas's nationalist paranoia, all movements of foreign origin were automatically suspect, including Brazilian Protestantism. Converts were simultaneously defined by him as subversive agents (i.e., American spies) and weak-minded people who succumbed to a foreign ideology (Pierson 1974). The timing could not have been worse. Vargas's suspicions of Protestantism arose as Brazilian Protestants developed strong native leadership and created self-sustaining churches that were far less dependent on foreign funding. Just then, their government decided to question their birthright. Vargas kept chipping away at hard-won Protestant freedoms until he threatened to ban all non-Catholic worship in Brazil. Under duress, Rev. Matatias Gomes dos Santos, president of the Brazilian Confederation of Evangelical Churches, met with the dictator to swear, on behalf of Brazilian Protestants, an oath of allegiance to the nation and unconditional support to his regime.

That might have been, perhaps, Brazilian Protestantism's most infamous moment—an unnecessary and cruel act of obedience, exacted by military xenophobia. And yet, here they stand—the Zumbi congregation. In broad daylight, under military rule, posing for the camera and struggling to hold on to their loyalties to Brazil and Protestantism, without surrendering either. I look at these faces and think back to when it all started, some sixty-five years earlier. The 1930s clash began with the arrival on January 15, 1873, of John Rockwell Smith, a tall, lean twenty-seven-year-old graduate of the Union Theological Seminary in Richmond, my hometown. A son of Lexington, Kentucky, Rockwell Smith was the first Southern Presbyterian missionary sent to the Brazilian Northeast.

After a thirty-three-day trip on the steamship *Ontario*, Smith landed in Recife, ready to share his faith. He rented a small room from a Scottish expatriate, got permission from the governor to start his ministry, and took to the field. James Bear's *Mission to Brazil* describes Smith's letters home, which paint a quaint view of my hometown: "The picturesqueness of the city as seen from the sea; its reefs; its size—a hundred odd thousand; its narrow streets; the foreign colony of two to three hundred who received him kindly but were not interested in religion; the quality of Catholicism he found there, and the conflict between the church and the state over Freemasonry. He found the climate not too bad, and recommended that the Boyles [the next missionary couple] come as soon as possible."[20]

He would preach his first sermon in August 1873, to an audience of ten—three locals included. Learning the language took longer than he expected. He studied Portuguese for at least seven months before he felt comfortable enough to preach in it. Unfortunately, the 1874 American economic depression cut off further mission funding, checking his initial plans to expand Presbyterian work throughout the region. Colleagues who arrived shortly after him had to be called home due to financial hardship or on account of tropical disease. It would take another six years before he got any reinforcements. In the meantime, Rockwell Smith taught English to supplement his meager income and as another way to meet locals.

As any immigrant would, he must have struggled to adapt to such a strange culture. The work was discouraging—on a good Sunday, he averaged ten to thirteen worshipers in a city of hundreds of thousands. It took five years of slow growth before twelve local converts would organize the First Presbyterian Church of Pernambuco.[21] Having lived in Kentucky, Tennessee, and Virginia for almost three decades now, and as deeply immersed in southern life as I am these days, I can't help thinking of how hard it must have been for Rev. John Rockwell Smith to make his way among Northeasterners in Pernambuco. What must he have thought of my people? How strange did the food taste? How odd did Portuguese sound? What would a southerner from a century ago have paid attention to in our ways of life?

More importantly, what part of our ways gave him hope? What about us challenged his resolve? I look at myself, living now in the same area where Rockwell Smith grew up, and recognize the bravery of his efforts. Nothing in Recife would have looked like southern culture or southern life. He gave up family, friends, and everything familiar for a place where he might never have felt at home. By the time I got to the United States, I was quite familiar with southern ways. By the time he arrived in Recife, everything must have looked completely strange: no one with whom he could celebrate American holidays, no one to sit down with for a Thanksgiving dinner, no one to share his love of American music or food.

And yet that man labored among us for twenty-three years—for a cause hard to translate and slow to adopt. In the process, and inadvertently, he turned us into immigrants in our own homeland. We would grow up singing American hymns, learning the Westminster Catechism, and avoiding all things Brazilian. So drastic was the change he effected that some sixty-five years later his spiritual descendants would face a military ruler who questioned their right to practice Rockwell Smith's faith in Brazil, a dictator deeply suspicious of the American culture they had embraced. One who had to wonder whether there was room in his country for people whose way of life was so distinct from the rest of Brazilians. To me that shows how drastically Rockwell Smith's work changed the Northeastern cultural landscape. We were as much American as we were Brazilians.

My paternal grandmother was a steadfast member of Rockwell Smith's congregation. One of his many spiritual heirs, she faithfully attended First Church till the day she died (she is the one who brought me along to her congregation). Her brother was a Presbyterian minister; her children would attend Protestant schools in town. First Church was the spiritual home of my teen years. My network of friends belonged to that congregation (they still do, as do their children). First Church also supported my candidacy to ministry. It was there that I preached my first sermon, 101 years after Rockwell Smith had delivered his fateful initial homily.

Leaving Self-Exile

So how does one deal with such double origins? American by faith, Brazilian by birth, it is a journey in search of balance. Since we had no way of sorting out what was American culture from what was Calvinism in our transplanted faith, we adopted the missionary worldview wholesale. As we did so, we also failed to realize that our "strangeness" to other Brazilians was more *cultural* than *religious* in nature. For the sake of an American God, we revamped our local habits and learned to behave as proper Southern Presbyterians. We never dreamed that along the way we would give up parts of our culture that had nothing to do with our search for religious integrity.

The end result was being forever caught between two worlds. I look at the old photo of the Zumbi Presbyterian Congregation now, and see people whose conversion led to cultural self-exile. Why would local folk so easily part with their own culture? Perhaps the need for greater spiritual certainty trumped the force of local habit. Confronted with what seemed to be the "true" faith, they willingly left behind the moorings of their social life. It is not as grim as it looks, though. Local Protestant congregations offered not only existential certainty but also surrogate families. My mother grew up surrounded by "cousins" who were related to her only by the faith they shared. Spiritual certainty guided us into "new tribes," if not into a bifurcated cultural territory.

But it is clear to me now that to be a Protestant in Recife when I was growing up meant cultural self-exile. Spiritual heirs to J. Rockwell Smith, we contended with the foreignness of our daily condition by telling ourselves that that was the price we paid for following the true path. Overcompensation helps, when you are culturally alienated. So we grew up convinced of the superiority of our faith and our lifestyle. All else gravitated around such firm a foundation. We went about our business trying to create in the midst of an Iberian Catholic culture a small religious island of Scotch-Irish American comfort. The irony is that those of us who "for the sake of the gospel" became self-exiled in our homeland ended up more alienated than the missionary who brought the foreign faith in the first place!

As converts we had to deal with the constant sifting, weighing, balancing of all activities and relationships, to keep the appropriate distance from the "failed" and "worldly" surrounding culture. There was a constant, if subtle, self-checking that went along with it. Is a certain activity or friendship proper for a Protestant? How about going to a soccer match? How close could we get to non-Protestant neighbors? (Dating an "outsider" was out of the question in my adolescence.) What local celebrations were allowed? Which ones crossed the line? We had to model a different way of life, without turning off fellow neighbors when we refused to join in their daily rituals. That was the pattern that followed me from grade school to college. A constant check on the sports I played, hobbies I practiced, and trips I took.

Such an all-encompassing way of life was reinforced every Sunday by "pie-in-the-sky-when-you-die" hymns like "A Poor Wayfaring

Stranger" or "This World Is Not My Home." How not to feel alienated in one's own land? How not to be estranged from one's own culture? Sooner or later the whole edifice of cultural self-exile has to come tumbling down. It is not possible to be completely insulated from one's surroundings, even for the most determined and persistent among us. Slowly, you find yourself giving in to the most Brazilian of temperaments, to the tastes, desires, and dreams of the larger culture. You relish street food, beautiful and exotic songs, even the relaxed pace of life so dear to us *Nordestinos* (Northeasterners). Plus, there is no way to fully avoid feast days—the colors and pageantry of Saint John's and Saint Peter's celebrations, the throngs that celebrate Recife's patron saint, Our Lady of Mount Carmel, the garish Christmas decorations.

By giving in here and there, you start your true *hybrid* life; you engage in that inevitable accommodation to the truth that you find in both worlds. As your world expands, you get pushed beyond the parochial circles of faith and region. As many people who grow up in other countries know, becoming a hybrid means loosening one's early parochial certainties. You realize sooner or later that there are valuable things in both worlds, that both are worthy of your attention and loyalty. And you cherish the parts of your life that resonate with both. But it is certainly not an easy path.

It helped in my case that my parents' generation was already moving beyond the insular confines of my grandparents' religious circles. I was lucky to grow up in a family who loved all things Pernambucan, Northeasterner, and Brazilian. So the liberal, middle-class leanings of my college-educated parents won out against the strict Calvinism of my grandparents. If the latter advocated strict distance from our larger surroundings, the former took a selective approach to the larger culture. I may not have celebrated Recife's Roman Catholic saints' days or prayed a novena with classmates, but my childhood was immersed in folktales and songs of my homeland—in other words, as a cultural hybrid.

Hybridization stretches you beyond faith, region, and sometimes class. It usually hits you around adolescence. Slowly, you realize that the universe does not gravitate around all that is precious to you, your family, or your social rank. That awareness hits you harder, if you belong to a more insulated religious/ethnic/or regional minority. All that once was certain becomes questionable, as you build the means to sort out the essential from the accidental. Sometimes, if you're lucky, there are good role models. Most of the time, you figure things out as you go along.

Becoming a hybrid in terms of faith meant facing the impossibility of a creator who designed the entire universe exclusively for a sliver of predestined people who alone would inherit it. That level of rabid exclusivity went against the grain of my larger Brazilian culture. Unlike the strict individualism found in America, Brazilian life is utterly inclusive. Plus, I found among other Brazilians a warm welcome, unlike the pettiness of my small Presbyterian circles. How could we be exclusive paragons of charity, faith, or hope when other Brazilians had those virtues in spades? Along the same lines, how could the dictates of a sixteenth-century northern European faith fit the world I inhabited?[22]

TV and telephone had reached Recife in my late childhood. Americans landed on the moon the year I turned thirteen. In California, Edwin Hubble's Doppler shift pointed to an ever-expanding universe, and to the Big Bang. Advances in medicine, science, and technology opened up so many secular explanations for our place in the universe. How to reconcile such different worlds? It seems that my everyday life constantly challenged the tenets of the Westminster Catechism. And yet, it was during this period of fast modernization in Latin America that Protestantism retrenched the most, still clearly wed to the orthodoxies of a bygone era. To this day, the leadership of my church refuses to acknowledge that faith, much like everything else in society, requires regular updating.

The Presbyterian Church of Brazil grew more insular as I came of age. It broke off ties with the World Council of Churches, with the South American Council of Churches, and even with its mother churches in North America. Eventually it stopped collaborative work with other Brazilian Protestant denominations. That lesson in insularity became a crucial focus of my academic work. It taught me that there is no such a thing as "generic" Christianity. The faith is always shaped by the times and places where it takes root. It is hard to confront your faith's inability to see religion as a product of its own time. In that sense, while tradition sheltered four generations of my family, it has given me no solace. And it failed my brothers and sisters as well. Along with our cousins, we are the first generation to give up on the ultimate certainties of our ancestors.

Moving beyond my region meant discovering that the Northeast, for all its vainglory, was the least developed part of the country. Regular childhood visits to my cousins in Rio de Janeiro and São Paulo, the industrial centers of Brazil, made that plain to see. Their towns supported superior cultural events, stronger soccer teams, and urban delights that my parochial Recife was years away from knowing. My cousins' schools were more connected to intellectual developments around the world. Their media brought more to their attention. More importantly, to me they seemed to live in the present tense, lacking that instinctive need of older regions to cling to the spoils of lost splendors.

Northeast Brazilian gentility, like southern gentility in the United States, sensed that time had passed us by and left us only with the dignity of bygone days. So we clung to the old ways, to the dignified manners of a fading imperial past, to a time when our region was Brazil's economic powerhouse. That past came alive when my parents entertained the extended family at dinner gatherings, and we assembled in the family music room after meals. The older generation would introduce us to all that glorious nineteenth-century imperial lore—street songs, serenades, and poems.

Today, I realize that those nights gave my generation a window into what was sacred to our parents as they preserved a culture precious in turn to their parents and grandparents. We were simply the next link in the chain of such holy heritage.

Thus, we grew up surrounded by an insular secular culture as well, one too fond of the old ways. Meanwhile, my uncles and aunts in south Brazil savored the fresh and sensuous sounds of bossa nova as they celebrated Brazil's modernity. My cousins danced to the Beatles, Rolling Stones, and Brazilian rock and roll. To me, they were the seduction of the new, they pointed to the promises and possibilities of future trends. It was harder to hang on to the Northeast way in all things. It got harder as I got older. These days, my bossa nova collection is a testament to my hybridization. And I have my (Brazilian) southern relatives to thank for it. Their "subversive" ways have stood the test of time.

Moving beyond my middle-class world meant giving up the silly notion that my country's interests gravitated around the concerns of my social station. Soon enough, schooling would introduce me to children of local elites and the conspicuous consumption of the better-bred. In similar fashion, my trips downtown revealed the foibles of Brazil's downtrodden. So I grew up squeezed between the two, pressed by Brazil's horrible income distribution. While the privileged 5–7 percent of the country enjoyed most of its riches, the rest of us were pushed downward, with the bulk of our citizens living in large pockets of poverty around the edges of large urban centers. All of that would become clearer after I bought my first record, at the tender age of thirteen.

Part of a series dedicated to famed Brazilian composers, the LP show-cased the working-class songs of Noel Rosa, a leading songwriter of the 1930s and '40s.[23] Rosa's music introduced me to a world that challenged my safe, ordered, middle-class, Protestant universe. His songs unveiled the realities of the Brazilian urban peripheries. The grimy conditions of Rio's factories would come to life in his music, along with the slums, the peddlers, the drunks, and the prostitutes. Rosa's songs described tragic lives, full of fateful breakups, economic destitution, lost ambitions, and twisted fates. Rosa himself had had a tragic childhood, followed by alcoholism and homelessness in adult life. A college dropout, an incorrigible bohemian, he lived for his poetry, for his music—for that beautiful turn of phrase, that melodic twist in the bridge of a song. He also lived for dancing, crazy loving, and cheap thrills.

As a clean-cut, middle-class Presbyterian, it astounded me that anyone could bear that much risk, pain, and sorrow in the pursuit of sheer beauty or pleasure. The notion challenged every middle-class fiber in my being. But if you ever listen to "Três Apitos" or "Meu Último Desejo," you'll find in Rosa a deep vein of wisdom about human nature, one that all catechisms in the world have yet to understand. The "poet of the dew," as he called himself, marveled at life's imperfections, at its smallnesses, daily indignities, petty injustices. From him I gathered that life was twisted and small (which made beauty or pleasure ever more precious). Things didn't always work out. People were complicated, even authentic ones. It was an eye-opener to find out how vices were so intrinsic to the human condition!

Slowly it dawned on me that one could not understand human nature by denying or repressing its darker side. Rosa made me realize that my *mestizo* Calvinism, obsessed with human perfectionism, could not fathom the hidden depths or sweetness of our tragic side. It would take me decades to fully decode Rosa's work. But savvy poet that he was, he planted the first seeds of my class consciousness. I would love to say that leaving early parochialisms was easy, just part of growing up. But the truth is that it was not. You "loosen up" a few of your early certainties, but you never reject your origins entirely, lest you deprive yourself of key parts of your identity. Ultimately, denying them would be denying who you have become.

These days I joke in my classes about being an "ethnic" Southern Presbyterian, or a "recovering" Southern Presbyterian. But I cannot deny that I still think of the world in very ordered Presbyterian categories. It's instinctive, pre-rational, almost limbic. Things *must* be ordered when you grow up with such an orderly God. What really changes as you stretch your worldview is your awareness of having a double soul. The sooner you realize you inhabit two distinct but equally valid worlds, the sooner you draw strength from your early moorings. Negotiating the two worlds, on the other hand—the early certainties versus the broader self—takes a lifetime. You live out your days holding the two distinct worlds in tension; asking yourself, "How much of who I was still matters to who I am now?"

But the reality is that I could no more deny my southern origins as I could reject my "larger" Brazilian self. Nor could I fully relinquish the early faith that led me to the latter questioning. The more global my experience has become, the more important it is to know the depths of my own roots. The positive side of living between two worlds is that they relativize your existence. You realize that standards created by human cultures are not carved in stone. They become less "real" and more "constructed." You come to see that people in different places and times organize their lives around different values to adapt to the conditions under which they must exist. Once that is understood, you are free to shape your identity with less fixed parameters—you pick and choose from both worlds, selecting which parts you wish to honor, which to struggle with, and which you definitely reject.

This is what I call "leaving self-exile." Once I fell deeply in love with my Northeastern culture, I discovered a wealth of art, music, and literature that moved me beyond my early religious proscriptions. Similarly, moving to the United States allowed me to dig deeper into southern art, song, and prose, and to break the insular walls of my early faith. In both instances, expanding beyond my roots was equally valuable. But there is no linear process to assimilation—one does not trade the first for the latter. There is no leaving behind João Cabral de Melo Neto's poetry for the sake of Will Campbell's wonderful tales. I can't abandon the songs of Catulo da Paixão Cearense just because I found Hoagy Carmichael's music.

A true hybrid knows that it is always both. It will always be both—whether it is the folk chants of street minstrels from Recife or the clever songs I heard at the Ryman Auditorium in Nashville. Your worlds expand outward, taking you with them. You keep adding things, and redefining your identity as you go along—rethinking your journey. Each new addition unsettles the fragile balance you have achieved in the past. It moves you to reconsider what matters, how it matters.

At Home in Homelessness

A Northeastern proverb says that "those who leave the homeland never truly settle anywhere else" (*quem sai da terra natal em outros cantos não para*). There is much truth in that statement. Leaving self-exile does create a sense of impermanence, of homelessness. You are never fully settled anywhere, not even in your supposed homeland. Life changes as your tastes and habits change. And wherever you go, there is always a part of yourself missing. My Brazilian family cannot "see" my American side (which seems so visible to me), just as my American friends miss my Brazilian identity entirely. One moves from being settled to being a sojourner, something that goes against the grain of Brazilian culture (my family has been in the same region of our country for almost five centuries).

Along the way, we relinquish the comfortable world we once knew for the sake of provisional homes. And again, it is not an easy process. There is a lot of certainty in the old worldviews. Thankfully, the change is gradual, and our homelessness does not hit us full-blast. We tell ourselves we are leaving temporarily, "just to see what is out there." And it does not feel that we are really leaving the old world for good; that we are giving up things so formative in our early days. Life just gets complicated in a good way, and we learn to roll with it. However, once we stretch beyond our initial certainties, we keep adding colors to our palette.

In my case, moving beyond my regional identity as a Brazilian Northeasterner meant discovering Brazil's larger culture, the wonders of the Paulista Modernist school of painting, the urban sadness of Minas Gerais poetry, or the bossa nova sounds of Rio de Janeiro. Similarly, moving to the United States allowed me to reach beyond my southern identity, to claim a culture of continental proportions, rich with the philosophical power of American pragmatism, with the soaring heights of New England's transcendentalism, and the larger aesthetics of American art. Who could ignore Emily Dickinson's sing-song verse, Robert Frost's sparseness, the raw power of Langston Hughes's poetic blues, or the rich energy of the Harlem Renaissance and the delights of the American songbook?

Those of us who live in these multiple worlds are drawn to the new; as if it holds the promise of shedding light on parts of our journey that still make little sense. We do so, even if leaving early certainties takes a toll on us, on our loved ones, and on our region, much as the African American exodus to northern U.S. cities drained the South of its rich heritage. Similarly, the Northeast of Brazil has lost plenty of workers to Rio de Janeiro and São Paulo since the mid-nineteenth century. Drought, lack of opportunity, and blocked social mobility all contributed to the exodus.[24] But so did the dreams of life in the big city, of cultural joys yet to be discovered. We leave to know, to become, though we mourn the consequences of our exodus.

Leaving creates a sense of dislocation, one always present in the songs of the Brazilian migrants. They sing of constant homesickness, of the harshness of the large southern urban centers. Northeastern migrants pine for their homeland, for their food, for relatives, for the pace of life, for indigenous celebrations. No matter how long the sojourn, they keep hoping that someday, as things improve, they might reverse the migratory process.[25] It is a sense of dislocation equally felt by working-class laborers and scholars. The Northeast of Brazil has lost writers, composers, and poets to the South; all left seeking fame and fortune.

We lost abolitionist poets like Castro Alves and Joaquim Nabuco, legal scholars like Ruy Barbosa, and classical composers like Paurillo Barroso, Alberto Nepomuceno, and Liduíno Pitombeira. They all migrated south in the nineteenth century. Writers like Jorge Amado, Manuel Bandeira, Ferreira Gullar, Rachel de Queiroz, Graciliano Ramos, and Nélson Rodrigues left for Rio de Janeiro in the twentieth century, seeking to hone their craft. In fact, Northeastern migration shaped the contours of Brazilian modernity. For more than a century the country's industrial areas flourished with a fresh supply of those *retirantes* (Northeastern term for those who leave our region).

Retirantes helped build Brazil's industrial base and added much to Brazilian culture. But the process took away much of what was valuable in our region. Talent exported under duress only contributed to our sense of loss. Those who left never stopped being *Nordestinos* (the term for those who hail from our region), but their newly gained world took them farther away from us. And it is impossible not to wonder what more we could have achieved as a region had we harnessed that much energy internally.[26] And those of us who leave pay a price as well. We know the comforts we leave behind. We know our contribution will be missed, that we do leave a gap in what could be accomplished in the long term.

But once you begin to stretch out, once you discover the possibilities of your double souls, you have to wonder—in the words Walt Whitman,

America's ever-expansive poet—whether you might be more, whether you might "contain multitudes."[27] Much as I found my larger Brazilian and American selves when I moved to America, I had to wonder how many more selves were out there to be discovered. "Do I contradict myself?" sang Whitman. "Very well, then I contradict myself!"[28] From humble Long Island beginnings, he would notate the virtue and value of a continental home and a continental self in a single lifetime. No wonder Latin American writers were so enamored of Whitman. They too struggled with their own "multitudes."

They too could not go home. Once they had moved beyond early certainties, they found in him a kindred soul. In his struggle to define a changing self and a changing nation they recognized their own struggles.[29] Poets like the revolutionary Cuban José Martí, or the Argentine Rubén Dário, who referred constantly to the words of El Gran Viejo (the Old Man) in their work; or the Peruvian José Santos Chocano, who was considered the "Whitman of the South," for the vastness of his verse. Whitman's verse structures underlined the poetry of the Uruguayan Alvaro Vasseur, and of the Mexican modernist Amado Nervo.[30]

It seems that those who leave parochialisms behind find larger homes in their apparent homelessness. I suspect that that is why the theme of multiple selves runs so deep in Latin American literature. Along with the Latin American theme of *alteridad*, of self and other that we find in so many of our novels, there is the ever-present sense that one can no longer hold onto the limited world of one's childhood. Identity becomes a journey, a travel of sorts—you move toward your true selves as you move away from the early certainties. That is why the Latin American writer must leave his or her country for lands beyond, in ever-expanding circles of cultural inclusiveness. The journey is an evolution of sorts, one best expressed in the poem "We Are Many" by Chilean Pablo Neruda:

Of the many men whom I am, whom we are
I cannot settle on a single one.
They are lost to me under the cover of clothing
They have *departed for another city*." (my italics)

Neruda is honest enough to present even the disappointing selves in his poem, those less honorable selves, the lazy selves. He ponders whether one can "single out [one's] self," or "put [oneself] together." "I never know just who I am," he pleads, "nor who we will be being." He longs for a bell to call up his real self, his true self. He fears that self

might disappear in the multiplicity now existing. The poem ends with
the secret for the multiple selves—they all spring from the work, from
the craft. He wishes for someone to research the problem, to make sense
of it all. I have been always fond of Neruda's poetry, of his clever, insightful take on life's journey. It is not always about self-congruence. It
is about coming to terms with a hybrid life, shifting wisely from self to
place and back, since the changes we experience come from moving, to
other homes, to other lands, and eventually to other selves:

While I am writing, I am far away;
And when I come back, I have already left.
I should like to see if the same thing happens
to other people as it does to me,
to see if as many people are as I am,
and if they seem the same way to themselves.
When this problem has been thoroughly explored,
I am going to school myself so well in things
that, when I try to explain my problems,
I shall speak, not of self, but of geography.[31]

2

Military Rule

These all died in faith, not having received what was promised, but having seen it and greeted it from afar, and having acknowledged that they were strangers and exiles on the earth. For people who speak thus make it clear that they are seeking a homeland . . . they desire a better country.

Heb. 11:13–16, RSV

Latin America's great tragedy is that there isn't a woman or man my age in the region who has not lived under military rule. In fact, the arbitrary and capricious use of military power in domestic affairs has been a hallmark of our homelands. While the American citizen enjoys the safety of the Posse Comitatus Act, which forbids the American armed forces from domestic law enforcement operations, Latin American populations are and have always been at the mercy of their own military's whims.[1] From one end of the continent to the other, always employing the latest in weapons technology and military training, Latin American soldiers have waged war on their own people since our countries' independence days.

Look northward from Brazil, and there is the bloody Guatemalan civil war, which destroyed 450 Mayan villages, killed 200,000 citizens, and displaced a million more.[2] Look south, where the so-called Dirty War in Argentina (1976–83) killed 9,000 to 30,000 citizens.[3] The numbers are still muddled by secrecy. Next door, some 2,279 Chileans were murdered during the Pinochet regime, which also tortured 31,947 and sent 1,312 into exile.[4] The astonishing thing about Latin America is not how often military rule has taken place, but how widespread the practice has been. In fact, with the single exception of French Guiana, which is still a French protectorate, every single Latin American country has had strong civilian dictators or military rulers for most of the twentieth century.

It is hard for my American friends to imagine the kind of relationship Latin Americans have had with their military. American citizens see in their armed forces a benign shield against the foreign foe. Since the U.S. military is seldom used domestically, the American public as a rule is quite grateful for their men and women in uniform. In fact, American soldiers are held in high esteem and many are afforded the highest civic honors for service to the country. Some go on to serve in national elected offices or state legislatures. Others are governors of their home states. A few who have seen battle have also become commander in chief at the White House; at least five come to mind who have served during my lifetime: Dwight D. Eisenhower, John F. Kennedy, Richard Nixon, Jimmy Carter, and George H. W. Bush.

After attending several Memorial Day concerts on the West Lawn of the United States Capitol, I can understand why. American soldiers are willing to die in the defense of freedom. They rise to protect the very heart of our democratic practice—the ability of a people to determine its own future, free of external threat. Since U.S. citizens are not usually on the receiving end of such might, there is great comfort in knowing that the most powerful military in the world is watching our back as a threat appears. And on Memorial Day we pause in gratitude for those who, in the words of President Lincoln, "gave the last full measure of devotion" for their country.[5]

Were that it was so for Latin American citizens. But there we need protection from our protectors. There is no bond of gratitude among Latin American populations toward their men and women in arms. Rather we cultivate a healthy fear of people in uniform. Consider this—*every* country in the region has seen its military used by a strong ruler or military junta against the local population. Since 1950 alone, seventeen out of the nineteen nations in Latin America have been under military rule. That is a rather sizable group. Just in the last century in Brazil, we had the Vargas military dictatorship from 1930 to 1946, and another series of military "presidents" from 1964 to 1985.

In other words, Brazilians spent some thirty-seven years out of the last century under undemocratic regimes, facing daily violations of their most basic rights—be it freedom of assembly, freedom of the press, or freedom from unreasonable search and seizure. To put it in personal terms, my grandfather's generation, my father's, and my own have all experienced life under military watch. Since Brazil became a Republic back in 1889, there has not been a generation until 1985 that did *not* experience periods of military rule. Out of thirty-six presidents the country has had, seventeen rose to power without being elected for office. Nine of our presidents were active officers in the Brazilian armed forces as they were inaugurated.[6] None gave up his active military duty while in office. That does not happen in democratic societies.

To make matters worse, sometimes the number of unelected rulers in a given Latin American country is so overwhelming one has to wonder whether that country is governable at all. Take Paraguay, for instance—between 1904 and 1954 Paraguay had thirty-one presidents. Most were removed from office by force. Venezuela saw its own string of dictators during the same period. The same can be said of a number of other Latin American nations. Since becoming independent from the Old World, we Latin Americans seem unable to break free from the cycle of one strong man (and it is always a man) replacing another strong man, except for the intermittent, brief periods of real democracy.

In the second half of the twentieth century alone there was not a region in Latin America untouched by military rule. In the Southern Cone, the Argentine military ruled from 1976 to 1983. In Chile, Pinochet reigned with an iron fist from 1973 to 1989. At the time of his death in 2006 he was facing three hundred criminal charges for human rights violations, tax evasion, and embezzlement.[7] Paraguay was ruled by two generals—Alfredo Stroessner (1954–89) and Andrés Rodriguez (1989–93)—for almost forty years. Uruguay was under military rule from 1973 to 1984. Odds are, if you were born in the Southern Cone since 1950, you have lived without civil liberties for a good chunk of your life.

The same can be said for citizens of the Andean countries. After a military junta ruled Bolivia from 1964 to 1969, General Hugo Banzer Suárez took over the country for another seven years. He was followed by General Luíz Garcia Meza Tejada, who ruled from 1980 to 1981. In the next fourteen months Bolivia had three separate military governments. Colombia fared no better. It was under the control of General Gustavo Rojas from 1953 to 1957, and under a military junta from 1957 to 1964. Ecuador had two rulers in the same decade: General Guillermo Rodríguez (1972–76) and Admiral Alfredo Poveda (1976–79). Peruvians faced General Juan Velazco Alvarado (1968–75) and General Francisco Morales Bermúdez (1975–80). From 1990 to 2000 the Peruvian president Alberto Fujimori created his own version of a police state.

One finds the same picture in Caribbean countries of South America. French Guiana's prefect, always a conservative candidate, is appointed by the French Parliament. In nearby Guyana, with full American support, Forbes Burnham ruled the nation for almost two decades, from 1966 to 1985. Dési Bourtese's de facto regime choked Suriname from 1980 to 1991 (Bourtese was eventually convicted in absentia in the Netherlands in 1999 for cocaine trafficking). Given the outstanding international arrest warrant against him, Bourtese can no longer leave his country.[8] And compared to Venezuela's previous dictators, none had the cunning, resilience, or tight grip on power as Comandante Hugo Chávez, who has ruled since 1998.

Our counterparts in Central America have endured similarly dismal fates. To defend against Guatemala, Belize has "hosted" a garrison of 1,500 British troops since its 1981 independence. Costa Rica, the most democratic of Central American countries, endured a short civil war in midcentury. El Salvador's civil war lasted for more than a decade, from 1980 to 1992. Guatemala has had the largest number of *caudillos*—five generals and two colonels—between 1957 and 1986.[9] The nation of Honduras saw its own string of dictators from 1963 to 1981. Nicaragua had three Somozas, a single family of dictators, ruling it from 1936 to 1979. In Panama, Colonel Omar Torrijos Herrera called the shots from 1968 to 1981 and was followed by the now infamous General Manuel Noriega from 1983 to 1989.

Dreams Deferred

Faced with such evidence, it should surprise no one that some of us choose to live in self-imposed exile. Eventually, a few of us even take citizenship in our host countries. The question in Latin America is not whether there will be military rule, but when. With every new military regime, a series of atrocities gets visited upon the local economies and local populations, and multiple generations of Latin Americans learn to live with dreams deferred. All of this despite the immense joie de vivre one finds in any nation of the region—lively cultures, beautiful folklore, tasty foods, and rich celebrations all. Tragically, were you to visit every single major city in the region during the past fifty years, you would also find a repressed but vibrant civil society—generations of college professors, doctors, engineers, architects, journalists, artists, lawyers, and judges all wishing for the civic virtues of mature democracies for their homelands.

But between the surrogate battles of the Cold War and the unenlightened self-interest of our own elites, those dreams remain deferred. Of FDR's four freedoms, we seem to enjoy only freedom of worship, when available.[10] To add insult to injury, when I was growing up, Latin America tended to be typecast in other parts of the world for its backwardness, political ignorance, and/or popular servility. Nothing could be farther from the truth. But it was hard to fight the stereotypes created by our own local tyrants. The term "Banana republics," once attributed to Central America, was also aptly used to describe other nations south of the Rio Grande.

But we too are cultural heirs to Greece and Rome. We too inherited the blessings of the Enlightenment.[11] Those of us who read law or politics in college have known well our Western heritage; we are conversant with the French *Philosophes*, the British moralists, and the American Founders, people who helped turn their countries into modern nations of laws, not rulers. Moreover, the solutions to our problems have been known since our independence days. Many a talented politician in the region has battled to create much-needed stable political institutions. Many a legislator has given his or her all to help form a "government of the people, by the people, for the people."[12] Many a dedicated journalist has risked life and limb to preserve a free Latin American press. Our professors hold degrees from the best universities in the world; our writers are translated into every major language;[13] our artists are celebrated far beyond their homelands.[14] All of them have been actively engaged in training our people.

It is not backwardness or ignorance that keeps us from extending the franchise to all, from creating an educated citizenry, or from raising the standards of living in our respective nations. It is a matter of surviving the historical role that the Latin American military have assigned to themselves in our countries. Unlike the United States, our independences were not wrestled from monarchical European powers by a citizen's militia. Nor were our governments built by a civilian cadre of political thinkers, indebted to the likes of Thomas Hobbes, John Locke, or Adam Smith. We lack this tradition of civic respect for political rights that emerges in societies created and led by civilian rulers.

When Brazilian immigrants arrive in the United States they are gladly surprised by the level of respect with which they are treated by the business community and the government authorities. They encounter a degree of civility they seldom knew back home from those in places of authority; and this despite the fact that the Brazilian immigrants may not yet be fluent in English or even citizens of this country. One of the scholars who researched the subject argues that their positive view of political and civil institutions in America is framed against the background of those institutions in their own society. They come to the United States after facing regular violation of their civil and human rights, after they realize the impossibility of attaining a life of dignity framed by the protection of those very rights back home.[15]

The limiting effects of the military grip on our civil societies are most evident during the few brief years when we enjoy democratic rule. In those short periods, Latin American societies respond with competitive party systems, independent judiciaries, and active legislatures. We assemble public services and voluntary associations to tackle the common problems that pester our nations. We challenge the oligarchic grip of old Latin American elites on our economies. We fight the worn-out reach of political nepotism and push for the emergence of local entrepreneurship, couched on meritocratic practices. Sadly, those periods tend to be the exception rather than the rule.

To aid us in such endeavors, we rely on our share of visionary leaders: statesmen like Juscelino Kubitschek, the founder of Brasília, the Brazilian president who more than anyone else modernized our country; or the beloved Guatemalan Jacobo Árbenz Guzmán, who pushed courageously for land reform in his homeland at a time of conflict and political tension; or the brave Peruvian Fernando Belaúnde Terry, who met the challenge of domestic guerrilla with an unwavering commitment to democratic practice.[16] Theirs is the example that reminds us of the possible in the realm of Latin American politics. I am convinced that those political periods reveal the true democratic potential of our societies.

Take Chilean president Michelle Bachelet, for example. She is perhaps the most recent model of a competent Latin American leader.[17] By the time she left office, she enjoyed an 84 percent approval rating, something never before seen in Chile. By creating a $35 billion reserve from copper sales revenues, she allowed Chile to ride the global financial crisis relatively unscathed (this despite a 30 percent devaluation of its exports). In her last year in power, the economy reached a 5 percent growth rate, with the nation's sovereign wealth funds building up to almost $20 billion. Few of her neighbors could have claimed equal levels of financial success.

Moreover, the economic surplus gave Bachelet the opportunity to invest in much-needed social reform. Under her leadership, alimony was institutionalized. She tripled the number of free child-care centers for low-income Chilean families. Her minimum pension for the very poor in Chile and for low-income homemakers allowed them to experience an impressive modicum of human dignity. On her watch, Chile replaced its perpetual shantytowns with modern, affordable housing. Watching this level of responsible governing, no one can tell me that Latin American nations do not know how to govern themselves. And Bachelet achieved all this in a country with a horrible military past.

Had someone told me at the height of General Augusto Pinochet's years that Chile one day would be such a full-fledged democracy, I would have questioned his sanity. And yet, at the dawn of the twenty-first century, a professed agnostic, divorced physician (divorce has only been legal in conservative Chile for the last six years) ran for the country's presidency and won with 46 percent of the votes compared to 25 percent for the runner-up. More importantly, Bachelet proceeded to address the problems of the country with the sensibilities of a doctor, a mother, and a woman who had survived one of the harshest military regimes in Latin American history.

This is why Bachelet's window of democratic rule is important. Under her guidance Chile reformed its health care system. Two new ministries were created, one for citizen security, the other for the environment. As she moved her country forward, she also found room to encourage the development and support of female leadership at the highest levels of public and private institutions. That kind of inclusive civil society is a recent development in the region. Her inaugural cabinet had equal numbers of male and female cabinet ministers, another unprecedented instance of political leadership in a Latin American country. Clearly, administrations like Bachelet's fill me, a self-exiled expat, with hope for the region.

The most moving part of Bachelet's accomplishments is that they did not spring from a sheltered life. Like other Latin American leaders, she experienced the brunt of military repression and exile. The daughter of an archaeologist and a Chilean Air Force general, Bachelet grew up around military bases in Chile and the United States. After finishing high school in Santiago, where she was active in music and theater, she started medical training with a focus on pediatric surgery. Her life, in that sense, was not that much different from the life of other Latin American upper-middle and middle-class women of her generation. That life, however, took a turn when Pinochet came into power.

Michelle's father was arrested for treason. Tortured by his uniformed comrades in arms, under the custody of the country he had sworn to defend with his life, he died in one of Pinochet's prisons. For a couple of years Bachelet was able to continue her medical studies in Chile, but in 1975 she was eventually arrested, interrogated, and tortured. After spending a year in a Chilean prison, she and her mother were allowed to go into exile—first to Australia and later to East Germany, where Bachelet persevered in her medical studies. She returned to Chile in 1979, where she graduated from medical school in 1982. Until 1990, she worked in a nongovernmental organization helping children who had been victimized by the Pinochet regime.

The return to democracy gave Bachelet a chance to do public service as she worked with Chile's National AIDS Commission. Later, she was recruited to serve as President Ricardo Lagos Escobar's minister of health. Ironically, she also became his minister of defense. Bachelet was in fact the first Latin American woman to occupy that post. It was her career in public service that garnered her credentials to run for Chile's highest office. And in an age when Latin American leaders are amending their constitutions to hold on to power, Bachelet was a model of democratic restraint even in exiting the presidency. Forbidden by the Chilean Constitution to serve two consecutive terms, she completed her time in office and vacated it willingly, without resorting to dishonorable or dishonest political trickery.

She did not use Chile's devastating earthquake to cling to the presidency; she did not call in political favors to guarantee the success of her party's candidate; she did not seek to raise a puppet regime. Her term served, her sense of duty fulfilled, Bachelet stepped down and left an unparalleled legacy of female political leadership in the region. Her example finds precedent among other Latin American leaders who experienced similar political repression. In Brazil, President Fernando Henrique Cardoso, the first sociologist to become president of a country, was also a former victim of military repression. Much like Bachelet, he served his term in office, developed similar kinds of projects, and exited gracefully when the time came to do so.

Public Intellectuals

Visionary civilian leaders are critical to a region like Latin America. In nations gripped by military rule, many of them are public intellectuals, people who represent a key segment of Latin American societies. As privileged men and women of letters, in countries with vast uneducated masses, they carry a special *cargo* (burden). By necessity, they must place the welfare of their countries above their desire for a life of literary endeavors. Given the lack of strong party systems, stable political institutions, or independent judiciaries, people like them must learn and promote the art of democratic politics. Writers, poets, artists, and journalists become prophets of civic virtues, as they rally against the use of arbitrary power.

As public intellectuals, those leaders fight for transparency in the res publica (in the common good). They question the usurpation of legitimate authority, sometimes at great personal risk and risk to their families. Some spend time in jail, some are exiled, a good number are killed. Obviously, their unenviable task as promoters of democracy places them squarely in the crosshairs of local political despots.

Brazil has had its share of public intellectuals, too many to list. But a few come to mind from my own lifetime. There is for instance Celso Furtado, the economist, who created the agency for the development of Brazil's Northeast. An avowed Keynesian, Furtado believed in the role of government in stimulating economic development and worked with Latin American governments to make that happen. More than just a prolific author (he wrote more than thirty books in his academic career), it was his work on behalf of Latin America in international agencies that set him apart as a public intellectual.

Furtado served in the Brazilian armed forces as they joined the American military in the Italian campaign during World War II. After the war, he earned a PhD in economics at the Université de Paris (Sorbonne). His first job, in the newly created United Nations Economic Commission for Latin America and the Caribbean, allowed him to tackle the problem of Latin American development from the start. Furtado returned to Brazil in 1954, where he was invited to lead the Brazilian Development Bank during the Kubitschek presidency (1956–61) and served as the minister of planning in the João Goulart administration (1961–64). Clearly the man of letters was also a man of action. As a founder of the United Nations Conference on Trade and Development (UNCTAD), he worked tirelessly to address the problem of asymmetrical international trade.

Unfortunately Furtado's service to country and region came to a halt with the 1964 military coup in Brazil. Exiled, he taught at Yale and the Sorbonne. It would be another fifteen years before he would be allowed to come home to serve as Brazil's ambassador to the European Economic Community. He finished his public service career as the minister of culture in the Sarney presidency (1985–90). His academic work, based

on his experience serving the region, would lead to Furtado's nomina-
tion to the Nobel Prize in Economics in 2004, the year he died.[18]

Furtado's career is by no means unusual in Latin America. Fernando
Henrique Cardoso, the sociology-trained professor, became president
of Brazil after being exiled during our military years.[19] The Costa Rican
Óscar Arias Sanchéz, who holds a PhD in political science from Essex
(UK), served twice as president of his country and won the 1987 Nobel
Peace Prize for stemming civil wars in neighboring countries.[20] Jaime
Roldós Aguilera, the lawyer-turned-president of Ecuador, stood for
human rights at a rough period of his nation's history.[21] His death, after
less than two years in office, was tragic and suspect. President Gonzalo
Sánchez de Lozada of Bolivia, a Chicago-trained man of letters and son
of a political exile, achieved landmark social, economic, and constitutional reforms in his nation.[22]

Then there are the Latin American intellectuals who become political
muses by the power of their academic or literary work. People like the
Colombian Gabriel García Márquez, Nobel Prize winner in literature in
1982, who worked as journalist, editor, and political activist back home
prior to retiring in his beloved Cuba.[23] Or the Chilean Pablo Neruda,
the 1971 Nobel Prize winner in literature, who sang in verse Machu
Picchu's majesty. After a long diplomatic career, Neruda served a term
as a Chilean senator.[24] My favorite Latin American author, Carlos
Fuentes, grew up all over the world as the child of a Mexican diplomat.
A diplomat himself, he served Mexico in London and Paris, from 1965
to 1978. But it is Fuentes's intellectual work that has affected Latin
American generations. He would go on to write some twenty-five novels
and nineteen political monographs during his career.[25]

It is hard to create a single, all-inclusive list of so many talented
scholars. Even today, a quick tour of the continent reveals key thinkers
who are still playing the role of public intellectuals. In Argentina there is
Ernesto Sabato, a man who courageously presided over the commission
investigating the atrocities of the military era. In Chile, Jorge Edwards
and Arturo Fontaine were voices of wisdom during Pinochet's rule.
These days Chileans benefit from the wisdom of Roberto Ampuero's
and Roberto Bolaño's pens. Mario Vargas Llosa, the 2010 Nobel Prize
winner in literature, was Peru's moral compass during the Fujimori
regime. The journalist Plinio Apuleyo Mendoza documented Colombia's
recent atrocities.

These intellectuals, well versed in their disciplines, reputed scholars
in their own right, bring the best of Western Civilization to bear upon

their countries' ills. Faced with tragic odds—rampant illiteracy, high unemployment, internal migration, discouraging infant mortality rates, large masses living at subsistence levels—they have to find creative solutions for centuries-old problems. They give their best to the effort. In some cases, politics may not be their calling, but who else is there to take on the job? They are critical to the enterprise of preserving open civil societies in their homelands. So they run these parallel lives, caught between their literary muses and the greater duties to their countries.

Tragically, they must do so within small windows of democratic rule that open up now and then in Latin America's long history of despotic regimes. They have only those precious few years or perhaps decades to push their nations forward, to fully address the same tired old problems over and over again before the next military ruler clamps down on their freedom of speech. The asymmetrical cycles of democratic and despotic rule generate their own political and economic distortions in our countries. Together they create a rather sad picture of the entire region. So the task of public intellectuals is a Sisyphean, never-ending, always interrupted civilizing process: one they are willing to engage in despite the odds; one their nations are only too fortunate to enjoy.

Life under Military Rule

I turned eight in 1964, the year the Brazilian military took over the nation. Their drab olive green uniforms looked just like the ones on my World War II GI Joe toys. Brazil was the only South American country to send troops to the European theater during World War II. The Brazilian Expeditionary Force (BEF), almost 26,000 strong, fought in Italy, alongside the U.S. Fifth Army and the U.S. Mediterranean Allied Tactical Air Force.[26] During the war, the American Air Force set up bases in the Brazilian Northeast for easy air connection to northern Africa. Similarly, the U.S. Navy VP-52 patrol squadron and Task Force 3 were stationed in Brazil, hunting German submarines in South Atlantic waters.

Working alongside the American military during World War II greatly contributed to the modernization of the Brazilian armed forces. The BEF was set up as a standard American infantry division (down to the logistical details of postal and banking services). After the war, the Brazilian military updated its training schools and sent its best to American military academies for graduate training. American military aid and matériel flowed freely southward to its Brazilian counterpart.

In fact, the American crowd-control military gear used against un-armed college students in my hometown in the early 1960s was funded by President John F. Kennedy's Alliance for Progress.

The Alliance for Progress was part of Kennedy's arsenal against the 1959 Cuban Revolution. Castro was a turning point in American foreign policy toward Latin America. Kennedy considered the region "the most dangerous area in the world."[27] He knew Latin American nations needed development aid more than anything else, but pressed to stop the spread of communism, Kennedy opted for building up the local military in proxy wars against the Soviet Union. So, the threat of communism gave the Latin American military the perfect excuse for staging coups with the full aid and support of the United States. If you are only eight years old, however, and completely oblivious to the geo-political chess game of world superpowers, a military coup is your worst nightmare.

You go to bed one night and wake up the next morning in a totally different world. And there is very little anyone can say to help explain the sudden change. On the eve of the coup, my father got home with food supplies to last us weeks. An upstanding businessman in the local community, he was obviously tipped off on the impending military takeover. I had never seen him so scared before. He boarded up the front door and windows of the house, and we cowered inside for almost a week. But living on a busy connector road, we could hear the military vehicles pounding the asphalt in all directions that night. When finally allowed to go back to school, just a block away, I found a soldier with a gun on almost every busy corner of my neighborhood.

By March 1964, Brazil's fragile democratic regime had hit a rough political patch. The progressive Kubitschek administration (1956-61) had been followed by a tragic compromise. Since neither the National Democratic Union Party (NDUP) nor the socialist Brazilian Labor Party (BLP) was fully capable of taking the presidency, an alliance was cobbled together to maintain the political status quo: the NDUP's Jânio Quadros would create a ticket with BLP's João Goulart running as vice president. Quadros, the former governor of São Paulo, Brazil's economic engine, was the elites' candidate. Once in power, Quadros's policies set him on a collision course with his own supporters, Brazil's corporate leaders and the armed forces. Pressured to conform to their interests, he resigned instead—after only seven months in office.

That precipitated a constitutional crisis. Since the Brazilian military was not about to let a socialist vice president take over at the height of the Cold War, the country became a parliamentary system with a strong prime minister under military control and Goulart as a weak president, a figurehead. The compromise lasted less than two years (in January 1963, by popular referendum, Brazil returned to its original presidential system). To his credit, Goulart tried to steer a nonaligned course despite the Bay of Pigs and the Cuban Missile Crisis. But pushed by organized Labor and left-wing nationalistic supporters, he eventually vowed to nationalize Brazil's key industries on March 13, 1964. By March 31 he was out of office, deposed by a military coup.[28]

Dressed in our Sunday best, my family celebrated Easter that weekend. The coup, still fresh in everybody's mind, was a forbidden topic in our downtown congregation. No mention was made of the soldiers in the streets, or the media blackout, or the early arrests of key political figures. Good southern hymns were sung, orthodox prayers said, and the collection plate was passed around as usual. My pastor's impeccable homily made the case that the real action took place in Jesus's time, not ours. Afterwards, we visited a bit with other upstanding Presbyterian families. Then went home, thankful the Lord had risen. To this day I have no idea whether the good-hearted Presbyterian missionaries who ministered to my family were informed of the American military presence. Had they been alerted? Were they aware of the situation? And if so, when, by whom?

Off the Brazilian coast that week, speeding toward Guanabara Bay, an American aircraft carrier group was at the ready to aid the Brazilian military with ammunition, gas, and other military supplies.[29] It would be decades before Brazilians would learn of its presence, after American documents were declassified. An eight-year-old boy, I had no idea my future and my country's were being shaped by special interests in faraway places like Brasília, Washington, DC, or Moscow. Off our coast, the American soldiers kept watch, while their ambassador monitored the coup. Somebody was helping write Brazilian history. Part of me wonders if the American sailors celebrated Easter too on that Sunday. I wonder if they sang the same hymns I did. I wonder whether their chaplains preached the same good news I heard in my Presbyterian haven. Probably so.

Thirty-five years later, in a workshop at George Washington University, I met the retired admiral who had led the military convoy that weekend. A short, fiery, resolute man, with a glint in his eye, he chatted amiably about his duties in my homeland. By then he was working with a Washington, DC, think tank to reduce reliance on unilateral military

Military rule, Brazil, April 1968 (Arquivo Nacional, *Correio da Manhã*)

power in the resolution of international conflict. Back in Brazil, his leadership of the aircraft carrier group was crucial to preserve Brazilian capitalism, protect Brazilian elites, and indirectly help create the world's worst income distribution.

After the coup, things went downhill quickly. Eager to preserve a semblance of democratic rule, the military kept Brazil's presidential system intact, if only on paper. A series of generals were indirectly "elected" to the country's presidency, while the Brazilian multiparty system was replaced by two closely monitored political parties. Through a series of the so-called Institutional Acts, the military gave the executive unchecked powers to change the Constitution, to suspend political and civil rights, and to declare a state of siege. Civil society's reaction against the coup was quickly restrained. The hardliners inside the military used it to stage a coup inside the coup. By 1968 all forms of protests were being violently suppressed.[30]

The repression would reach my extended family. My uncle in São Paulo, a publisher and a poet, the intellectual of my parents' generation, was detained and interrogated for his political activities. I suspect he was tortured, though he never discussed the matter afterward. Decades later I would find the record of his military arrest and interrogation in a book about military torture in Brazil.[31] When he was temporarily released on his own recognizance and went underground, the military placed my aunt and cousins under house arrest. Only with the help of a neighbor were my aunt and cousins able to escape. They drove 1,300 miles to hide in our house for almost a year. At great personal risk my dad eventually smuggled my uncle into Uruguay, where he had to remain for a good while.

Happy to have my São Paulo cousins around, I still couldn't figure out why they did not go to school or leave the house much. Life would remain out of joint for the rest of my childhood. An immediate conclusion I reached in the aftermath of my uncle's escape was that if my parents could not protect my uncle, aunt, and cousins from the military, they certainly could not protect me. My cousins felt the same way. The repression took a toll on all of us. One cousin never fully recovered. Despite having degrees in philosophy and mathematics, she remains — for all intents and purposes — a reclusive ward of my aunt. Two cousins left Brazil entirely, making new lives for themselves in Switzerland and Germany. My uncle eventually returned to Brazil but had to start a new professional life in middle age.

The military's grip on power lasted two decades. And I came of age under its close watch. In September 1966, as a ten-year-old, I witnessed firsthand a brutal and bloody cavalry charge against a peaceful student demonstration in downtown Recife. That was the first time I observed people bleeding on the streets. I watched as college and high school student leaders were thrown into military stockades for their activism.[32] College campuses were regularly surrounded by shock troops to repress student assemblies.[33] As a teen I helped another uncle to rescue a cousin, who was hiding in the chemistry building of her university, from tear gas and police batons.

For most of those twenty years military death squads brutally murdered journalists, professors, union leaders, even priests to quell civic discontent. Father Antonio Henrique Pereira da Silva Neto's brutal assassination was a case in point. A talented young priest in the Roman Catholic Archdiocese of Recife and Olinda, Father Henrique was kidnapped in 1969, tortured, mutilated, and killed in retaliation for the progressive policies of the local archbishop.[34] The photo of Father Antonio's remains was on the front page of our town's newspapers and in the local news. His death hit me hard—when priests are murdered in a heavily Catholic country, no one is really safe.

By the end of it all, a Brazilian blue ribbon commission investigating the military atrocities tallied 339 dead under the regime (many families chose not to come forward with the names of their missing loved ones to the commission, for fear of retaliation).[35] The Roman Catholic Church documented another 1,781 deaths in its own report, while the Landless Workers Movement registered 1,188 deaths for the period.[36] A thorough review of the regime's military records indicates that 7,367 Brazilians were "officially" arrested and at least 1,918 tortured under interrogation. Some 10,034 individuals were interrogated without detention, and 6,385 were imprisoned, though never tried.[37] The military nightmare lasted too long, and as always, its final accounting was much too light.

The Surrealism of Military Regimes

The surreal side of military rule is the rulers' assumption of having ultimate control, of establishing ultimate order. They overestimate their ability to turn populations, societies, and nations into regimented military battalions driven by the same logic and precision of military drills. The right amount of coercion, the right amount of force, they hope, might create an obedient and well-regulated public. So legal and extra-legal mechanisms are developed to "pacify" all forms of unorthodox reaction, and legitimacy is quickly sacrificed for the sake of expediency, until no one is safe anymore. Sadly, in the Brazilian case, the military's obsessive need for control was greatly influenced by French Positivism.

Our military came into full power at the height of that philosophical school's popularity in Brazil. Positivism had represented a secular breath of fresh air in Brazil at the last quarter of the nineteenth century. Until then, Brazilian elites had been schooled in a heavily medieval Roman Catholic view of social order; one based on the distorted form of Iberian Thomism that was exported to the New World. By century's end, Brazil's growing urban centers offered social mobility and cultural opportunities that pushed our emergent middle classes beyond that Iberian worldview.[38] Newspapers, cultural associations, and theaters broadened their tastes, and they turned to Europe and North America for information, lifestyle, and political ideas.

Attracted by the material progress of Europeans and North Americans, the Brazilian middle classes mastered French, English, or German for direct access to news from those countries. Newspapers carried accounts of what was happening in the leading nations of the Western world, and programs of learned societies and cultural associations featured discussions of the technical advances they made. Members of the urban classes traveled abroad, returning to Brazil with nostalgia for all things European (particularly Parisian), and the desire to reproduce its modern way of life in their own homeland.

This surge of new ideas owed much to our improved communications with the rest of the world and the interests of our rising urban middle classes. Once Brazil opened up to new ideas, ideologies like Social Darwinism or Positivism gained influence in urban circles. Those were the theories that inspired the Brazilian middle classes into activism and social reform. Intellectuals, professionals, and military officers created voluntary associations to promote liberal causes such as abolitionism, mass European immigration, federalism, separation of church and state, campaign reform, and a republican form of government. Newly minted military officers came to believe that reason and discipline could ultimately impose rational order on all aspects of life. And they proceeded to take Positivism's tenets to heart as they crafted their role in Brazilian history.

Sizable enough to exert real influence for the first time, flexible enough to welcome innovations, and strong enough to challenge the traditional aristocratic powers, Brazil's middle classes played an important role in opening the nation to modern times. And military officers figured prominently among their leaders. Fresh out of professional schools, open to European ideas, more vocal and influential than their predecessors, they assigned themselves the task of modernizing the nation. If merchants, managers, bankers, industrialists, lawyers, doctors, and teachers talked about effecting social change in their cultural associations, military officers saw fit to deliver it.

So it was that Brazil's armed forces deposed our emperor, D. Pedro II, in 1889, launching the country's republican era. Our first president, Deodoro da Fonseca, was an army marshal. So was the second one, Floriano Peixoto. The Brazilian republic was born under the auspices of Auguste Comte's theory as interpreted by the military. Comte's ideals even adorn our flag. To this day, the Brazilian flag proudly displays the Positivist motto "Order and Progress."

Another irony of military rule in Latin America was the drive to control even the "public morals." Under the guise of preserving public decency, military rulers stretched their tentacles into all forms of media and artistic production. Plays were censored, songs forbidden, news heavily redacted; nothing escaped their scrupulous attention. At the height of the 1960s Brazilian military regime, its censors had developed quite an elaborate index of secular heresies, one that included among other things forbidden books, movies, music, and other "morally subversive" items. Of course, the problem with ultimate control is that life is irrepressible, especially in a region so varied with such multifaceted social life. Latin America's ethnicities, cuisines, festivals, and regional differences all mingle constantly in disorganized ebullience.

There is too much life in the region to be curbed by military design. Musicians do not stop composing, sculptors do not halt their work, and playwrights do not withhold productions for fear of censorship. The flow of creativity remains despite the threat of harsh repression. Latin America's irreverent soul continued to pulse through its artistic creations. That is why one finds brilliant protest songs, such as Chico Buarque's "Apesar de Você," taking over the country by surprise at the height of military censorship, or lyrical odes to life such as Violeta Parra's "Gracias a la Vida" ("thanks be to life, for giving me so much!") reaching a new flair when sung by Mercedes Sosa during Argentina's military rule.[39] Her singing defied the junta's push for control. Exiled, she pressed on from Paris; brought home, her popularity remained unabated. Similar examples abound for every country in the region—life's beat goes on, even under duress.

The Personal Side

As a Protestant, the military pressure to conform hit me twice as hard, for a simple reason. While the Brazilian military ruled the country with an iron hand, the right-wing leaders of my southern faith ruled our denomination in similar fashion. The military need for ideological control gave the religious leaders the perfect excuse to take over the church. Siding with military leaders, they used their newly gained political influence to purge the church of political "heretics." Though the Presbyterian need for order sprang from a different source, the end result was the same. The military censored the media for its criticism of political repression, just as my church censored journalists for promoting liberal ideas that subverted its orthodoxy. The regime saw the creative arts as a threat to their imposed order even as my faith condemned their depravity with equal zeal. The military arrested protestors, while my church conducted its own witch hunt to discipline those who questioned its decrees.

Growing up under these conditions, I felt my life was overregulated for political and metaphysical reasons. It would take me three decades to "exorcise" this absurd need for control—first by leaving my church, then by leaving my country. When I decided to study theology, I enrolled in another denomination's progressive seminary and I chose ordination in the Free Church tradition (the left wing of the Protestant Reformation). My first professional publications as a sociologist exposed the unholy alliance between the Brazilian military and the right wing of the Brazilian Presbyterian Church,[40] documenting the church's use of military connections to deport progressive missionaries, close a liberal seminary, and purge enough congregations and presbyteries to create a separate denomination.[41]

Eventually I would discover that simply running from one's roots is not the answer (no matter how much distance I put between myself and what I perceived to be the source of my oppression, I could no more stop being Brazilian or Presbyterian than I could stop breathing). My roots followed me wherever I went. There is something deeply formative in our childhoods. Not the things we remember—the walks in the parks, the zoos, the family trips—but the things we can't shake loose. But it took me a long time to figure this out. Back then, running away was more appealing, especially in coming to the United States, where Americans have the freedom to reinvent themselves, multiple times if need be. Here I was free to practice reinvention. And practice it I did. Nevertheless, at some point you realize that making peace with your own roots is less psychologically draining. You come to terms with those defining parts of yourself, the parts that run deeper than you first imagined.

The irony, in my generation's case, is that the same America that supplied the Brazilian military with extra gas and ammo also gave us our first taste of freedom. Despite censorship and repression, we Brazilian baby boomers came of age by rebelling against our parents in the same fashion American baby boomers did. Going through adolescence under a state of siege is trickier, but doable (you worry about your parents' curfew as much the military's). But if rock and roll contributed to the American generation gap, it certainly defined my generation. We dodged the close scrutiny of military censors by growing up with Crosby, Stills and Nash, the Turtles, CCR, the Mamas and the Papas, the Byrds.

It was Ana Regina, the older cousin who fled the military siege at the chemistry building, who introduced me to rock and roll. Her earlier boomer wave had discovered it in high school. I was still in middle school when the British invasion hit the United States. She was the one who gave me my first Beatles single. No band has influenced me more. Their songs are as life-giving today as when I first heard them under military rule. Listening to "Let It Be" or "Imagine" under military rule is quite different from watching the Beatles on the *Ed Sullivan Show*. But those songs gave us strength to hang on. They remain incredibly healing to this day.

Unlike my cousin's, my middle school generation came of age to mellower rock and roll sounds. We grew up with Carly Simon, Carole King, Janis Ian, Cat Stevens, and James Taylor. Some of us even found solace in the nature-driven music of John Denver. The year I was a foreign exchange student in New Mexico, his "Rocky Mountain High" hit the top of the charts. John Denver made this urban kid fall in love with the West and the Rockies, a part of America I didn't know yet. He was the first environmental influence in my life.

For the more politically aware in my generation, American folk was the genre that offered the best resources to cope with life under military rule. Simon and Garfunkel's "Sounds of Silence" was prophetic in 1969 Recife, when Brazilian students were being silenced by repression. "Bridge over Troubled Water" was truly an anthem of solidarity (I even got married to that tune!). It comforted an entire generation of Latin Americans persecuted across the region. In college I discovered Joan Baez, then Bob Dylan, then Peter, Paul, and Mary, and through them Woodie Guthrie, Pete Seeger, Ronnie Gilbert, and the Weavers—all fellow comrades in the trenches of my activist youth.

The American protest songs gave us a renewed sense of the possible. Bob Dylan's "Blowing in the Wind" rallied us to hope. Pete Seeger's "Where Have All the Flowers Gone?" showed the futility of military solutions at a time when military solutions were all that we had in Latin America. Phil Ochs's "I Ain't Marching Anymore" called us to pacifism when the Brazilian urban guerrilla was trying to recruit middle-class college students. Finally, Joan Baez's "Gracias a La Vida" reconnected me to Violeta Parra and Mercedes Sosa, a rare instance when my two worlds touched expressively, united by a common struggle against the "rational" war machine.

Of all American music genres, folk hit closest to home. The protest against the Vietnam War paralleled our own struggle against the military in our region. Seeing the picture of an American college kid offering a flower to a soldier in front of the Pentagon was electrifying. Obviously, we could not stage similar demonstrations at the height of the repression, but we lived vicariously through the freedom of our American peers. Their songs were hard to censor since our military censors were not exactly fluent in English. For all their professionalism, our armed forces were not sophisticated enough to distinguish folk from rock and roll. It was all American music, and our military were allied with American business interests. If only they'd known . . .

A New Beginning

I remember well the anniversary of the Brazilian military coup the year my son turned eight. It was a cloudless sky on that March 31 evening. By then I was out of graduate school and we were living in Richmond, Virginia. As always, we followed our nightly ritual—I read him a story before bed, kissed and tucked him in, then turned off the light in his upstairs bedroom, and sat a while by the window. Gazing at the quiet street outside, bathed by the light of a single lamp post, I could see our nearby neighbors going about their usual business. A few living rooms were lit by TV sets; some folks were having late dinner. We lived in a peaceful neighborhood in Henrico County, next to the Tuckahoe public library.

My son, Gui, was a bright, affectionate boy. Born in Nashville, Tennessee, during my graduate school days, he grew up far away from everything that scarred my childhood. His days were filled with science projects, after-school soccer practices, and classmates' birthday parties. We both loved science fiction. I introduced him to the first *Star Wars* trilogy on video, and we eagerly watched weekly episodes of *Star Trek: The Next Generation*. A voracious reader, he was a constant presence at public library events. It thrilled me that he could have a normal childhood, away from the things I had witnessed when I was his age.

It dawned on me that night, as I gazed out the window, that I had never taken the time to introduce my son to my Brazilian roots. Despite our common interests, I never felt pressed to lead him back "home." We never discussed my growing up, or the things I liked to do back then. We never talked about my own family that much. That made me realize I had built a childhood for him that could not be stolen by another Brazilian military coup. Unconsciously, I had built a life for him in America that did not look back to my own country. His childhood could not have been more different from my own, more removed from that tragedy.

Gui would not hear the military trucks pounding the street outside his home as I did as a frightened eight-year-old boy. He would not see the fear in his father's eyes that I witnessed in mine. His uncle would not be arrested, nor his cousin rescued from a campus under military siege. He would not witness a cavalry charge against unarmed student demonstrators. He would not come of age under strict press censorship, lacking the most basic political freedoms. As an American, he would be fully vested by those freedoms from the time he was born. Right then, as I pondered those things, my whole life under military rule came flooding back. Thankfully, by then Gui was sound asleep and could not see my tears. His life would be my family's new beginning in a new world.

3

Naturalization

I have an idea that some men are born out of their due place. Accident has cast them amid strangers in their birthplace, and the leafy lanes they have known from child-hood remain but a place of passage. They may spend their whole lives aliens among their kindred and remain aloof among the only scenes they have ever known. Perhaps it is this sense of strangeness that sends men far and wide in the search for something permanent, to which they may attach themselves. . . . Sometimes a man hits upon a place to which he mysteriously feels that he belongs. Here is the home he sought, and he will settle amid scenes that he has never seen before, among men he has never known, as though they were familiar to him from his birth. Here at last he finds rest.

W. Somerset Maugham, *The Moon and Sixpence*, 1919

Somerset Maugham's words aptly describe those of us who leave homelands in search of more familiar places. It is a search not wholly driven by financial need. Ambition alone cannot explain it. There is more to it. Something else animates the impulse, something about our lives back home feels misplaced, slanted. We cannot explain the strangeness of our birthplaces, nor account for the familiar feel of our destinations. Our families do not understand it. That we do not fully belong to our own befuddles friends and acquaintances, people quite comfortable with their surroundings. But we know better. We sense that there is another place elsewhere, beyond what we have experienced so far, where we will at last find our rest.

I have witnessed such conviction before—in the eyes of my Scottish pastor, during college days. He arrived in Brazil soon after his ordination and never looked back. Decades later, at the end of his career, home was the warm tropics, among a people who could not be more different from his Gaelic roots. That same instinct drove an Italian anthropology professor to find his place in the colonial city of Salvador, Brazil, amid descendants of African slaves. Meeting him at a lecture here in the United States, I had to marvel at how more Brazilian he was than I. Then there was the German seminary professor in Recife, who left his country to escape Hitler. Brazil was not just a point of destination; it became his true homeland. Peregrines all, they came seeking a birthplace among other tribes.

I remember well the first time that sense of the familiar overtook me. Climbing down from an airplane onto the hot New Mexican tarmac as a high school foreign exchange student, I was surprised by how things finally made sense, how life was finally fitting, and how right it felt to be in that place. It is an eerie feeling. I knew no one yet, had found no shelter in this alien plot of land, and there were no assurances that things would work out, that the whole experience might be enjoyable. But I found I could navigate the place as if I had been born and raised in it. Somehow there was something in this society that felt completely natural, astoundingly "familiar."

The same sense of familiarity would return when I made my way back to the United States for graduate studies. My arrival in Louisville, Kentucky, in 1981 felt like a homecoming of sorts. The colonial Williamsburg architecture of its houses and churches could not be further removed from the Iberian wide-walled, red-tiled homes and sanctuaries of my birthplace. Louisville's manicured lawns were a long shot from the dense, chaotic urban architecture of my three-million-people metropolis. In that sense, Recife was more like New Orleans. And yet, Louisville's urbane environs felt right, in ways I could not fully explain at the time. From the first time I was driven to the seminary campus I knew the place "made sense" just as it was.

The interesting thing to me in that familiar feeling is that many of us enjoyed it prior to the fast-paced globalization of today—where ideas, tastes, and consumer goods crisscross the world at lightning speed. Before the era of smart phones, electronic tablets, or the Internet, some of us were already finding homes away from home. Prior to the globalization of fast food, for instance, the taste of American meals felt strangely familiar, desirable, and satisfying to me. Some of the things about my home church in Brazil, about my Presbyterian habits growing up, and about my family's lifestyle became more understandable in Louisville, more real to me, as I immersed myself in the life of the city. I did miss the hustle and bustle of old Recife, my relatives, but there was a clear feeling of being home. This was not a place where people were "of another sort," as the Brazilian sociologist Ana Cristina Braga Martes puts it.[1]

In New Mexico first and later in Kentucky I understood that ever-so-Protestant push for personal autonomy, for operating outside of the grid of kinship connections, of tribal affiliations. While I enjoyed the interactions in the Protestant community of Recife, our sense of solidarity never felt as organic as the Catholic connections I observed among my friends and neighbors, or in the public life of my town. My Catholic friends seemed more burdened by the duties and responsibilities of a tribal life. As a Protestant, I could timidly strike out on my own and have my own world. Coming to America only expanded that space. It was in New Mexico and Kentucky that I affirmed my greater appreciation for self-reliance, for problem solving—alien concepts among my Brazilian peers.

Brazilians grow up under the auspices of the Iberian patronage system, a colonial heritage of asymmetrical relations that coat all aspects of life. Whether in politics, the economy, religion, or family life, people are connected through strong hierarchical ties. Favors are dispensed on the basis of fealty to one's patron. In Latin America all power once flowed from the king to the colonial governors to local powerbrokers, who sustained people's loyalty at all levels by dispensing arbitrary favors and privileges. As Latin American nations became independent, the system was carefully preserved by their new leaders and passed down to us through the generations.[2]

The biggest byproduct of patronage is powerlessness, that lack of self-efficacy that is found among members of any given Latin American community. Solutions for all kinds of problems—large and small—must come from "above," from the rightful "authorities," or they must at least be sanctioned by them, whenever it suits them to do so. Taking charge of local matters, even personal ones, means crossing fealty lines, insulting one's patron for doubting his or her ability to provide for your well-being. That could lead to ostracism and loss of perks and privileges—something few dared to test. The end result is a great deal of inertia when it comes to problem solving in Latin American communities.

Since one must wait upon one's patrons to have problems fixed, people learn to tolerate an enormous amount of indignities, rather than deal with problems as they arise. Those in charge, on the other hand, feel no great sense of accountability toward their "dependents" either.

They do not feel pressed by the needs of others. They are free to solve whatever things they wish to solve, whenever it is convenient to do so. Nothing gets fixed on time, if anything gets fixed at all. The quality of life suffers, things are in a constant state of disrepair, and people make do as much as they can with half-baked "solutions"—emergency fixes of a rather temporary nature.

Patience becomes the ultimate virtue in the Latin American patronage system. One must be able to trust one's patron, to see that in time he will provide the appropriate relief. All will supposedly be taken care of eventually. It is just a matter of things getting prioritized. One should not press for quick solutions. That attitude pervaded people's lives in Recife when I was growing up. There were long lines to pay bills, to get access to health care, or to deal with maintenance of roads, residences, or utilities. As we say in Portuguese, we all had to face life "with Job's patience!"

No wonder I fell in love with the American take-charge approach of my Louisville neighbors. They took matters into their own hands. They found solutions to pressing problems. In doing so, they were never afraid to tinker, to try other things if results were not fully satisfactory. Somehow, despite growing up in Brazil, that approach seemed quite familiar to me. It seemed to affirm something deeply held within me since childhood days. For whatever reasons, I grew up thinking that there had to be better ways to organize life in a community; there had to be better ways for taking charge of one's own life. Life in the United States confirmed my suspicions—it was possible to develop a stronger sense of agency.

Back in Brazil, though, people had to develop creative responses to their waiting-for-your-patron game. When pressed by need, they would rely on their "tribal" connections to create whatever temporary relief they could muster. Extended family or friends in the neighborhood or at work were recruited to find a temporary solution to a problem, one that did not insult the powers of the patron, of course. So if your electricity was cut off by the power company, a neighbor could hook you back up into the grid through his home's connection. Temporarily, of course. That way, daily living was ameliorated without jeopardizing one's loyalty or questioning the patron's ultimate power to fix things.

I can see why my sense of familiarity with American ways tends not to be the predominant reaction of other Brazilian immigrants to this country. Brazilians who arrived in New York in the 1980s and 1990s were put off by the American need for privacy, for personal space, for

autonomy. To Brazilians, this came across as reticence, un[...]
personal distance, or simply rudeness. They found no tribal connections
in the Big Apple, no self-appointed patrons. Their constant complaint
and disappointment was that in the United States the favored disposition was every man for himself, even among their own compatriots
(they might tolerate practical Americans—who did not know any better,
but had no use for the practical Brazilian expats!). Americans seemed
impervious to the Brazilian need to establish a lattice of favor exchanges,
so typical of our tribal ways.

Of course, these immigrants were immersed in a web of close
connections back home. They saw their extended families on a regular
basis, almost daily in fact. Relatives tended to live near each other, and
social life revolved around frequent family interaction. It was not (and
still is not) unusual in Brazil for people to drop in on one another un-
announced. Favors were exchanged constantly. That was the stuff of
everyday life. As they arrived in New York, my fellow Brazilians were
turned off by the simplest things that implied personal distance, such
as the avoidance of eye contact among Americans in public spaces. That
loss of intimacy led them to find Americans cold, lacking in human
warmth and empathy (I would say, cynically, less "reliable"—should
the need for temporary solutions arise).[3]

Nevertheless, despite the wisdom of Maugham's quote, no one
leaves home simply driven by the draw of the alien place. Exiting comes
at too steep a price. No one gives up on her own culture lightly, nor
easily turns her back on family and friends. Leaving home is a painful
process, painful in ways that never abate—no matter how long one has
lived abroad. You keep trying to go on with your life with half of it
missing. It's like putting a giant jigsaw puzzle together without the
appropriate pieces. The Brazilian sociologist Ana Cristina Braga Martes
has perhaps the best description for the process:

> Emigration is a highly selective process from the individual's perspec-
> tive. It requires courage and a willingness to face new risks coming from
> an unknown situation. While Brazilian immigrants show sufficient
> courage to face adversity, they also experience, perhaps in equal mea-
> sure, an unfamiliar personal situation: a feeling of fragility imposed by
> having become a foreigner. This sense comes from the perception that
> they will have to face situations they have not yet deciphered and in
> which they see themselves as lacking, emotionally and otherwise. The
> Brazilians lose much of their previous ability to handle a whole set of
> basic information relative to daily life involving both written and oral

communication—reading a simple street sign, knowing how they should do their jobs, or how to handle a new currency—at the same time that they experience the absence of friends, of family, of their hometowns, of a place where people are "of another sort." Almost everything has to be learned again.[4]

Martes is quite perceptive in her description. Moving to a foreign place means losing the basic coordinates of your everyday life. You face a different language and deal with different food, different pace of life, different norms and etiquette, and different networks at home, work, church, or leisure. No matter how familiar you are (or become) with your host country, you are still out of your full-fledged comfort zone. There is still a good deal of translation to be done even in the most basic of transactions. The move is never complete and never easy, even when things go smoothly.

Then there are the other risks. For instance, one has to deal with the financial toll and interruption to one's career. Not to mention that the kind of money required to migrate is not easy to come by. After obtaining a full scholarship to an American graduate school, I still had to sell all my furniture, wedding gifts, and car to afford a couple of one-way plane tickets for my wife and me. Moreover, fresh out of law school and seminary, my two potential careers had to be put on hold. Rather than applying for a position with the D.A.'s office or seeking employment at a Recife law firm or even considering ministering to a midsized congregation, I arrived in Louisville in 1981 facing the prospect of living on $250 a month for as long as it would take to get a master's and a doctorate before heading back to Brazil.

If there is one thing I learned from being an immigrant and from studying immigrants in this country it is that migration is perceived by others as intentional. But people do not carefully map out every step of their exodus with great precision. None of us has that kind of control over our lives, or the migration process, for that matter. We can't even predict how much being elsewhere will change us. And none of us leaves home thinking that we will not go back. We always assume the foreign sojourn will be temporary, done for a certain time. It takes a long time for that feeling to dissipate. In reality, migration happens in fits and starts, with more twists and turns than most people can imagine. I never planned to stay in the United States; most immigrants do not (at least that is the case for Brazilian immigrants and a good number of other Latinos as well).

At the time I left, there were no doctoral programs in Brazil. The path to a scholarly life led, by necessity, to Europe or North America. And I was not alone in my dreams of returning home afterward. Half of the foreign born who got graduate degrees from American universities in the mid-1980s planned to go home.[5] We all saw ourselves as temporary guests of the United States. There is plenty of evidence that immigrants never see their initial migration as more than provisional.[6] Studying Brazilians in the United States, Maxine Margolis, professor emerita of anthropology at the University of Florida, found that many failed to fill out the 1990 Census forms (and were therefore undercounted) because they planned on a temporary American stay and saw no need to be counted.[7] Think about this—after all the struggle to get to the United States, those folks still saw their status as "here today and gone tomorrow!" A similar sense of temporary stay is found among other immigrant groups, who took a similar approach to being counted by the American Census.[8]

Another important lesson about migration is that it is never a predictable process. Some who move to a foreign country to settle down end up having to return to their homelands. Others come desiring to go home eventually and do so quickly after graduation. Still others travel abroad thinking of returning home but end up overseas for the rest of their lives. When it comes to migration, neither intention nor desire suffices. One needs job opportunities to match one's life chances (either at home or abroad). One needs the right credentials, possibly family connections, and a host region that welcomes immigrants, among other factors.

Take the case of Brazilian hopefuls who arrived in the United States during the last twenty years. They came wishing for a permanent home, perhaps a business of their own, even some financial security; yet now they find themselves returning to Brazil. The economic recession left them stranded as much as it did other Latin American migrants.[9] Thousands of Brazilians left Massachusetts recently, many after losing homes in the subprime mortgage crisis. Some left after a decade of trying to obtain legal status ("You can't spend your entire life waiting to be legal," said one of them). The exodus was not limited to Massachusetts. Many more left from New York, South Carolina, Florida, and California.[10]

The unpredictability of an immigrant's path persists regardless of class, gender, age, income, education, race, or ethnicity. To be sure, there are indeed broader patterns that can be ascertained among certain categories of migrants. Those who live closer to the host country, for instance, may find it easier to have transnational lives, remaining connected at the local level to both home and host nations. But at the individual level, those patterns are not quite as clear, or perhaps they do not hold as stable. White-collar workers face as limited control over their migration process as those seeking asylum or engaging in temporary guest work on American farms.

As for the broader patterns, according to Alejandro Portes and Rubén G. Rumbaut's masterful book on immigration, there are at least four types of migrants who reach our shores: laborers seeking menial and low-paid jobs, professionals following career opportunities, entrepreneurs setting up ethnic businesses, and refugees fleeing political persecution.[11] The migration pathways for all four categories are riddled with uncertainties. Laborers must obtain temporary visas or guestworker permits with no certainty they will be allowed to stay once the job is done. Even those who arrive through the Family Reunification Act might get too homesick to linger here after all. Professionals may find similar attractive employment back home once the economy picks up. While well paid here, they can afford similar lifestyles in their own nations. Entrepreneurs may or may not prosper in their American businesses. And political refugees are always at the mercy of their country's relationship with America.

However they may enter the United States, all four types of immigrants must start at the bottom rung of their respective occupational ladders. Success takes decades of steadfast work and patient climbing, assuming the right doors open at the right time. There are no guarantees. Meanwhile, things back home may get better, or opportunities may appear elsewhere in the United States or other countries. When you're on the move, no situation is ever permanent. Furthermore, your immediate family might have a hard time adapting to local conditions or your children may connect to the host culture in ways you did not expect, nor approve. And you may go for decades without finding a network of expats.

If the process is so unpredictable and uncontrollable, why come to America? Why bother? Besides the impulse described by Somerset Maugham's quote, the answer for Latin Americans is quite simple: the United States still offers opportunities that we cannot find in our own countries. When I left Recife in 1981, Brazil was still under military rule. Had I pursued one of my dream fields, constitutional law, I would have found little room to practice it, since significant sections of the Brazilian constitution had been gutted by the military regime. There were fewer opportunities for freshly minted lawyers—I remember a friend who graduated from law school with me who was driving a taxi to pay the bills. I needed a postgraduate education.

Economically, in the early 1980s, Brazil was beset by endemic problems. Low wages, underemployment, high cost of living, and financial insecurity were the hallmark of my childhood and young adulthood days. My dad worried constantly that the family business would go under. It was hard to develop long-range plans in an economy plagued by tenacious inflation rates. Moreover, for twenty years after my arrival in the States things did not get better back home. In fact, between 1980 and 1992, Brazil went through four currencies, five wage and price freezes, and nine economic stabilization programs. At the end of the period, Brazilians were facing an inflation index of 146 million percent.[12] Those are not exactly favorable conditions to start a career, or to build one's dreams of a middle-class life.

Needless to say, the harsh turn in Brazil's economy took a toll on the middle class. The higher prices of middle-class services fueled Brazil's hyper-inflationary situation. By 1994 middle-class Brazilians, my family included, were facing an upsurge in rent that was over 200 percent. The cost of domestic service rose by 150 percent. Restaurant meals were hiked 66 percent. Medical costs increased by 60 percent.[13] And school fees reached nearly a 50 percent rise (given the precarious conditions of Brazil's public school system, most middle-class families in Brazil send their children to private schools). Faced with such dire conditions, Brazilians left their country in droves for the first time in its history, starting in the mid-1980s.[14]

A key finding of Portes and Rumbaut's study is that the very poor or unemployed seldom migrate, legally or illegally. They lack the resources, the conditions to leave home. In that sense, those who do migrate are positively self-selected in ambition and drive. They are more likely to trade proximity to family and friends for the uncertainties of a new life. They are also more influenced by the advanced conditions of consumption and lifestyle of their host country. And they may be more aware of the opportunities available for those who dare to cross the borders. For instance, prior to coming to the United States for graduate studies, I had already spent six months here as a foreign exchange student.

Portes and Rumbaut's findings resonate with research on Brazilian migration to the United States as well. Margolis's survey of Brazilian immigrants in New York found among my expats a good number of middle-class professionals—psychologists, economists, lawyers, teachers, social workers, and agronomists. These were people who simply could not find adequate, full-time jobs back home. In fact, 34 percent of the Brazilian population was in the middle and lower-middle classes in the early 1990s, compared to 79 percent of the Brazilians in New York. The poor accounted for 60 percent of Brazil's population but only 10 percent of the Brazilian immigrant population Margolis interviewed.[15]

Land of Opportunity

Once here, the opportunities for the driven are real. All you have to do is look at the number of international students who fill up the graduate engineering programs in America. Fifty-five percent of the PhD students in engineering in 2004 were foreign born. So were 33 percent of the students who received PhDs in science and engineering that year. Other fields benefit from the wave of newcomers too. Forty-five percent of PhD physicists working in the United States are foreign-born. Between 1980 and 2000 the percentage of foreign-born PhD scientists and engineers employed in the United States jumped from 24 percent to 37 percent.[16]

No other country in the world offers these kinds of opportunities. According to the *Survey of Earned Doctorates*, out of 43,354 doctorate recipients in 2005, 14,424 (33 percent) were non-U.S. citizens. A 2006 study by the *National Science Foundation* found that international students comprised more than half of all doctorate recipients in the fields of computer science (57 percent), electrical engineering (57 percent), civil engineering (54 percent), and mechanical engineering (52 percent) in America.[17] Those statistics match my own experience. With Vanderbilt's Harold Stirling Vanderbilt Scholarship, I got tuition and living expenses covered to pursue an MA and PhD in Sociology, and was able to complete both programs successfully unencumbered by student loans or school-related debt.

Moreover, some of us who obtain an American graduate education are fortunate enough to find employment in the United States once our training is complete. As fewer Americans choose to go to graduate school these days, the tendency is for the academic job market to absorb a greater number of foreign-born professors. For example, by the early 2000s, 32 percent of geography professors in America were foreign born.[18] In 1987, 98 percent of history faculty in the United States was American-born compared to 89 percent in 2003.[19] The American high-skilled job market continues to attract workers from literally every part of the world. They come because the prospects are here. Although the pathway to American citizenship is uncertain and unpredictable, opportunities for the foreign born in America are quite real.

In return, the United States profits from attracting highly motivated and talented international workers. Twenty-seven out of eighty-seven American Nobel Prize winners in medicine, more than 30 percent, were foreign born.[20] In the mid-1970s one-fifth of all U.S. physicians were foreign born; by 2000 they represented almost 30 percent.[21] The American space program was launched by Werner von Braun's German team, relocated to the United States after World War II. Albert Einstein explored theoretical physics from the comforts of a Princeton home, in New Jersey. The Frankfurt School of Social Sciences relocated entirely to Columbia University to flee the Nazi regime, expanding several fields of scholarly research in the United States at once.

And the benefits brought by foreign workers are long lasting, for the most part. There isn't a scholarly field in America that has not profited from the long-term work of foreign-born professors, whether by their steady intellectual production over many decades or their training of generations of American scholars. Foreign-born intellectuals can be found in the natural sciences, social sciences, and the humanities in America's academia. In social sciences alone, one finds giants like the German political scientist Hannah Arendt, the Austrian sociologist Peter Berger, or the Polish anthropologist Bronisław Malinowski. Their work had a lasting influence, and the generations they trained are still building upon their scholarly legacies.

Even my modest career exemplifies the advantages of attracting international scholars to the United States. By my calculations, since 1986 I have taught close to five thousand American college students, supervised eleven graduate students, published four books and twenty-five articles, and made forty-four scholarly presentations in professional conferences. But my contribution pales in comparison to someone as prolific in his field as Dr. Mohamed S. El-Aasser. Dr. El-Aasser, an Egyptian professor of chemical engineering at Lehigh University, has advised more than one hundred fifty master's students, doctoral students, and postdoctoral fellows. He also authored five books, produced four hundred scientific articles, and holds nine patents in his field.[22]

Moreover, academia is not the only area benefitting from immigrant contributions. Take the U.S. military, for instance—foreign-born troops have defended the United States since the War of Independence. In the Civil War alone, 500,000 immigrant troops fought in the Union Army. Noncitizen American soldiers in World Wars I and II and the Korean War benefited from Section 329 of the Immigration and Nationality Act, which allowed 174,000 of them to become naturalized. Today, there are more than 60,000 immigrants on active duty in the U.S. armed forces, making up nearly 5 percent of all enlisted personnel. Of the 3,406 Congressional Medal of Honor recipients, 716—more than 20 percent— were immigrants.[23]

American business also depends on immigrant contributions. Immigrant labor sustains a number of industries in our diversified economy. Hispanics alone, as the second-largest group of U.S. workers (some 13 percent of the labor force), will account for half its growth between now and 2020.[24] The U.S. Small Business Administration calculates that immigrants represent almost 17 percent of business owners in America, generating $67 billion of $577 billion total annual income. Immigrants are responsible for a quarter of all business income in California and nearly one-fifth in New York, Florida, and New Jersey.[25]

Even temporary low-wage jobs in America depend upon the drive and preparation of incoming immigrants. According to Maxine Margolis's New York sample, more than three-quarters of Brazilian immigrants who did menial work in the early 1990s had at least a high school education (at that time only 32 percent of the Brazilian population had graduated from high school). Nearly half had some university training, and close to one-third held college degrees. The levels for Brazilians in the greater Boston area are quite similar.[26] Ironically, menial jobs in America paid better than professional jobs in Brazil. Almost none of the Brazilian immigrants working in New York had been employed in manual labor prior to arriving in the United States.[27]

Immigrants like that drive up American productivity. The New York Brazilians compensated for their low wages by working multiple jobs. Almost a quarter of those interviewed held more than one job at the time of the study. A fair number had two full-time jobs, getting very little sleep along the way. They did so despite the temporary condition of their dead-end jobs, which kept them constantly looking for new sources of employment. Pursuing their dream of success, like other Latino immigrants in the United States, the New York Brazilians kept hopping from job to job, seeking better wages, better hours, and better working conditions.[28]

Long and Winding Road

If migration benefits both migrant and host country, why aren't more outsiders moving to the United States? The answer is simple—given the large volume of applicants, even when done by the book, immigration and naturalization are slow and cumbersome processes. All travelers to the United States need an entry visa to come legally into the country. The types of entry visa range from family reunification to studying to opening a business to being a temporary worker or even a refugee. Once here, of course, the next step is to obtain a legal permanent resident visa, a green card. Green-card holders are allowed to work, to travel abroad, to own property on U.S. soil, and they can eventually request American citizenship.

But the immigration logjams start at the entry visa point. By 2004 the total backlog for entry visa applications to the United States stood at 4.7 million petitions. Meanwhile, family reunification visas that year were capped at 480,000, employment visas at 140,000, and the White House set the limit for refugees at 70,000.[29] It is not hard to see why the logjam keeps growing. The funneling effect starts at the entry level. Once here, immigrants come up against further backlogs. By law only 140,000 green cards are issued annually. So the backlog for green-card requests is equally staggering, with a waiting period that runs up to five years or more.[30] By one estimate there are currently 615,000 people waiting for their green cards.[31] Then you have the backlog for citizenship, too. Some 1.4 million green-card holders sought to become U.S. citizens in 2007, double the number of requests for 2006.[32]

As you clear each logjam, be prepared to pay a series of hefty fees to change your immigration status. The application for employment authorization costs $340. The fee for a green card is now about $930, with an $80 separate fee for collection of fingerprints and associated biometric data. The final step, the application for naturalization, costs $595. Those fees are expected to go up soon.[33] If you are an employer, sponsoring an immigrant could cost you from $3,000 to $5,000 in fees. But if his green card is delayed for six years or more, the employer has to apply for extensions.[34] Of course, the fees do not include the immigrant's own legal expenses. Successful immigration cases, managed by competent immigration attorneys, can range anywhere from $5,000 to $20,000.

Obviously, the logjams and time delays complicate the immigration and naturalization processes, exacting quite a toll on those waiting for a status change. I entered the United States in 1981 on a student visa (F-1), planning to finish my MDiv and PhD programs at the Southern Baptist

Theological Seminary and return to Recife for a career in theological education, possibly ministry. Upon completing my MDiv, I discovered that the mission board sponsoring my U.S. studies was altering our agreement. I was told to return to Brazil for two years prior to requesting a renewed sponsorship for the PhD. Not willing to postpone my doctoral studies, I decided to transfer to a secular university.

When Vanderbilt University accepted me into the PhD program, my immigration status changed to that of a visiting scholar (H-1 visa). That visa allowed me to work on campus for a maximum of twenty hours a week. The campus job paid my bills except for large-scale expenses (you pray you won't get sick or need hospitalization, or that the car will not break down, etc.). But I never dared to travel abroad from 1983 to 1994, since there were no guarantees that my Certificate of Eligibility for Non-Immigrant Student Status (I-20) would be renewed. The inability to go home was an added hardship causing me to miss a number of critical events in the life of my extended family. I missed the funerals for my father, my grandparents, and my aunt. When Dad passed away, I had my green card but could not get the appropriate paperwork done in time to go pay my final respects.

There were missed joyous occasions as well. I missed my brothers' graduations and weddings. I missed the births of my nephew and my cousins' children. Each time my family moved into a new home, I missed the housewarming parties. Each time they took a new job or started a business, I missed the appropriate celebrations. Family reunions were not frequent, thus ever more precious. I missed them all. Waiting for a green card or a final naturalization ceremony makes for a lonely exile. True, life here gets better, you finish school, you get a good job, you start your career, but at the cost of being unavailable to your loved ones back home. I dedicated my PhD dissertation to my nanny, but I was not there to pay my final respects to her, a woman who was such an important part of my childhood.

My path to a green card came through teaching at a community college during my dissertation-writing days. That school became my job sponsor with the Immigration and Naturalization Services. To hire me, they had to prove to the American government that they could not find any qualified Americans who could do my future job. Thankfully I had enough graduate credits in counseling, philosophy, ethics, and sociology to make me a unique candidate for the position they advertised. Nevertheless, what was supposed to have been a thirty-six-day process took four years to complete. By the time the green card was issued I was already on my way to a tenure-track job in Virginia.

After clearing all the hurdles in my green-card application, I bumped into one further step. Foreign students who complete graduate studies in the United States are expected, due to international agreements between the United States and their countries, to spend two years back home prior to accepting an American job. This has to do with preventing brain drain, with keeping the United States from "stealing" highly qualified workers from other nations. Never mind that the Brazilian government did not contribute a dime toward my graduate education. Never mind that they had offered me no jobs had I returned. I still had to request a waiver from the Brazilian authorities in order to finalize the green-card process.

Since there is a five-year waiting period before green-card holders can petition the American government for naturalization, it took me a decade to finally become an American citizen. After my son was born in Tennessee, I had decided to stay in the United States, and that led to the community college job offer. The school applied for my green card in 1989. It arrived in 1993. But I would not become a U.S. citizen until 1999, literally ten years after my initial application. In my case, doing everything by the book meant that I would spend those ten years of my life in suspense, waiting to find out whether my American stay was temporary or permanent. And that did not include the previous eight years I had spent in graduate school on student visas.

Requiring someone to put his life on hold for ten years is a hardship. Looking back now, I realize that I risked a lot. The consequences would have been severe had I not gotten the green card and become naturalized. Professionally, it would have meant going back to Brazil to restart my academic career after spending those ten years in the United States. Starting again in Brazil at the age of forty-three would have been difficult to say the least. My son was born in 1986. By the time I became an American citizen, he was an eighth grader and the United States had been the only home he had ever known. By then I had been divorced for two years. Thankfully, his Brazilian mother got her green card through my employment application. That way she did not have to return to Brazil while I stayed here with our son.

The irony is that I consider my personal immigration and naturalization experience as one of the most successful I have known. At no time was I required by American immigration authorities to leave the country and restart the process with the American Embassy back in my homeland. At no time was I deported or denied re-entry for overstaying my visa (something I took great pains to avoid). At no time did I breach my legal welcome, or was forced to go underground due to missing documentation or misunderstanding between my immigration attorney and the U.S. authorities. Despite the fact that U.S. immigration authorities lost all the original documents I submitted to them three times, documents difficult to produce in a pre-digital-era Brazil, I still managed to get through the whole thing without major disruptions.

I can't imagine what the process must be like for immigrants who come to the United States in other visa categories. The backlog for those who migrate through the Family Reunification Act, for instance, has reached approximately 4 million applicants in 2010. The average wait for a sibling of a Filipino American to be issued an entry visa is twenty years.[35] The delays for business immigrants, guest workers, or those seeking asylum as political refugees is quite lengthy as well. As Judy Golub, the spokeswoman for the American Immigration Lawyers Association, put it, "Legal permanent residents often wait up to twenty years to reunite with their spouses and children." To her, "Such long separations make no sense in our pro-family nation and reflect poorly on us."[36]

One thing is certain. Migration is not for the faint of heart.

Becoming an Alien

Those of us who, in the words of Somerset Maugham, go "far and wide in the search for something permanent," fail to realize something crucial in our quest. Simply settling in a new land does not a native make. Our drive to seek the familiar abroad and our sense of comfort upon arriving at our new destination delay our perception that our hosts may not be welcoming us with open arms. Though we may feel that we belong to this new place, the feeling may not be reciprocal. Though familiar with our new country, we may still be seen as outsiders. It took me a while to discover that. Language fluency, American mannerisms, and awareness of local etiquette do smooth social relations. And time-in-country aids our seizing of local ways. But none of that accomplishes tribal inclusion. All along, there remains an invisible line, which cannot be easily crossed. We live among them, but are still not of them.

Newcomers to the land, we might not see the barrier at first. After a few mishaps, we grow wise in sensing its boundaries. In a way, that is the dark side of Somerset Maugham's wise quote. We may be home in the new place, but we settle amid alien scenes, and we live among folks we may never fully know. Tragically, the longer we are here, the less our loved ones in our country of origin will understand us. They remain forlorn with our departure and eventual transformation. And our new relations will constantly measure our performance in their culture by their own standards. Thus, the price of "coming home" is to remain strangers—to our homeland folks and to our hosts in the new country.

Very few migration studies explore this duality of strangeness. But we immigrants know it well. It comes up whenever we gather, at work or leisure. We are constantly reminded of what it takes to navigate both worlds. We know which parts of us are missing when we visit home, and which are missing as we return to our new nation. We identify with certain things local residents of one place or the other do, and dislike others. We dwell in that netherworld created by the cherry-picking of elements from disparate cultures. Our identities always carry this mix of traits that are appreciated by both, and also traits that make us strangers to either group. Wherever we immigrants are, we share the same sense of wonder and frustration with the way we fit our surroundings.

We ponder what it must be like to be fully home in a single world. The questions multiply—why are certain virtues more cherished by one society than another? Are there any truly universal tastes? What social expectations are non-negotiable in a given society; which are flexible? Why? What social markers attest to one's "native status?" If so, why are natives unaware of their own markers? Things that seem so obvious to us easily escape folks who fully inhabit a single culture. For them, their way of life is just "the way things are." They are blessed with a healthy dose of ethnocentrism, that marvelous belief that their society's ways are superior to those of others.[37]

Ethnocentrism is critical to group survival. The deeper one believes in the merits of her own society, the more she has a stake in preserving it. So, ethnocentrism fosters group solidarity. Without it, social cohesion (and social order) might collapse. In that sense, a nation's values represent the ultimate commitment its citizens make to each other as a group. Their norms set the baseline for appropriate and inappropriate behavior among its members, and for belonging or not to that particular community. Those who grow up in that group pick those norms up as part of their "natural" world. And their adherence to those standards engenders among them a deep sense of commonality, of group loyalty.

Ethnocentrism is formed over time, of course. In its daily dealings, a community generates the values and norms it needs to organize or smooth in-group relations and interactions. Children born to that community acquire those ways as they become fully functional members of the group. To group members, their behavior is the only appropriate way to live. "Insiders" don't distance themselves much from their group standards, lest they incur the group's penalties for deviating from "normal" behavior. This is why ethnocentrism leads group members to use their shared values as a yardstick by which to judge outsiders—people who do not follow or fit in their ways. Learning to recognize outsiders is important, because it helps members of the group reaffirm its boundaries, acknowledge its common identifiers.

Ethnocentrism works as the internal glue of a community. But it does little to prepare natives to positively appreciate or engage with the ways of other cultures. Ethnocentrism can smooth relationships within a group, but not as easily relationships between groups. As a result, members of a group develop cultural blinders as they gaze upon the ways of outsiders. Their ethnocentric approach to culture keeps them from realizing the relative nature of their customs, of their value judgments. They don't immediately assume that what they hold dear is simply a collective statement of preference. Instead, the question becomes, "the way we do things is the right way—who would not want to be like us?"

Since all communities have unique histories, their histories create different ways to address unique local problems. The value judgments of a given group simply represent the way it chooses to handle certain aspects of its common life. Other societies may find equally acceptable but distinct ways to reach the same goals, but the members of a given group are not aware of that. For instance—not every culture practices monogamy, not every culture raises children inside nuclear families, and not every culture recognizes kinship on both the mother's and father's side. And yet children in all those societies grow up fully acclimated to their ways and continue to perpetuate their values and norms without any major social disruption.

For group members, however, their norms and ways of life are not an option. They are the ultimate markers that set the insider apart from the alien in a given culture. Those of us who have lived in more than one society know that norms or values are not fixed. Monocultural folks are not so quick to buy that. So, learning to adapt to a host culture means understanding what it prizes and why. For outsiders, this adds a "layer," a second lens with which they now must perceive or interpret their new world.

But unlike a child born in that culture, we know we are adopting it. We know ours is an optional, intentional act on our part. We must learn to reason differently about the way we do things; we must develop different aspirations. Becoming ethnocentric in a new culture is a demanding process—one that feels very natural if you grew up in that community, but very artificial if you are picking it up later in life. And between those two cultural layers lies our tribal exclusion. Somehow, natives can tell when our adopted behavior falls short of the mark, when it comes across a bit artificial. They know it does not come naturally to us to act like them. So living abroad means engaging in constant rehearsals, in constant practice at being like people of our adopted country.

Furthermore, what makes learning a new culture even more difficult is that often the values prized by folks in a particular country reflect deep, contradictory social undercurrents. For instance, immigrants learn that Americans prize individualism even as we watch them work really hard to fit in, to conform at the same time—be it at work, in the neighborhood, or at the club. A nation's values are not necessarily logically ordered. They betray the group's internal conflicts, tensions, fissures. The values may contribute to the group's survival, but that does not assure their ultimate congruence. For those coming from the outside, that nuanced reading of an alien culture takes time, sensitivity, and a deep desire to belong.

Pledging Allegiance

If you are my age and grew up in Latin America, you are probably un-familiar with the Anglo-Saxon need to swear public oaths. Pledge-making was part of our private lives, of course; but not public oaths, and never as an outward display of patriotism. We learned our national anthems in grade school, perhaps the state anthem, and a few assorted civic hymns. We lined up every morning at the school patio for the hoisting of the flag. And we pulled for our countries during international games and tournaments. But pledging allegiance was never part of our cultural vocabulary. We simply were our country's citizens, period. There was no choice but to ally ourselves with our own tribe. To us, pledging allegiance made no sense, since everything we did was im-mersed in our Brazilian-ness, Chilean-ness, Uruguayan-ness. Allegiance was implicit.

Only as a teenager in New Mexico did I discover the Anglo-Saxon need to swear public oaths. A foreign exchange student, I was confronted with the school ritual of the pledge of allegiance since the pledge was a constant presence in school activities. At first, the ritual felt very odd, very alien to me. That any natural-born citizen would be required to swear an oath of loyalty to his own country seemed a bit of overkill. But I could tell that those around me took it seriously. As a hallowed practice, the pledge was done willfully and without reservation (many times out of sheer force of habit). Only later, as a trained sociologist, would I dwell more carefully on the need for public displays of tribal allegiance. Back in New Mexico, the thought of pledging allegiance to one's own country seemed excessive.

Who else could my classmates pledge allegiance to, I wondered? Mexico? Canada? Born here, they knew no other way of life; they had lived in no other culture. Who could they be loyal to other than the only place they had ever known? And the more I learned about the pledge itself, the more puzzled I became. That it was written in 1892 by Francis Bellamy, a Baptist minister and Christian Socialist, to foster patriotism among readers of a popular children's magazine made little sense.[38] The hallmark of the Baptist faith in the European Continent had been the separation of church and state, especially the freedom from oath-swearing! Why would a Baptist minister in the New World be so concerned with children's loyalty to their own country?

This is what I mean by cultural blinder. Something that makes perfect sense to a native is quite befuddling to the outsider. To a Latin American, who witnessed waves of military regimes break their promises to citizens, oath-swearing was simply meaningless. It cost nothing to mouth off words. It reminded me of what Dietrich Bonhoeffer, the German theologian, called "cheap grace," a promise devoid of any sacrifice. No self-discipline was required, no follow-through. The promise itself was the end goal. Nothing further was asked of those who swore it. By comparison, for us in Latin America, the point of living right seemed to be the faithful discharge of one's duties, not the pledging of it.

But if you grew up in an Anglo-Saxon culture, public oath-swearing was simply part of your larger civic life. Even British monarchs swore a coronation oath upon ascending to the throne, promising to govern their subjects according to the laws and customs of the land. Parliament passed the Coronation Oath in 1688, but an older version was already in use in 1660.[39] British kings demanded the same swearing of their subjects. The Oath of Supremacy established by King Henry VIII in 1534, repealed by Queen Mary I, and re-established by Queen Elizabeth I in 1559, was required of anyone taking public or church office. The subject had to swear allegiance to the monarch as "Supreme Governor of the Church of England." Later on, the same oath was required of members of Parliament and those attending English universities. Failure to comply could lead to indictment for treason, as Sir Thomas More, the Roman Catholic counselor to King Henry VIII, discovered. He was tried and executed in 1535 on that account.[40]

Clearly, the practice of public oaths transferred to the British colonies in the New World. To this day, an oath of office is still a common observance in the United States at all levels of government. Presidents, members of Congress, and Supreme Court justices are all sworn in at the beginning of their terms in office. That carries through to the state and local levels as well. Every citizen who registers to vote in Vermont is required to swear a Voter's Oath before a notary public. Vermont established the practice in its 1777 constitution.[41] So, there is something to public pledging among people of Anglo-Saxon descent that almost rises to the level of the holy, something akin to civil religion.

Back in New Mexico, I never knew what to do as the occasion arose to pledge allegiance. On the one hand, I was not a citizen. Those around me knew that quite well. On the other, the pressure to conform was intense. Nothing feels more isolating than to be caught in a public ceremony as the only nonconformist. When everyone around you stood up and recited the oath, you had no choice but to follow them. Yet, what a strange experience it was, to pledge allegiance to another homeland at the tender age of fifteen. Part of me knew this was only a formality, a cherished rite of an alien culture. But there was something terribly amiss in the exercise. The rights and privileges covered by the oath did not apply to me. That may have been my first exercise in tribal exclusion.

Public oaths in the Anglo-Saxon world are meant to divide, to sift, to make visible distinct categories. When King Henry VIII demanded an Oath of Supremacy from his subjects, he used it to screen out the Roman Catholics in his kingdom. The oath bestowed advantages to some, and dispensed—in Sir Thomas More's case—deadly consequences to others. In the United States, the oath of office segregates the office holders from the rest of us. In Vermont, since 1777, it sets apart those who are eligible and willing to vote from those who are not. In the Anglo-Saxon world, oaths preserve the tribal boundaries of restricted communities. Thus, I should not have been surprised that the final step in my naturalization process would be the swearing an oath of allegiance to the United States at a public ceremony in an American court.

In fact, oath day is supposed to be the festive part of naturalization. Local papers and TV stations drop by the courthouse to cover the proceedings, while the Daughters of the American Revolution festoon the court chambers in civic motif to welcome the new citizens. Some ceremonies are even scheduled for important civic holidays, like July 4. Or they take place in hallowed locales like Independence Hall in Philadelphia or Mount Vernon, Washington's home in Virginia. This is the country welcoming brand-new citizens, so the red carpet is rolled out at last. As the final step to becoming an American, the oath carries tremendous symbolic meaning. But its demands make for quite a somber day for those of us who must swear it, for it separates us permanently from our birthplace and loved ones back home. Before an immigration judge, we swear the following:

> I hereby declare, on oath, that I absolutely and entirely renounce and abjure all allegiance and fidelity to any foreign prince, potentate, state or sovereignty, of whom or which I have heretofore been a subject or citizen; that I will support and defend the Constitution and laws of the United States of America against all enemies, foreign and domestic; that I will bear true faith and allegiance to the same; that I will bear arms on behalf of the United States when required by the law; that I will perform noncombatant service in the armed forces of the United States when required by the law; that I will perform work of national importance under civilian direction when required by the law; and that I take this obligation freely without any mental reservation or purpose of evasion; so help me God.[42]

All of us who swore the oath that day had no problem supporting and defending the U.S. Constitution or the laws of the country. Nor did we have problems with bearing faith and allegiance to them. The pacifists among us might have struggled with the notion of bearing arms to defend our adopted nation, but the noncombatant service option would have assuaged them. I do not think that any of us pledged the oath with mental reservation or purpose of evasion. After all, we chose to become Americans; no one forced us. It was the first part of the oath that weighed heavily on our minds. Publically, in front of representatives of our adopted community, we were asked to absolutely renounce our homelands, to forfeit all allegiance to our birthplace, and to turn our backs on the home where we were raised.

This was not an easy promise to make, and no one I know did so with a light heart. Of course, we were glad to have become American citizens. Many of us had waited decades for the ceremony. Our friends honored us with their support at the occasion. But something very dear was given up that day. As immigrants, we understood the need for such an oath. We understood that we could not serve two masters. We understood that we had to start our citizenship in a new nation unencumbered by former loyalties. But the choice is neither easy nor joyful. The Daughters of the American Revolution present at our ceremony failed to comprehend that deep sadness, focusing instead on our bright future ahead. But we said goodbye to our past that day in such a public and irrevocable fashion.

Ironically, after I became a U.S. citizen, I was informed by the Brazilian Embassy that Brazil's constitution had been changed to recognize dual citizenship. It was now possible, at least on the Brazilian side, for me to remain a citizen of both countries. "But should you prefer to keep only your American citizenship you will have to request from the Brazilian government the divestment of your rights as a Brazilian citizen," instructed the embassy website. So, it turns out that my country of birth allows me to fully forsake it, but only in a public statement, one that has to be published in the official acts of the Brazilian Congress. Even Latin American countries now have ways to segregate their former citizens.

A "Hyphenated" American

Not long after my naturalization ceremony one of my Anglo professor friends asked in half-jest, "How does it feel to be a Hispanic-American now?" Despite living in the U.S. for eighteen years and teaching about race and ethnicity regularly, I was not prepared for the "joke." Only then did the importance of ethnic boundaries finally dawn on me. In my new homeland, I was not simply to be an American. I had to be a "hyphenated" one. Never had I felt with such clarity the full force of ethnic divide. In return, I mentioned something self-deprecating and stumbled back to my office. But the remark eventually prompted me to start a line of research on immigration studies. I needed to find out who else shared my ethnic niche. What other folks were assigned the same label?

So I turned the experience of exclusion into a professional project—a five-year study of Latinos in the greater Richmond area, as far as I know the first survey research of Latinos in Virginia.[43] Looking back now, I realize the research was my way of coping with being culturally pigeonholed. In truth, my family came from Italy to Brazil, bypassing the whole Spaniard heritage. But in the United States, for all intents and purposes, I was Hispanic.[44] That is the tiresome thing about migrating—that ever-present feeling that you will never reach home. You swear allegiance to a host country only to find out that your Zion remains quite elusive, a receding horizon at best. Sure, there are places for people like me in this country, that is with our own kind and long history of exclusion.

The niche was there all along, lurking. Studying Latinos in Richmond fleshed out, experientially, its dynamics—the construction of "safe" American cultural ghettoes. As part of the immigrant experience, they shelter minorities in a solidarity and dignity of their own, while keeping them simultaneously apart from the dominant group. In other words, hyphenation means always dealing with feeling "almost there." In a sense, no matter how long you live in the place, how well-integrated you become, you are still an outsider. There is no solace for that kind of parsing out. One puts up with it, but it is not a chosen manner of living.

Nevertheless, among other Latinos in the greater Richmond area, I found a rich tribe of sorts. We hailed from many countries. We had diverse tastes. But here we were, lumped together under one large cultural umbrella, one easily recognizable by the dominant group. So we danced together, shared joys and sorrows, and tried to make the best out of the situation. Our kids attended the same schools. We shared a few neighborhoods in the area. There were ethnic associations that sponsored soccer leagues and cultural events. We tried to create a pan-ethnic identity as part of the effort to integrate ourselves into this patchwork society.

Traditionally, citizenship was established by birth (*jus sanguinis*) or soil (*jus soli*). *Jus sanguinis* is the "right of blood." It is an inheritance—as citizens of a nation, your parents bestow their same citizenship upon you. *Jus soli* refers to citizenship from place of birth, or "right of soil." Those born in a territory are by right its citizens. Most countries, in fact, use a mix of the two as criteria for legal citizenship. My son, born in the United States, is an American citizen by *jus soli* and a Brazilian citizen by *jus sanguinis*. In modern times *jus matrimonii*, citizenship by marriage, has become another common tool of incorporation, just as with naturalization—which allows one to choose his own nationality.

In medieval days, a person's political identity was determined by the lord he served. The connection between lord and subject was permanent. One could not simply choose to relocate to other lands. Vestiges of that legal straightjacket are still found today in failed communist countries like North Korea or Cuba. But in modern times, nationality is more portable. It represents someone's legal tie to the state insofar as it concerns the rights and privileges appertaining to citizenship—the freedom to reside permanently in a given country, the right to work, to vote, and to run for office. Of course, along with it come the duties of citizenship—serving in the country's armed forces, paying taxes, performing jury duty, and the like. That it is possible nowadays to obtain those rights from a place not of one's birth is the real novelty.

Finding Rest, at Last

Sociologically speaking, the novelty springs from the loose connection between nation and state. As modern history shows, the boundaries of nation and state do not always coincide. The ties of nation tend to be more tribal, more tinged by ethnicity, by cultural difference, by local flavor. They reflect a similarity of language, faith, habits, customs, and origin—aspects that play the more important role as people sort insiders from outsiders. A country like Yugoslavia, for example, could house multiple nations—sometimes with horrible results, like ethnic cleansing. Nevertheless, given the tribal connections, it should not surprise us that there are more nations than states in the world.

For me, as a sociologist and an immigrant, these tribal ties reach deeper than any certificate of naturalization, passport, or ID card. Tribal connections are more basic, more instinctive. No public ceremony fully rends them asunder. We belong to those who birth us, who raise us, who shelter and nourish us above all else. Parts of that may happen in our country of origin, parts may take place in our adopted land. That we may choose other shores and acquire other nationalities is a blessing, but knowing who our people are provides the ultimate anchor. We are theirs and they are ours, for good or ill. They provide the foundation for our journey; their affinity normalizes our sense of being, our sense of identity.

There is an elegant nomadic tribe in Kenya, the Gabra, who practice a beautiful ritual of mutuality called *dabare*.[45] Gabra families down on their luck can ask neighbors whom they once helped for a gift in return. Gift-giving in pastoral societies usually involves livestock. The Gabra's gift exchange serves as a form of community trust, a stock of goodwill that will not allow any of them to fall into destitution. They have a powerful proverb that says, "If someone cries out and no one responds, is there a person crying?" There must be those in our lives to whom we are that accountable. Hearing that proverb for the first time, I finally understood why ostracism was the worst form of punishment for the ancient Greeks, one worse than death. We ache to belong, to be known as we know.

But lest I give the impression that I'm an unhappy hyphenated American, let me once again claim Maugham's quote in saying that here in the United States, at last I have also found rest. Despite the hardships, delays, and ups and downs of immigration, migrating does free you to choose your basic ties. Among Americans of all walks of life, I have found ties as strong as those I shared with my folks back home. My connection with them transcends race, ethnicity, or any other form of social distancing. These are the people in the United States who grieved with me in the death of a parent, and who celebrated the joyous birth of my son. Somehow, they chose me as I chose them, for the long haul.

And therein lies, perhaps, the hidden grace of migration—the wondrous surprise of finding, amid strangers, those who belong to you. With them you mark the seasons of your life, and share theirs as well. They do not reach you out of utility. You do not seek them for profit or gain. There is nothing practical in your meeting. Somehow, the opportunity appears, and they and you decide to share the journey. With them, at last, as Somerset Maugham predicted, you are home. With them you make a tribe that breaks the insider/outsider mold.

By fortune or circumstance, during graduate days in Nashville, my wife and I ended up with two sets of adoptive parents, generous people, who, knowing little about us, decided to look after us as if we were their own. They opened their homes and families to us. There followed regular Sunday dinners, much-celebrated birthdays, and delightful vacations. It is hard to explain why those four people would take in a couple of Brazilian strays and turn them into kin. But that is exactly what happened. With them, there were no emotional barriers or distance. They confided in us and shared our concerns about our respective extended families. They helped us survive the resettlement issues and the early stages of our American sojourn. We followed one couple to the end and still visit their graves every time we are in Nashville.

I met a PhD candidate in graduate school who became my older brother. Despite our different origins—he was the only child of a blue-collar factory worker in Memphis—we quickly bonded. There was much that we shared—we both struggled with the point of graduate school, with our dads' expectations for us, with our marriages, and with finding our place in the world. Harmon Wray had a deep commitment to inclusion. He was equally at home with graduate students and with death-row inmates he ministered to. He spent more than three decades ministering, attending to their spiritual needs. His work became so important to him that he never finished his dissertation.

To me, Harmon embodied the southern notion of radical grace that I had found in Will Campbell's writings. He deepened my knowledge of the Radical Reformation and schooled me further in all things southern. Most of all, our relationship was really one of family—no matter how much time had passed between us or how busy we had been, we were always on the same page every time we visited.

So many other "self-appointed" kin have impacted my American journey, such as the seminary professor who taught me Christian social ministries. She grew up in a denomination where leadership positions for women were few. And yet that never deterred her from doing the work, from pursuing her calling. She was the first person who highlighted the importance of a cultivated life to me, especially for those of us committed to a lifetime of social activism. A social worker and an artisan, she modeled the pursuit of justice as well as beauty, and spent her entire career training men and women to work in children's homes, social service agencies, elder care, nursing homes, and hospices.

Then there was the cosmopolitan PhD student, specializing in biblical art and archeology, who turned the Bible into an intriguing piece of literature for me, one full of human passion and emotion. Or the divinity school friend, a rising Methodist minister, who taught me that fellowship and solidarity were far more important than orthodoxy (not an easy lesson for a recovering Presbyterian!). There was the community organizer who introduced me to civil rights activists all over the South, and who remains a sister for life. And the Presbyterian minister who visited Recife and sponsored my graduate work in the United States and who accompanied me, step by step, during graduate days.

At Vanderbilt I would find my fair share of fellow travelers, such as the African American philosophy professor who guided me through two semesters of reading Marx. Or the German émigré, who shared my notions of self-exile and supported my transfer to the graduate program in sociology; and the Jewish scholar, who touched me with his commitment to labor studies and who has remained a lifetime mentor. Finally, I was fortunate enough to arrive at Vanderbilt at a time when the university was hiring a young expert in Brazilian history. UCLA-trained (UCLA had one of the best Brazilian Studies programs in the United States), he helped me piece together parts of my country's history that had been censored back home. He also shared my bicultural condition, for he spent his life between two cultures. Sometimes talking to him was like looking at an inverted mirror.

At my first professional post, the University of Richmond, I was fortunate to find fellow travelers as well. Two of them were central to my early career—the senior anthropology professor in my department and the fellow assistant professor in communications and rhetoric. The senior prof took me under his wing, and patiently modeled the life of a scholar and caring, but exacting teacher. He took me on hikes and canoeing, but most of all, taught me to delight in the life of the mind. There was a practical and intellectual curiosity about that man that inspired emulation. He remains my benchmark for academic excellence. The fellow assistant professor shared the hard grind of tenure track with me, along with a similar childhood faith and the desire to do good, meaningful work in this world.

Then there is the larger circle of friends, fellow travelers in this self-imposed exile: classmates from graduate school who stay in touch, senior profs in my first department whose wisdom and care made such a difference, the university campus ministers at Richmond who graciously helped me sort my faith journey, my coauthor in the study of Latinos in Richmond who, more than anyone else I know, deeply understands the heart and soul of immigrants in ways that still move me. There were the other parents in my kid's schools who shared parental joys and pains. And finally, my martial arts students whose love of an ancient Japanese art form sustained me for a whole decade.

Some of us are indeed born, as Somerset Maugham waxed philosophically, out of our due place. Our homelands are but places of passage. Though not fully aware of it at first, in time our strangeness does send us far and wide. In my more cynical moments, I doubt that we will ever find "something permanent," as that writer craved. Once in motion, we tend to remain aloof. I have learned that migration detests permanence. But in my more optimistic days, I do hope that we eventually find a place to belong. Life abroad is never all-inviting or all-welcoming. But, if we are lucky, settle we will, as though familiar with the surroundings from birth. The many kindnesses of adopted family and friends will make the place our home. We may struggle with certain cultural boundaries, with issues of inclusion—but here, ultimately, we find our rest.

4

Immigrant Parenting

Your children are not your children. They are the sons and daughters of Life's longing for itself. They come through you but not from you. . . . You may house their bodies but not their souls, for their souls dwell in the house of tomorrow, which you cannot visit, not even in your dreams.

Kahlil Gibran, *The Prophet*, 1923

We late boomer suburban parents probably raised the most over-scheduled bunch of American kids ever. With Mom and Dad busy at work, taking turns with after-school activities, our kids grew up at the Y, the children's museum, the science museum, the dance studio, the martial arts studio, the local public library, and other assorted sites. They signed up for chess club, language club, robotics club, jazz band, orchestra; or enrolled in soccer leagues, baseball little leagues, basketball intramurals, swimming teams, or track teams. Summers found them at science, computer, math, dance, and music camps. As Neil Howe and William Strauss found out studying our children, they were raised by parents who placed a high value on activities.[1] Unstructured free time among kids ages three to twelve decreased 37 percent from 1981 to 1997.

We told them we kept them busy (too busy actually) so they could sharpen their skills and talents. In truth, we also overstructured their lives to protect them from the harsh world we knew growing up. So our children worked hard for accolades and learned too soon to link effort and reward. They trusted the institutions responsible for their oversight in ways our generation never could, and grew up pressured to excel. Told they were "special" and gifted, they came of age second-guessing those abilities, hoping never to disappoint their progenitors. To confirm our hopes of their brightness, we scrutinized every transcript, test score, and school activity—pushing them to excel in everything they did.

They learned to carefully plan their activities, quickly becoming experts in time management. Team-oriented, the only way to survive such brutal regimen, they were far more afraid of failure than we ever were at their age. We watched them become self-fulfilling prophecies— young achievers, driven repeatedly by the draw of their own success.[2] Only now we wonder if the overachieving came at too hefty a price. On the one hand, they love their triumph—four in five teens now believe they will be more financially successful than their parents. On the other, they grew up too fast. High school students these days walk around with detailed five- to ten-year future plans. Rather than a means to an end, success has become the summun bonum, generating further effort, harder work.

They know how to win the game they are playing, and know that victories will lead to a better life (the more reason to keep playing it well). But my generation wonders whether our kids will find real intrinsic rewards in what they do. My guess is that the intrinsic satisfaction came in the in-between moments, in person with friends with whom they could bear their souls, their insecurities, their pain; or perhaps online with like-minded people who shared their questioning. While highly programmed to excel, they probably do not know other forms of excel- ling besides the conventional ones laid out on their path. My generation experimented, dropped out, and freaked out parents and friends. Our children only knew one way to be successful—the highly competitive, winner-take-all game.

My only hope is that they remain optimistic, upbeat, and civic minded. And well they should. Their generation's achievements are impressive already. They and their peers drove down all kinds of rates associated with troubled adolescence. The number of teen suicides is significantly down, as are teen pregnancies and abortions, as well as rates of violent crime and drug use. These are good kids, who responded to what they perceived as narcissism, self-absorption, and iconoclasm in our generation by keeping their acts clean, trusting the system, and truly caring for each other. As a result, their aptitude test scores kept going up with each grade level. Never has admittance to a top university in this country been so competitive. The *Washington Post* recently ran an article on a high school student who coauthored a science paper with a college professor![3]

Fortunately, our children are less biased than we are. After all, this is America's most racially and ethnically diverse generation. By 2002 minorities made up 37 percent of the under-twenty population in the United States. One in five kids had an immigrant parent; one in ten had a non-citizen parent. So, this generation's interests are truly global. Their music comes from around the globe. They enjoy exotic foods my generation never dreamed of. Their habits and activities truly reflect a global sense of identity. They are open to more flexible lifestyles and more tolerant of their peers' diverse interests.[4]

But I can just hear my mother now: "That's fine. But when do you teach them the importance of family, the roots that should ground their other interests? When do they learn to delight in family tradition?" My answer, and I suppose the answer of most parents in my generation, is, "Mom, there wasn't time! We were just too darn busy keeping up with all their activities!" I suspect that for U.S. parents of my generation, time for relatives was quite limited. If our parents' generation was the first to leave ancestral places, my generation perfected that mobility. Schooling meant opportunities elsewhere. So did jobs, leading us to follow other work opportunities or career promotions. At this point, a Norman Rockwell family scene seems quaint to us, something irretrievable, impossible to duplicate in our rushed world.

Family, the Latino Way

If preserving family connections is hard for the average American, for immigrants the lack of family ties is a fact of life. My kid's relatives on both mother's and father's sides lived some 4,200 miles away. There was no going home for Thanksgiving or Christmas. We sent pictures and videos, keeping the grandparents abreast of Gui's victories. But the reality was he did not grow up around them. He saw them twice on Brazilian vacations that lasted a little less than a summer. It is hard to build a sense of extended family for a child so far removed from every living kin beyond his parents. But my mother's questioning points to a loaded meaning of family. Families are everything to Latin Americans, so it behooves her to ask the question.

In Latin America, extended families are far more important and more controlling than the average U.S. family. By comparison, members of

American families enjoy far more freedom and privacy. For Latin Americans the family unit, its well-being, and its honor represent the very glue that holds everyone together, the basis for our individual and collective identities. No matter where you were born in the region, your family's interests came first, never your own. We lived for our families, not the other way around.[5] That message was constantly reinforced for my generation as we were growing up. Family commitment came first and was non-negotiable in all matters of life.

There is reason for such loyalty. In a region of weak political institutions and corrupt economic structures, your family is your ultimate shield. Your family alone protects you from the outside world and takes care of you when you need help. But you have to do your part; you have to be loyal to kin. Your family mediated all conflicts, internal or external. If any two of us were having a problem with each other the matter became a group concern. Family members stepped in to resolve it, reminding the warring parties of their mutual responsibility and pushing them to make up. Solidarity was always the norm, always the expectation (ironically, when Brazilians migrate that sense of solidarity seems to weaken[6]).

Unlike the typical post–World War II American family, Latin American kinship reached far beyond the nuclear unit. Our families were multigenerational—grandparents, children, and grandchildren sometimes lived under the same roof. They also stretched horizontally, reaching blood and marriage relatives to the second and third degree. Finally, family ties even included folks related by informal adoption (it is not unusual in the region for a family to take in children whose parents are going through tough times and cannot provide for them) or by godparenting.

Godparenting—*compadrazco* in Spanish, *apadrinhamento* in Portuguese—is a Catholic ritual kinship, extended to people not legally your kin. Godparenting bonds unrelated families, by creating religious ties of mutual obligation. Your godparents provided life-long mentoring and the kind of moral instruction most Americans expect only from parents.

Of course, life in an extended family of this sort offers no sense of privacy. To put it mildly, your business is everybody's business. There is little to no individual liberty. Your well-being concerns all those who surround you. Everyone has an opinion of how you should best live your life. Relatives meddle avidly in your studies, who you should date or marry (sometimes the two are not necessarily the same), who you should befriend and why, and which careers were most appropriate for someone of your family lineage. The last item is critical, because in Brazilian culture, your family lineage locates you within a system of privileges that sorts out the "well-bred" from their social "inferiors."[7]

A rank-based society, with far less social mobility than the United States, Brazil has often allowed the powerful to enjoy benefits those below them could never hope to gain. We truly lacked the American egalitarian ethos. Political and economic perks were clearly tied to family heritage, and, of course, to class and race. Brazilian elites (almost always white or light-skinned) expected special treatment from those they outranked (mostly brown, black, or poor white).[8] So your family was also the foremost source of status and esteem. Therefore its hold on us never abated. Our personal needs remained aligned with our family's interests, our decisions made within those parameters.

Family loyalty carried into the smallest details of everyday life. For instance, unlike American college students, Brazilians never leave to pursue their studies. Few Brazilian universities have dorms. You remain with your parents until the day you marry, and then settle within a short distance from them. In adulthood, you are expected at your parents' (or grandparents') home for weekly family meals, celebrations, and for regular interaction. The family continues to play a role in all major decisions of your life, impacting your personal choices and aspirations to the day they die. Only as a foreign exchange student in New Mexico was I able to marvel at the whole construct from the outside. My "adopted" American siblings enjoyed a freedom to pursue their own interests that I could only envy.

On a curious note, the Latin American family pattern tends to be stronger among Catholics than Protestants. Within the Catholic communal worldview, one's loyalty is tied to the well-being of the larger group. So, there is no need to strike out on your own, to leave your mark, to seek your place in the world away from the close scrutiny of relatives. This is a culture that predates the individualism of modern capitalist societies. Among the children of Calvinist merchants in Northern Europe, for example, individual fame and fortune were expected in all manner of enterprise. As a result, Protestant individualism trickled down to family matters. Their Iberian counterparts, on the other hand, even those who roamed far away as seafarers, did so for their families, their church, and their Catholic kings.

Nevertheless, given the prevalence of Catholicism in Brazilian culture, Brazilian Protestant families are not as individualistic as their American counterparts either. When I was growing up, my mother followed the more communal Catholic pattern, while my father leaned toward the individualism brought by Protestant missionaries. He waxed eloquently about the merits of the self-made man, of the entrepreneur. His universe was filled by books from Dale Carnegie and Henry Ford, pushing the Horatio Alger rags-to-riches myth to the max. That, of course, makes for a confusing childhood. My father approved of my early efforts to discover the world on my own, while my mother mourned my independent streak.

As a teenager I spent every summer at youth conferences and camps (common here in the United States, not so much in Brazil those days). Of four siblings, I was the one who chose to participate in a foreign exchange program, away from the family's support network. To this day I'm the one who settled the farthest away geographically. With few exceptions everybody else, despite our Protestant leanings, stayed home. It befuddled my relatives that I seldom consulted them for anything, that I always solved problems on my own. I chose my hobbies and extracurricular activities. They were not consulted when I picked a college or a wife, topics usually requiring a great deal of input in most Brazilian families. My father never understood why I took up theology instead of business. He imagined his eldest son a captain of industry someday.

Sometimes it was hard to be so independent. But personal freedom certainly defined my growing up and set me apart from siblings and peers. Emotionally, this mixture of Protestant and Catholic affections still complicates my life as an immigrant. I cherish my independent life in the United States, but there is a sadness that hangs over my chats with family back in Brazil. My noted absence is a constant source of disappointment for them. None of my relatives can fathom why I remain abroad, especially now that I have reached a certain level of stability in my professional career. None see the point of a life away from the homeland. And none appreciate my need for personal liberty or privacy.

So in my interactions with folks back home they find me reticent, "distant." They wonder why I do not require, or seek, the same kind of intimacy and busybody connections that are so essential to their well-being. They long to keep me updated on the smallest details of their lives and expect me to do the same in return. When that fails, the sense of loss is rekindled in their voices. Perhaps I was always a bit removed, I want to say, while reminding them of my independent youth. Perhaps this individual streak has been part of my life all along. But clearly, they seem to notice it more these days.

"Congratulations, It's a Boy"

My countercultural sense of independence was only shaken up by the advent of parenthood. As a child I could always count on my parents and adult relatives to empower my flights of fancy. They supported my interests and praised my accomplishments. What I did not realize then was that my carefree disposition was made possible by their careful and constant watch. In their selflessness, they cleaned up my mistakes and quietly contributed to my successes. I claimed all the credit, of course. But there was always a safety net; I just never took the time to see it. Until my own son was born. Having a baby abroad, away from my entire family, quickly became downright exhausting and scary. His mother and I were his only family, with no help from relatives.

When I was born, my parents had the constant aid of grandparents, aunts, and great-aunts. As my son came into the world, he had his mom and me as his entire support system. As Brazilians, my wife and I were worried about raising a son without relatives. In fact, his birth exposed our lack of connections in the United States. For the first two years of his life we did not go out in the evening because we did not know any babysitters. Our few friends were either college students or coworkers who happened to be single or childless. We lacked a support network for parenting tips, or shared duties, and other issues like finding a dentist or a pediatrician. We met a couple at the Lamaze class, but they were busy professionals, pressed for time.

For two Brazilian immigrants, having a child in the United States raises the question of operating as a nuclear family. Prior to Gui's arrival we were simply a couple whose extended families happened to live elsewhere. We remained our families' children, with no responsibility for creating our own family traditions. We traveled, enjoyed life abroad, and studied. Nothing pushed us to rethink our family unit as Gui did. All of a sudden, every child-related holiday begged for a new family tradition. Of course, living in a foreign country, our family traditions were built around "borrowed" holidays, since we celebrated what other families in the neighborhood were celebrating. We kept track of American rather than Brazilian holidays.

In the process, we ended raising a very American son, in a very American family unit. His childhood was unlike our own. Halloweens were huge at the Cavalcanti residence, though Brazilians do not celebrate Halloween. Gui loved the costumes, the trick-or-treat rounds. Neither his mom nor I had the heart to tell him we had never celebrated Halloween until he came along. Christmas meant decorating the Christmas tree, his treasured ritual. But we did not grow up with Christmas trees, carols, or snow. Christmas came at the height of summer in Brazil. Instead of Rudolph and Santa Claus we had beach picnics and street festivals at night. The Easter Bunny and the traditional egg hunt were a huge part of our son's calendar, though Easter was not celebrated that way in South America either.

The absence of a large Brazilian expatriate community made it hard for us to observe Brazilian holidays at home. To this day our son has no idea what a real Brazilian Carnival is like. He never learned the *Frêvo*, the most typical of Recife's Carnival dances. He never celebrated St. John's and St. Peter's Days eating corn-based country food and square dancing around the neighborhood, like his mother and I did when we were growing up. He never learned the mellow rhythms of a *Ciranda*, the gentle fishermen's round dance from my hometown, one that beautifully highlights their way of life.

But there was no way to raise a Brazilian kid by ourselves in the United States. And so much had changed about parenting since our childhood days! Our kid was part of the American millennial baby boom. So he rode the wealth of activities that businesses and community agencies created for his cohort. For instance, his mother and I did not grow up around public libraries. Back in Brazil, there were no public library branches in our respective neighborhoods. But Gui's weekly visits to the Tuckahoe Public Library were a huge part of his growing up. After-school activities and summer camps were unlike anything his parents ever experienced as kids. We grew up self-entertained, surrounded by siblings and cousins. He grew up shuttled instead.

I have the feeling that our childhood was more leisured, more spontaneous. It had to be. Our extended families were a moving feast. As parents of a kid in the millennial generation we did not have that luxury. Not even our language survived the pressures of suburban American life. The initial plan was to speak Portuguese at home and English elsewhere, so as to raise a bilingual child. That lasted till he started day care. Then he simply refused to speak Portuguese. So I quickly switched to all-English-all-the-time. His poor mother waged a losing battle to keep Portuguese alive, despite his insistence on replying in English. When he did speak in Portuguese, he had a curious southern accent that he never showed in English.

To be sure, all immigrant parents face the issue of language loss. As the first generation, they struggle to acculturate into a new language and new customs. But the second generation, the American-born generation, is fluent in English and often answers their parents' remarks in their mother tongue with English replies. Our case was not so different from that of other immigrant parents. In fact, it is not unusual for English to become the language spoken at home.[9] Moreover, large-scale studies of immigrant children show that few remain truly bilingual. Portes and Rumbaut found that only 28 percent of their sample was fully bilingual by the time of high school graduation.[10]

How to explain this American life of our kid to relatives back home? Our parents expected frequent reports. Siblings were curious about Gui's latest doings. And cousins bugged our immediate families for news from America. We reported on what we could. But our families had no frame of reference for our "small" (by Brazilian standards) suburban nuclear lifestyle. We sent photos and videos, but they lacked the cultural translation. All in all, there remained a persistent gap in our ability to explain how our little nuclear family deviated from the traditional Brazilian standards.

School Days

Another thing we did not realize, prior to having a child in the United States, was that American schools would need to find the right ethnic pigeonhole for Gui as part of his education. As a professor, I had taught sociology of education multiple times, lecturing benignly on the virtues of multicultural classrooms. As a parent I discovered that by honoring my kid's Brazilian identity, the school accentuated his difference, making it far more visible. In doing so, it turned him into an outsider in his classmates' eyes. The last thing my son needed was to be an outsider.

For someone who preached respect for cultural diversity in the classroom, that was a tough lesson to swallow. But what I had failed to realize was that family membership deeply defines a child's ethnic identity in America.[11] Schools are perhaps the first governmental agencies to classify our children on the basis of an official ethnicity. Gui spoke fluent English without any accent. In every way that mattered he was a thoroughly American child. Nevertheless, his parents' ethnicity became the ultimate criterion for his cataloging at school. Sadly, immigrant children, whose social markers ascribe them a minority status in school, spend their days seeking to normalize their condition, to rejoin the larger crowd. The need to be "normal" makes them spend a great deal of time and energy mimicking the modal responses of the dominant group.[12]

The irony is that my son did not know his home culture was foreign. We spoke Portuguese and dabbled in Brazilian food from time to time, but he had no way of comparing that to anything else. Given the somewhat segregated residential pattern of American cities, most children do not fully realize the stereotypes attached to their ethnicity until they reach school age. Once they become aware of them, they work hard to "blend in." They compare themselves with those around, sorting out similarity and dissimilarity, especially in relation to their reference groups. Pressure from peers and parents create an impossible tug of war throwing competing loyalties against each other, contributing to the kid's sense of marginality.[13]

By going to school, Gui finally encountered his foreign condition. All of a sudden, my son became painfully aware that our home culture had a label, and that label placed him squarely on the outside, looking in. Following the pattern of other immigrant children, Gui tried desperately to "normalize" his identity. Since *Guilherme* means *William* in Portuguese, he insisted that his classmates call him Will. But he was bullied repeatedly during second grade on account of his weird-sounding surname. Eventually the principal agreed to transfer him to a smaller school. There, he finally made lifelong friends among kids of other ethnic minorities and those who were part of the dominant group.

A unique part of Gui's struggle had to do with the issue of multiple identities, something that is commonly experienced by American minorities. When immigrants first arrive in the United States they are still wedded to their nationalities. As they settle down, those nationalities undergo a transformation. They become ethnicities. Eventually those ethnicities end up grouped into a larger umbrella. Let's say a Vietnamese refugee enters the United States. She will first be seen as an outsider, only to later be described as Vietnamese American as she becomes naturalized. Down the road her identity will be further conflated into the larger category of Asian American. This process happens continuously as the American society adds new ethnic groups to its composition.

In Gui's case he had to juggle "Brazilian," "Brazilian American," and "Latino." The more he tried to look like everyone else, the more he struggled with the Brazilian side of his identity, the more the larger society limited his options due to his parents' ethnic categories. He spent his entire childhood trying to belong. By the time he reached high school he refused to be boxed into the condition of Brazilian American, or the ultimate pan-ethnic category of Latino. In their study of immigrant children, Portes and Rumbaut found that over 53 percent of them identified themselves as American or "Other" American in 1992, but only 34 percent did so three years later.[14]

The struggle followed Gui to college. When he was exploring his college options, he was offered full scholarships to two top engineering undergraduate schools in Massachusetts. One school made the mistake of awarding him what would be their first Latino scholarship. The other gave him the regular, run-of-the-mill full ride. Needless to say, Gui chose the latter, partly on the basis of getting that all-American, merit scholarship. His father's lectures on the importance of opening doors to other Latinos were of no avail. And to this day he refuses to be boxed in.[15] Mind you, he is proud of his heritage—he speaks Portuguese and has taken Italian in school. He is not ashamed of who he is. But he wishes to honor it on his own terms.

One thing we failed to realize as "ethnic" parents was that once school started, our son's loyalty to us and our Brazilian home would be seriously tested by his classmates. Loyalty to family of origin only heightened his outsider status in their eyes, whereas loyalty to things American would improve his chances of becoming an insider. So, Gui sided with his peers. By the end of high school, his loyalty to his parents' culture was almost nonexistent. He opened up to the promises of the dominant culture but did so at our expense. Considering the other choices available to immigrant children—to stick to their ethnicity or hopelessly try to straddle both—Gui's option made sense.

Andrew Fuligni, Gwendelyn Rivera, and April Leininger, in their study of ethnic identity among teenagers, found that teens in Gui's generation attending urban schools had cast their lot with their ethnic side—perhaps because their schools had larger minority populations, perhaps because they had stronger minority markers. Nevertheless, those who chose the ethnic route had a stronger sense of ethnic identity as teenagers and felt a stronger sense of obligation toward family.[16] They were more likely to take their parents' wishes into account in their decision making. And their loyalty to family became an asset during adolescence. Following the Latin American mold, in their adult years, these students were more likely to assist parents and siblings than those who left their ethnicity behind.

The interesting thing is that those adolescents did not necessarily feel more emotionally close to their parents. Rather, they felt a deeper sense of belonging to their unique ethnic group. Loyalty to group defined them above and beyond what their classmates might say. That kind of family attachment is common among immigrants from Latin America. Comparing children of immigrants from the Americas, Europe, Asia, the Middle East, and Canada, Portes and Rumbaut found Latin American nationalities to have the most cohesive families and the lowest levels of parent-child conflict. Most Latino groups had the lowest proportions of kids who reported being embarrassed by their parents.[17]

Nevertheless, they also found that those children's successful acculturation weakened their family cohesion, leading toward a more individualistic orientation. Needless to say, that happened to our son. Rather than choosing his Brazilian side, Gui went on to adopt his classmates' culture, growing up in ways his parents could never have imagined as Brazilians. To us, love of family and loyalty to kin were essential ingredients in a healthy upbringing. We could not imagine not needing or wanting our parents' friendship when we were growing up. That kind of expressive bonding was critical to our sense of well-being. They affirmed us with their ties—their love was an emotional asset helping us navigate adolescence.

Our son never felt as strong a need for our company. Mind you, he didn't dislike us. He never rejected our instruction, nor doubted our care or concern for his well-being. But there was something a little more American about him, something that pushed him to strike out on his own. As any suburban American kid, Gui piled up laurels in a highly successful academic career, all spent in magnet schools from second grade on. He was active in school clubs, busy with school projects, and seemed to enjoy the opportunities that came his way. His college career was equally successful. These days he owns his own business in Boston. He just never needed the Brazilian closeness we grew up with.

Much like his peers of other nationalities, Gui showed high levels of self-esteem and independence throughout middle and high school. That is not unusual among children of immigrants. Nearly 58 percent of Portes and Rumbaut's total sample had high self-esteem scores. In follow-up surveys from junior high to high school, their level of self-esteem jumped ten percentage points. But that does come at a cost.

Sadly, much like his ethnic peers, Gui also experienced bouts of depressive symptoms. In fact, in Portes and Rumbaut's sample, the depressive scores of children of immigrants remained stable from junior high to high school.[18]

Our case clearly represents the paradox of immigrant parenting. Gui's successful acculturation was purchased at the expense of close family ties. When his mother and I were growing up in Brazil, closeness to family was foundational. Our son, on the other hand, took on the cultural traits of his suburban American generation. And like them, he grew up with a healthy sense of entitlement, a sense that parents existed solely to provide the needed resources for setting out on their own. I imagine that for Gui, the parent-child relationship was never a mutual giving and receiving. He knew he had a solid home base and knew he could count on us to support his efforts. Once he took off, however, there was no looking back.

I take comfort that Gui's choice, from the point of view of acculturation, was not altogether a bad one. The prospects for the average children of immigrants in the United States these days are rather grim. First of all, they struggle with invisibility. In 2007 about 16.4 million children—more than one in five children in America—had at least one immigrant parent. I doubt the average American would be familiar with that statistic. Moreover, that number had doubled since 1990, with the share of immigrant American children jumping from 13 to 23 percent of the population. They also struggle to fit in, lacking the cultural capital to fully integrate into the American economy or to avoid discrimination as my son did.

More than half of those children were of Hispanic heritage; though only 17 percent had parents from Central and South America or the Spanish-speaking Caribbean.[19] Many faced serious obstacles trying to make it in the States. Their parents lacked legal status or citizenship, as well as access to public services for their children and families. A good number lived in linguistic isolation—19 percent of those aged five to seventeen had limited English proficiency; one or both parents of the 61 percent had limited English-language skills as well. A quarter of the parents lacked a high school degree. Some 82 percent of the children lived in large families with limited resources—51 percent had family incomes twice the poverty level, while 22 percent were poor.[20]

The children of Brazilian immigrants in the United States face similar difficulties. Like Gui, they make their parents more committed to a future in this country. But studies of Brazilian teenagers in America show that they tend to reproduce the career path (i.e., menial jobs) of their parents. Sadly, for them, schooling is not a path to social mobility. The fact that the parents are engaged in multiple, dead-end, low-wage jobs means that schooling becomes secondary to survival. The children need to work to help with the household budget. And the parents' long hours give them little time to oversee the children's schooling. For them education is a means to learn English, but not much more. So very few of their children move up in the occupational ladder.[21]

What we find, when we take a closer look at the lives of these children, is a process of segmented assimilation.[22] Not all immigrants find full integration into American society, nor do they experience similar kinds of social mobility. Race and ethnicity, social class, labor market demands, and the context of the receiving nation affect immigrant access to resources and a successful pathway to integration. Immigrant children who attend better schools and whose parents have more human capital will experience assimilation in the same fashion as did the children of European immigrants during the first half of the twentieth century.[23] Immigrant children whose parents' race or low socioeconomic status places them in disadvantaged settings face the same limitations of other American working-class minorities, with the same reduced opportunities.

Parents and peers can have a profound effect on the aspirations and expectations of immigrant children. Since aspirations and academic performance are strongly correlated, children who do well and attend better schools will take advantage of this country's best educational opportunities. Their parents' level of human capital will assure that they will acquire the needed social skills to be successful in their endeavors. By contrast, the children of immigrants who enter the labor force at the bottom are more likely to reproduce their parents' status. They will learn the language and culture better than the parents ever will, but will still face serious difficulties climbing up America's social ladder.

Moments of Grace

Notwithstanding the pangs of an empty nest, and the ethnic struggles of our child, what an adventure to raise a kid in this culture! American public schools delivered quite a gifted childhood: advanced science, art and music classes, performance opportunities, and varied field trips. His mother and I had none of that growing up in Brazil. Gui's field trips took him to Washington, DC, Atlanta, Houston, and Orlando. In middle school he played trumpet in the jazz band and French horn in the orchestra, performing regularly around the greater Richmond area. In high school he was active in national robotics tournaments and advanced swing dance lessons. We were busy, but what a time!

In many ways, Gui's experience betrays the hope of every immigrant parent. Nashville and Richmond, the two cities where he grew up, had remarkable child-oriented programming. Both boasted children's museums. Both offered much in parks and recreation. Both had elaborate botanical gardens with a variety of child-related activities. Both had theme parks within driving distance—Opryland in Nashville, King's Dominion in Richmond. There were fine zoos within driving distance as well. Both metropolitan areas had respectable orchestras with child-appropriate concerts throughout the year. Children's theaters were available in both towns as well, with reasonably priced season tickets.

Within a short distance of our residential areas there were plenty of other educational opportunities. From Nashville we visited the huge Chattanooga Aquarium, the Memphis Zoo, and the Louisville Children's Museum. In Richmond we spent considerable time exploring the Smithsonian Institution museums in Washington, DC, the Baltimore Aquarium, and the Virginia Beach Aquarium. Virginia also offered historical locations like Jamestown, Monticello, and Montpelier, not counting regular trips to Renaissance fairs, summertime open-air concerts, and seasonal festivals. Gui's summer vacations at ages four and eleven took him to Disneyworld and SeaWorld, to Brazil when he was seven, and to New York when he was in middle school. It was thrilling to watch him discover this wide world.

Then, there were moments that made me think, "Only in America!" When Gui was eleven, he participated in a Civil War pageant at school where he played the role of Ulysses S. Grant. Watching my Brazilian American son don the uniform of a Union general and sing Lincoln's praises in Richmond, once the cradle of the Confederacy, was beyond surreal. There were also those sublime times when his middle school orchestra would be tackling a difficult piece of classical music, and I would watch kids from public housing playing right next to my son. Coming from a rank-based society, I could see how this might be the land of opportunity for many, that egalitarian new nation dreamed by our Founders.

Gui's best friends from grade school to high school are another telltale sign of the promises of this nation. One was a white, Italian

American kid from one of the most affluent neighborhoods in town. The other two were children of Indian immigrants who, like Gui's parents, lived in less affluent suburbs. The kids' close bond remains strong to this day. They grew up together, celebrated each other's birthdays, went to the same camps, attended the same proms. In what other country could the path of four kids with such different ethnicity converge? They found each other in public school and together became very American children.

These days, I wonder if we should have done more to help our son understand the privileged life he led in America. To him it was just growing up. To us, given our childhood in Brazil, his life was amazing. Despite the fact that we both came from middle-class backgrounds in Brazil, neither his mother nor I ever had the opportunities that Gui encountered in school. He grew up in a much more meritocratic nation, one truly willing to invest in its citizens. Virginia's standards of public education are quite impressive compared to those of any country in this hemisphere. He got a full scholarship to college. Such level of commitment to the next generation is simply hard to fathom for those of us who come from Latin America.

In this sense, the Anglo-Saxon political tradition of the United States is light years ahead of its Iberian counterpart in Latin America. An educated citizenry was always a precondition of American democracy. It was part and parcel of the American Revolution, deeply woven into the checks and balances that created this new nation. Timothy Ferris, in *The Science of Liberty*, summarizes its importance, as championed by John Locke, as "the kit of what was to become the democratic revolution—liberal governance based on natural rights and the consent of the governed; free intellectual, religious, and scientific inquiry; equal justice under law; and universal education designed to nourish individual capacity rather than mass servitude."[24]

College Days

As a professor, I could hardly wait for my son to go to college. I chalked up his emotional distance during high school to teenage students being predisposed to ignore parents at this stage of their lives. They were still trying to create a separate identity, I told myself, still developing their own tastes and personae. College, on the other hand, might be the time when they could fully appreciate what they had in common with their parents. Since we were no longer a threat to their freedom at this stage, I had hoped for kinder treatment then. Moreover, after eighteen years of college teaching, by the time Gui left for college I felt fully prepared to accompany him during his college career.

My reasons for expecting the closer bonding were simple—he would be living and studying in the same environment in which his father made a living. We could discuss his classes, go over his discoveries in poetry, literature, or history, even talk about cultural events. I couldn't wait to hear Gui's take on college life in America, since I thought it was vastly superior to my own college experience back home. I tried to picture him out there in Massachusetts, making his choices, learning lessons big and small, trying out stuff. I could see him figuring out what worked and what didn't, trying on different aspects of his personality, developing his own sense of manhood. What an awesome time he must be having.

That year, since I was surrounded by first-year students of his age, I paid closer attention to their interests—as if to distill from their experience my son's own. I spent more time with them outside the classroom, listened to their doubts, their concerns, thinking about Gui's own issues. However, as luck would have it, my son did not attend a liberal arts college. He fell in love with robots in high school and chose an engineering school instead. While I had dreamed that he would discover the wonders of Shakespeare as a freshman, the Greek and Roman roots of Western civilization, or the unique aspects of his country as a brand new nation, he actually spent his first year studying the hydraulics of robotic joints.

All the academic knowledge I amassed over a career gave me no entry point into my child's college world. I had always imagined him taking English, history, or philosophy classes. He would e-mail or call after class, and we would have these long-winded conversations about the stuff he was processing. Instead Gui was boning up on mechanical systems, vector calculus, and materials science. I had no way to respond to any of that. I had readied myself for chats on Plato's theory of love, Aristotle's take on human nature, and perhaps a discussion on the root causes of the Industrial Revolution. Instead I had to watch my son from afar, in wonder, with no clues as to how his college experience was going.

With his usual millennial disposition, Gui threw himself at engineering classes, leaving little time to process how they were actually changing him. Once again, he was mastering the skills he needed to succeed at what he was doing. But I could see that he lacked the wisdom to figure out why he was doing it, what the point of college was besides landing a great job. Since he did not have the regular load of humanities or social sciences classes, I could not see how he would figure out the reasons humans develop the way they do. His days were filled with mechanical contraptions—robotic snakes, water-propelled bottle rockets, nature-mimicking artifacts that required great technical problem-solving skills.

Sure enough, he crashed and burned by the end of his junior year. He took his senior year off to figure things out and spent the year working as an engineer at a local company. He returned to college a year later to complete his requirements and graduate. The irony is that his life still had a clear sense of direction by graduation time, but little meaning to go along with it. And I had to watch all this from afar, simply hoping for the best. Oh, I wrote e-mails, tried to catch him on the phone, and bugged his poor college advisor. But Gui was determined to figure things out on his own, without my help, and I finally respected his wishes.

Throughout his crisis, I wondered if he ever thought about the way his engineering skills were affecting his sense of self. I knew that being skillful increased Gui's confidence, his sense of agency, efficacy. I knew that engineering gave him the means to be very assured about who he was.[25] But I was not sure that it provided him with a deeper sense of his place in the universe. So I watched my son flounder around, looking for that higher meaning. To me, his college experience did not offer him time to ponder the shape and size of his emotions, or to pursue those qualities of his soul that would make him a more delightful person. The whole crisis seemed so wasteful, so unnecessary.

This is an area where, as a Brazilian, I felt I had an edge over Gui. People in America tend to justify their existence in rather utilitarian ways, on the basis of what they are good at, be it an engineer, a lawyer, or a doctor. In Brazil we define ourselves and others on the basis of who we are as human beings. So we focus on the quality of our selves, rather than our social functions. I may be a college professor, but that certainly does not define me completely. In that sense, Latin Americans face career changes with less trepidation. I am not sure that my American son could look at his life with equal wisdom. He talked plenty about the doors that engineering opened for him, but not enough about his trajectory as a human being.

This is when I realized that in my rush to schedule his life, to outfit him for success, I failed to teach him how to look at the world the way a Brazilian would. Ironic, isn't it? In hindsight, reviewing his and my time in high school and college, I could see how our paths diverged when we were the same age. For instance, in Recife, schools provided only classroom instruction. The extracurricular activities were found in the social clubs that dotted our lovely city. We explored the world of sports, parties, and social interaction outside school walls. And that taught us to prize other aspects of life, beyond the academic standards that so impressed our teachers.

In Gui's schools, extracurricular activities reinforced the academic game. From sports to theater to dance to fine arts to academic clubs, his schools defined what was useful for our kids. Students were valued on the basis of their functional adaptation to the demands of a post-industrial society. Even their leisure time reflected the students' compunction to keep climbing the social ladder. "Well-rounded" kids were polyglots, played chess, sang in the choir, and took part in school orchestras, while improving their SAT scores and GPAs. But where would our kids go to find their intrinsic worth? If worth comes from jumping academic hurdles, is it real, lasting worth?

Ironically, college in the United States is meant to be the time when students explore questions of meaning. Through their general education curriculum, they are provided with the collective wisdom of human civilization. Supposedly this should help them acquire the needed tools to gaze into their souls, to ponder the shape of their lives. College in Brazil, on the other hand, was strictly utilitarian. When I was growing up, the bachelor's was a terminal degree based on career requirements rather than self-exploration. You learned a trade and proceeded to pursue it. My two bachelor's degrees—law and theology—afforded me little introspection and much professional practice.

Here in the United States, Gui's college experience should have given him time to explore the purpose of life. But instead, it simply allowed him to become a well-accomplished technician. The school offered functional rather than contextual training. Sadly, as more American universities are pressured to create technicians, the liberal arts have become relegated to an ancillary function. So those of us in the humanities and the social sciences provide general education credits for people who are majoring in more "practical" disciplines. Given my son's experience, I have to wonder what kind of human beings we are forming with this kind of curriculum.

Saying Goodbye

My son's college days marked the end of our regular interactions. Shortly after we dropped him off, his mother and I were informed by e-mail that as a college student he needed his own space to figure things out. We were not to expect regular e-mails or phone calls. For the most part, he remained true to his word—no regular phone calls or e-mails were forthcoming. While other college kids were figuring out how often to call their parents, our child simply chose to leave us behind. And no amount of cajoling on his mother's part or whining on mine solved the problem. He seemed determined to start charting his own life from the time he started higher education.

The Brazilian in me was furious! "Why, that spoiled brat," I thought. "Who does he think he is? He's still on my dime, and as far as I'm concerned he better change this attitude." So I found myself sounding more and more like my old dad, something I had sworn never to do to my son. That was quite sobering. But his ingratitude and sense of entitlement hit us very hard. As immigrants we had sacrificed everything for this kid, left our families and culture behind to give him every advantage this country could offer. We put many of our dreams on hold for those eighteen years so that he could take every opportunity that life here afforded. And this is how he repaid us? It was as if he really wanted a clean break from the parents and culture that had made him an outsider in second grade.

Obviously, his mother and I went into deep mourning over his decision to remain aloof. And of course as immigrant parents, we could never "translate" his decision to our families back home. There is no such thing as an empty-nester in Brazil, just as there is no such thing as a child's "need for my own space." How to explain a son who took flight and left the nest to folks in whose land adults never emotionally leave their families of origin? Our relatives were astounded, puzzled. Cutting off one's ties to his family of origin in Brazil is the equivalent of committing social suicide. Your family grounded your social world. It held the platform for your future opportunities. They could make all the difference for your future life chances.

Here in the United States, on the other hand, we really had no leverage over our son's future. He had more contacts in robotics and engineering than we could possibly muster. And since he had a full scholarship to college, he only needed room and board money. But even that could be financed by his summer work at engineering companies around Boston. In other words, his connection to us was completely optional, fully voluntary. He realized that sooner than his parents did. So, throughout his college career we felt quite obsolete. We attended a few parents' events, but for the most part, our kid was on his own and doing quite well for himself.

I realize that this situation is not unique to immigrant parents. Much of it is really generational. Those of us who are late boomers (born between 1955 and 1965) raised very independent children, self-starters ready to fly the coop at the first chance they got. When I look at the parents of Gui's friends from high school, they did not fare any better in keeping touch with their children. A few of the kids from Gui's magnet school remain in touch with their home base, but the majority (especially Gui's closest friends) took off without looking back. With rare exceptions, they all went to out-of-state colleges, leaving Virginia right after graduation. They have also chosen careers in other states as part of their overall strategy.

But for immigrant parents this sense of abandonment is very difficult to handle. When you are raised in a culture where family devotion is a gift to be savored over a lifetime, the shock of the empty nest is unbearable. Children are not supposed to become that independent that early, if they are to become independent at all. Parents are not supposed to become obsolete after eighteen years of hard work and close attention to their kids' well-being. Immigrant parents take longer to get used to the idea of an empty nest, and longer still to move on with our lives. And yet, this pattern seems to have worked for *this* country for as long as children have been going to college.

The Cat's in the Cradle

Had my father lived long enough to see his grandson graduate from college, he would have been the first to remind me of the poetic justice of my condition. That the most independent-minded of his children would end up raising the most independent-minded of his grandchildren would not have surprised him at all. In all honesty, it should not have surprised me, either. Of all my siblings and cousins, I am the one who immigrated; I am the one who made a new life for himself. But it does. I thought things would be different between Gui and me. I was never close to my dad, but I adored the man. He was not good at demonstrating his love. And he could be quite hard on us, "toughening us up" to face the outside world.

As a result, the first time I heard Harry Chapin's song "The Cat's in the Cradle," I was miffed that it was not available in Portuguese so I could send it to the old man. The ever-so-busy businessman, he was never around when I was growing up—too many deals to close, too many places to go. The song, I thought, would be the perfect way to tell him off. And yet, despite those long years of trying to be more present in my son's life, I find myself ironically in his same shoes. The reality is that kids do grow up and have lives of their own. Gui went on to Massachusetts for college and never came home, not even during summertime. Research opportunities with his professors and in engineering firms took care of his summers.

There were no Thanksgiving or Christmas visits, and as far as I can remember, only a couple of spring breaks when we saw each other. His mother and I did not realize when we dropped him at school that he was leaving for good. I'm sure our divorce when he was only eight years old hurt him deeply, especially because we were his only family in America. It must have certainly sped up his emotional departure. But in our defense, we did the best that we could to shelter Gui from our own pain. We wanted him to know he would not be abandoned, so we both remained in Richmond until he graduated from high school. And our joint custody guaranteed that Gui would spend half a week with his mother and the other half with me.

For the next decade of Gui's life, we remained as deeply involved in his school and after-school activities as we had been. I even coached his soccer team in grade school and taught judo lessons to him and his friends in high school. But I guess life gets busy, and we had to make a living as well. My being on tenure track at a selective liberal arts college proved demanding, and his mother was equally busy managing a store in a mall. Try as we might to keep Gui's sense of family intact, I don't think he ever got over our separation. Perhaps the overscheduling, the summer vacations, and the host of after-school activities were our own ways to overcompensate for the pain of the divorce. I don't know. But I cannot imagine raising him in any less busy ways.

The truth is, I never figured out how to reach my son's soul in that place where things got so emotionally fractured. If not as absent a father as my own dad, I still ended up equally distant from him—despite my best efforts to always be a part of his life. I never missed a birthday, never missed a game or a play, though I may have missed a few daytime events. In the end, Kahlil Gibran's wisdom about parenthood applied equally to my father and me. Our children are never really ours to keep, though we certainly think so at their birth. They are "sons . . . of Life's longing for itself." They may spend a few years in our care, but eventually they chart paths of their own making.

Dad and I could have had quite a conversation on this topic. We could have told each other about how we housed our sons' bodies for a while, but how we failed—try as we might—to fully reach their souls. We could have described how we glimpsed our sons' futures, but somehow knew we would not be playing a large part in that tomorrow. My father would probably have enjoyed that chat. He would have reminded me that tomorrow, as Gibran says, is a place we cannot visit, "not even in our dreams." He would also have told me that I had become like him, despite choosing a different fatherhood style. Much like the lyrics of the song "The Cat's in the Cradle," I turned into him, as my son turned out just as independent as his own father was at his age.

5

Pledging One's Life

And for the support of this Declaration, with a firm reliance on the protection of Divine Providence, we mutually pledge to each other our Lives, our Fortunes, and our sacred Honor.

Declaration of Independence

To me, the final paragraph is the most moving part of the U.S. Declaration of Independence. Picture the scene: it is July 1776 in Philadelphia; the Second Continental Congress gathers in the Assembly Room of Independence Hall. On the second of the month, a vote of twelve of the thirteen colonies (New York abstaining) starts the deliberation on the Declaration of Independence, as written by the Committee of Five. Now on July 4, signers ready themselves for the final vote. They know the risks. This is no small feat they ponder. Here they are, representing a small group of assorted colonies on the Eastern Seaboard, about to face the brunt of the most powerful military on earth. A yea vote would break the bond that had defined the colonies from inception. Moreover, once free, they could no longer count on the protection of the most powerful navy at the time.

The document eloquently proposes a rationale for breaking away from British rule, with a long list of grievances that plainly states the reasons for such a political act. But it is the closing paragraph that truly shows the heroism of the Founding Fathers. To the future of their new nation, they "pledged their lives, their fortunes and their sacred honor." For the sake of their new nation, they were willing to lay it all on the line!

The repercussions were immediate. The British sent an armada to New York to crush the rebellion, so many ships indeed that their masts were said to make the harbor look like a forest. Some 23,000 British regulars were onboard, along with 10,000 German mercenaries—troops that would trounce George Washington's army on August 27, 1776.[1]

But as the colonies' representatives gathered in the Assembly Room, they had no way of knowing the magnitude of the punishment they would face, nor the final outcome of their rebellion. Declaring themselves free from Britain would be considered high treason by the Crown, a crime punishable by death. And the response would be swift and steady. All their earthly goods could surely be confiscated by King George in light of their vote, throwing their families into abject destitution. Everything laid in the balance on that bright, sunny, but cool Philadelphia day. Their votes would certainly upset their livelihoods and safety for the remainder of the Revolution. But by late afternoon, church bells rang out throughout the city marking the Declaration's final adoption.

Not only had the members of the Second Continental Congress approved the Declaration of Independence, but they ended it with a powerful statement of faith in their new nation. All they deemed precious hung in the balance, for the sake of their future country. They were ready and willing to invest all they could muster on a cause still uncertain at the time. Ever since, those who cast their lot with this country have done no less. All of us who come to these shores bring an equal disposition to pledge our existences, energy, talent, and efforts to the service of our new homeland. And for many of us, it may take a lifetime to accomplish it, amid the constant doubts from the natives.

There is something about America that draws you in, something that simply cannot abide half-measures. A country whose first citizens cast aside centenary royal traditions to create a brand new nation has to be a harbinger of human freedom. Here, new ideas are tried out on a regular basis. The Lockean empiricism that so influenced America's early endeavors has enabled this nation to keep searching for new, workable solutions. From the beginning, Americans were willing to try out new technologies in every area of human endeavor. Their ability to scrap something as they develop a faster, more efficient replacement was critical to producing the high standards of living they now enjoy. In the words of President Barack Obama: "From our earliest days, we have reimagined and remade ourselves again and again. Colonists in the

1750s couldn't have imagined that forty years later, they would be living in a nation, independent of empire. Farmers in the first decades of the nineteenth century couldn't have imagined that forty years later, their continent would be crisscrossed by a railroad linking Eastern ports to Western markets. More recently, my parents' generation couldn't have imagined, as children, a world transformed by the Internet."[2]

A Brazilian by birth, it does not escape me that at the end of the eighteenth century my homeland was ahead of the United States in every area of national development. We had more natural resources, more modern cities, higher rates of export to Europe, and fewer social problems. In fact, at the time, Brazil boasted the largest economy in the Americas. Nevertheless, despite the U.S. Civil War and the ensuing economic recessions in the United States, by the nineteenth century's end, Brazil's GDP was only one-tenth of America's.[3] The Brazilian inability to innovate, to adopt its most talented citizens' novel ideas, played a role in slowing our overall progress. We remained tied to past technologies while the United States burst forth into the industrial era.

More importantly, American innovation is not the monopoly of any creed, race, or class. The nation is driven by results. The first American to become the wealthiest man in the world was only a poor Scottish immigrant with little more than a grade school education. Yet Andrew Carnegie revolutionized America's steel production, and reaped fame and fortune along the way.[4] There is not a single ethnic group that has arrived on American shores that has not significantly contributed to the country's success. Whatever limited these immigrants' imaginations back home ends as they alight on their new nation. As Thomas Ferris argues: "Technological innovation put cash in the pockets of persons excluded from such traditional sources of prosperity as inherited lands and titles, creating a social mobility that undermined old political structures and strictures. Applied science amplified and accelerated the pace of technological progress, offering not only a source of labor-saving devices in the home—a better loom or plow, a more helpful farmer's almanac—but a way to make money and move up in the world."[5]

Perhaps this is the key to sizing up the courage of our Founders on July 4 in 1776. They were moved by daring prospects, creating a nation where citizens had inalienable rights, where they were free to pursue life, liberty, and happiness. To this I attribute the United States' successful rate of acculturation—here newcomers are free to reinvent themselves, their talents are not limited by caste or rank, and their intelligence is not muffled by class distinctions. Under these conditions, anyone—immigrant or not—can step past the social grooves that defined her parents' lives to create a path of her own making. It is an exhilarating prospect, whether you were born here or anywhere else in the world.

Of course, America's bounty does not translate into ultimate equality of opportunity for all. I am not naïve about the great inequalities and indignities that have been visited upon minorities in the United States. Their toil has built this country in its fields, mills, mines, rail yards, plants, and construction sites over two centuries of history. Many of those who built this nation got little to show for it most of the time. And they were not the ones who were flogged to death or enslaved to their dying days. These were only latecomers to the task of nation-building. Much iniquity was visited upon Native Americans as well, whose land was lost, bit by bit, in one of the most uneven struggles in human history.

Nevertheless, I know of no other land with more favorable odds to newcomers. The large waves of immigrants from every corner of the world who have settled in the United States for more than two centuries attest to those odds. Despite violent nativism and periods of strong anti-immigration moods, at no time in the history of this nation has it lacked a fresh influx of talent from abroad. Think about this—it is possible to find Americans who are fluent in just about any language. As President Kennedy set up the Cuban blockade, back in 1962, American sailors of Russian descent were shouting instructions in Russian to the arriving crews of Soviet ships. When President George W. Bush declared war on Iraq, we had plenty of Arabic-speaking translators to facilitate the invasion. There have been translators at every foreign intervention in American history—many of them bicultural American citizens.

A Nation of Laws

Another factor that draws immigrants to American shores is the possibility of life in a nation of laws. Though this may seem too stale a point to make in the twenty-first century, it should not be easily discounted. Living in a nation of laws makes a huge difference. It affects every aspect of one's daily life. I grew up in a country whose government did not trust its own citizens. All Brazilians had to have valid ID cards on them at all times and be prepared to produce them constantly in all our dealings with law enforcement. We had to prove who we were before getting any public service. To request services of any kind—from utilities to health care—we had to produce a series of documents that proved our identity.[6]

But presenting full documentation that proved we were legitimate citizens did not result in the relief we sought. We might still have to bribe the official in charge to obtain services that were legitimately ours to claim. We might have to engage powerful patrons to loosen up the bureaucratic red tape. I grew up witnessing my father bribe cops, business inspectors, bank managers, notary clerks, and judges, along with other higher civil servants. When I applied to become a foreign exchange student in the United States, Dad had to bribe the attending official to process my passport in a timely manner. It was clear to me even then that I lived in a nation of arbitrary, capricious rule—we were a nation of small rulers, never a nation of laws. There is no redeeming for that kind of civic powerlessness.

We even have a term in Portuguese for these sorts of "transactions:" *jeitinho*. The closest translation I can think of is "finding a way." If someone in a government agency tells you he cannot help due to strict guidelines, the correct reply is "será que não dá para dar um jeitinho?" ("Might it not be possible to find a way?") That will open the door for a possible bribe, circumventing the obstructing rules. Brazilians find *jeitinhos* for everything—reconnecting utility services, getting a new phone line, opening a business—you name it. My mother's first driver's license came from a *jeitinho*—Dad had to bribe the inspector after she flunked the road test. It makes you wonder how safe it is to drive on Brazilian roads!

Such lack of transparency, combined with the jumble of red tape created by arcane legal systems, saps the initiative and entrepreneurial spirit of Latin Americans. Hernando de Soto's research ably shows the tragic consequences of our *jeitinhos* and red tape. The Peruvian economist estimates that it would take 289 days for someone setting up a small Lima garment-making shop with only two sewing machines to have it legalized. With the help of a capable attorney, the whole process would only cost thirty-one times Peru's monthly minimum wage. Getting the legal title to a shack would take more than two hundred bureaucratic steps and twenty-one years of effort.[7] This legal apartheid constantly sabotages the chance of success for most in the region.

Ironically, *jeitinhos* and red tape deprive countries that tolerate them, since they push business into black/informal markets, which generate fewer taxes and fewer above-board economic inputs. By de Soto's estimates, 90 percent of Peru's small industrial enterprises and 60 percent of its fishing fleet and food stores operate illegally. Most of the new jobs created in Latin America are part of this informal economy. In fact, by one estimate, almost 80 percent of Mexico's population operates in the informal economy, producing the equivalent of a third of the country's GDP.[8] If you wish, you can blame Latin American blight on a number of international factors. But until we build sound legal and economic institutions based on the rule of law, nothing will change.

On the other hand, living in a nation of laws does change you. To operate within its parameters, you have to become more disciplined, more organized, more willing to function in a prompt, efficient manner. It demands planning, being accustomed to follow guidelines. You can no longer twist or bend every rule for your own convenience. People who can bribe their way around life have no reason to meet deadlines or to follow instructions. If they fail to do their homework, they can still bribe the official and get the desired results. What reason do they have for personal accountability, if they can mold the world on a regular basis to fit their whims? That is not the case in a nation of laws, at least not for the common citizen.

I am not alone in my appreciation of American transparency and legal efficiency. Researchers have found high praise for American institutions among other Brazilian immigrants, especially when compared to their Brazilian counterparts. My compatriots applaud the egalitarian treatment they receive in business transactions. They are surprised by the respectful tone they find when dealing with local authorities. They are impressed by the efficiency of American social services and law enforcement, and charmed by the easy-going relations between employers and employees.[9] They enjoy all this despite their lack of English fluency and possible questionable legal status. Coming from a highly ranked society, they should know what they are talking about.

Perhaps the most important civic reward discovered by those who move to a nation of laws is simply the joy of being treated as a real citizen, someone with rights. Brazilians in Massachusetts were pleasantly surprised to find that despite their lack of citizenship in this country, they were treated as people who had basic rights. In the greater Boston area, they enjoyed a dimension of citizenship that they never had known at home—the idea that citizens are owed respect by those in authority positions, that their needs are taken into consideration by government clerks, that those who do provide services ought to be accountable.[10] Brazilians are not used to this kind of treatment back home.

These are the same Brazilian immigrants who when they first arrive continue trying to pull *jeitinhos* because they are still operating with a Brazilian mind-set. But here in the United States, they find out very quickly that this is not a land of *jeitinhos*. That culture shock takes a while to fade. Here, if you get a permit to operate a grocery store, you cannot add a hair salon or a small restaurant in the back (as people do in Brazil). Permits are honored. If not, people are fined. And if violators are not fined, inspectors are arrested and tried for dereliction of duty. It does pay to follow the rules in a nation of laws. In fact, it sets you free to operate without having to constantly cover up your infractions.

While some may attribute the American system to higher morals or puritanical origins, I am more inclined to say that operating by the book is simply a more efficient way to get things done. Americans are a practical people by nature. And a basic principle of pragmatism is that contracts are honored and guidelines followed. Americans are no saints. Their corporations bribe their way into other nations' markets just as corporations from other parts of the world do. But bribes add to the cost of business and cut down on profits. The same principle applies to government—a town or state that constantly breaks its own rules will not attract many businesses. So we live by the rules because that expedites results.

The irony is that living in a truly regulated and transparent world frees you to follow your own ambitions. When you follow the rules, you spend less time and energy patching things up. You are free to pursue your interests directly. In the Recife business community where I grew up, it was common to use all kinds of subterfuge to get ahead. People kept double accounting books ("one for the tax man, the other for us") and withheld commercial information from the government on services rendered. You never got your receipt when you bought things. That allowed the owner to avoid paying taxes on the transaction. You could pay more for an object with the sales slip, or less without it.

It is a relief to live in a country with transparent practices. To be sure, the practices alone do not keep you from harm. Business people may still try to cheat you, and you may find certain town practices, like speed traps, terribly annoying. But there is a baseline, there is a yardstick against which you can claim damages, seek legal relief, and obtain redress. That makes a huge difference. Take the U.S. lemon laws, for instance. Purchasing a car is still an adventure in this country, and you always end up paying more than you should. But you have rights that allow you to rectify dishonesty in sales. You learn that the world does not have to operate by arbitrary, bendable rules.

It is amazing to see how quickly immigrants adapt to these standard operating procedures. They quickly grasp the built-in advantages of playing by the book. The red tape for setting up a business, or applying for a job, or pursuing an education is minimal compared to the systems left back home. The costs are lower as well. So it doesn't take long for them to realize the potential returns from doing things aboveboard. In Latin America today there are still people who think that prosperity is a function of luck, of knowing the right people, or getting special treatment from the authorities. Let them come to America and see the millions of immigrants who set up shop in this country and prosper by following the rules.

A second key aspect of living in a nation of laws is being able to elect the people who create the laws that will affect your life. Many American-born citizens may not realize this, but those they put in office do represent their interests. Again, it is all relative—but compared to politics in other countries, the American system is far more efficient. Public discontent with an elected official can certainly end his or her career. The first time I voted in Brazil we were still under military rule. Afraid of possible negative results, the military "pre-selected" a good chunk of our House Representatives. Those of us voting knew the whole thing was rigged, and we knew that we were simply rubber-stamping the military's choice. There were absolutely no guarantees that those we "chose" would legislate on our behalf.

This form of "election" takes place regularly around the world. In Iran, the clerics pre-approve those who can run for office on the basis of their religious allegiance. People who fail that test cannot aspire to serve.[11] Technically Cuba has staged "regular" elections during the Castro regime, but no one in Latin America or the rest of the world for that matter believes them to be true or legitimate.[12] The same applies to all the Latin American *caudillos* who have clung to power for decades on end, winning hollow re-elections. The semblance of democracy does not make for a representative system. All Brazilian "presidents" from 1964 to 1984 were generals appointed to office. None was chosen by the Brazilian people; none represented anyone's rightful interests.

In the United States, on the other hand, the political system must respond to local pressure. As Thomas "Tip" O'Neill, the longtime Speaker of the U.S. House of Representatives, once said, "all politics is local."[13] When everyone is free to participate in the process, the local issues and local interests drive elections as much as national concerns. In the eleven years since becoming a U.S. citizen, I have voted and contributed to political campaigns of all sorts in Virginia—from local town council to U.S. senatorial bids. Politicians running for office come through town on a regular basis. Their campaign staff knows you, e-mails you often, and organizes local meetings to rally the troops.

More importantly, whenever I contact one of my representatives I feel truly heard as I get his response. I feel that my opinion has been taken into account. The representatives may not always vote the way I would like them to, but I understand that they are not representing my interests alone. They have to consider the interests of all the people who put them in office. That they do so, that they respond to my queries and deem to explain their positions to me, still amazes me. In so many countries the interests of the majority are not necessarily the guiding lights by which powerbrokers set their compass. There, arbitrary rule perpetuates the personal hold on power. Look to the Southern Hemisphere—the examples abound.

During the period when I was researching Latin American immigration in central Virginia, local and state politicians contacted me to learn more about the state's immigrant communities. I had the honor of briefing the mayor of Richmond and two Virginia governors on data I collected. I also presented my findings to the Virginia business community, and to local agencies and police departments and health clinics in nearby counties. I cannot imagine replicating that in my country of origin. First, I would have no access to those in power. Second, they would have no interest in my findings. Here, my expert input was valued and it informed policy. *That's* the difference of living in a nation of laws.

Political scientists have long known that a sense of political efficacy is crucial for voter participation. Citizens must feel that their government listens to them, cares about their concerns, and that their interests affect political results if they participate. Absent that, political apathy sets in and voter turnout declines. In the words of one scholar, "as one participates in politics, one acquires political skills and perceptions of self-competence, qualities thought necessary for popular self-government and effective control over one's environment."[14]

This form of political participation is at the heart of real democracies. It empowers their citizens to interact productively with the political system they have created. This kind of political accountability was fully tried for the first time, at all instances of government, in the United States. There is a reason why political scientists consider our country "the first new nation."[15] The United States set up clear standards for democratic practices, and that is critical, according to Seymour Lipset, because political forces take different historical shape on the basis of the electoral systems that they create. America's political system was built on representativeness, on that frail balance of egalitarian participation and practical achievement.

Personal Accountability

Political efficacy is, of course, a function of personal accountability. Only a people who take responsibility for their actions can seek to collectively alter the course of history, to influence their nation's future. Personal accountability is based upon the notion of agency—the idea that those in charge of their own lives are responsible for the consequences of their behavior. Moral action demands agency—one cannot be blamed for acts performed under duress or coercion. It is precisely those free to choose a particular course of action who are therefore responsible for the outcomes. America was founded upon the premise that its citizens had the power to freely choose the means by which they would be governed.

In countries with low levels of political efficacy, the general public does not see power as emanating from the people. Individuals see themselves as subjects of the regimes that rule them. Power lies elsewhere: with the country's elites, its military, perhaps those few who control most of their nation's resources. Under such conditions, it makes little sense to talk about civil society or personal accountability. Those traits are squelched by the coercive circumstances under which citizens exist. Many Americans would be surprised to find out that the term "personal accountability" might not even have a direct translation in some languages around the world. For instance, I know no direct translation for "personal accountability" in Portuguese. The closest may be "being in charge of something." But that is not being accountable.

The ability to be self-governed requires personal accountability—the foundational notion that we as citizens are responsible for the institutions we build. That is why a nation of laws works only if its citizens are well-schooled in their civic duties, in being shareholders in the nation they help create or sustain. That is a far cry from Latin America's Iberian heritage, one whose institutions were imposed by an absolute monarchy, with no input from their subjects. Writing the Declaration of Independence, Thomas Jefferson wisely replaced the term "subjects" with "citizens," to clearly signal to the world that in America, political institutions would be of its citizens' own making.[16]

Despite such powerful beginnings, nation-building in a nation of laws is a never-ending task. Our founding documents speak of forming "a more perfect union." And from the beginning, this country has struggled to bring all its citizens into the body politic. It is one thing to advocate a government by the people in theory, quite another to allow everyone to partake in the effort. Not all Americans were enfranchised at the time of our nation's founding. Not all voices were heard. As Abigail Adams, wife of our second president, so aptly reminded her husband a few months prior to America's independence:

> I long to hear that you have declared an independency. And, by the way, in the new code of laws which I suppose it will be necessary for you to make, I desire you would remember the ladies and be more generous and favorable to them than your ancestors. Do not put such unlimited power into the hands of the husbands. Remember, all men would be tyrants if they could. If particular care and attention is not paid to the ladies, we are determined to foment a rebellion, and will not hold ourselves bound by any laws in which we have no voice or representation.[17]

There is no denying that the early moments of the American republic left out significant segments of society—white women, slaves, and the native tribes—upon whose toil much of the country's early wealth was built. Their later inclusion would be required for at least two reasons. First, because democratic rule depends upon the personal assent of the governed, and second, because exclusion creates diminished and biased political institutions. The assent of the governed demanded that those who were ruled be represented in the rule-making process. Institutions created by only a particular gender or race would, by necessity, reflect that gender's or race's biases and privileges.

In time, America's early political contradictions had to be corrected, its biases redressed in a Bill of Rights. That is precisely the genius of America's founding, the need to strive for that more perfect union. The only way to address the country's early injustices was political inclusion and that more perfect union demanded the input of the many voices who were initially left out of the conversation. So, as America expanded culturally and geographically, the pressures for inclusion increased as well. To be true to the self-governing model of their institutions, Americans had to fine-tune the republic, even to the extent of a bloody Civil War.

But democratic inclusion has been one of America's key strengths as a nation of laws. Its diversity in unity is ever proclaimed as *E pluribus unum.* It is precisely our capacity to incorporate the many distinct ethnic groups that have arrived on our shores into a single, self-sufficient republic that bodes well for the future of our nation. Our Founders' vision—their pact of self-governance, of a nation ruled by laws, based upon the personal accountability of its citizens—continues to entice newcomers to this country. Those principles are perhaps more critical for their acculturation than the simple demand that they use the English language.

Pledging One's Life

If the previous sections seem to depict America as an idyllic nation, let me hasten to add that there are no earthly paradises. Things were messy at this country's birth and remained so throughout its history. The same enlightened republic that crafted the Declaration of Independence exterminated or expelled the Cherokee, Creek, Seminole, and Choctaw nations westward. The liberal nation that fought a Civil War over slavery tolerated the KKK and Jim Crow laws in its aftermath until they could no longer be ignored. The progressive body that approved the Bill of Rights saw fit to intern Japanese Americans during World War II. Alas, the Founders' checks and balances were built for a nation of fallible citizens, not saints.

That is why pledging one's life, fortune, and sacred honor to the United States is a complicated process. Not every aspect of American life is genuinely infused by its mythical qualities; not every American trait is necessarily a virtue. The city upon the hill, the shining beacon of freedom has had more than its fair share of less than honorable moments. It is not clear, for instance, that the American process of political inclusion is complete. Old prejudices and fears are as alive in today's Tea Party demonstrations as they were in the rallies of the Know Nothing Party of the 1840s and 1850s.[18] Economic depressions, joblessness, and glum prospects for the future always incite nativism, leading people to rely on the same tired scapegoat rationales to make sense of their hard times.

Every immigrant who reaches these shores sooner or later realizes that she has traded one set of troubles back home for a new set in the United States. No matter how long you live here, you remain to some degree an outsider, and outsiders are expendable. Your children might fare better, but they too will face their moments of exclusion. It is a tiresome proposition to spend one's life educating people who should know better when it comes to immigration, especially given their enlightened political origins. But when Arizona passes a punitive immigration law, one must remind its citizens that eight signers of the Declaration of Independence and seven signers of the American Constitution were not born in the United States.[19]

To be fair, a few immigrants bring their own foibles and dishonorable motives to this land. When ethnic gangs are as perilous as the home-bred kind, one wonders what must be done. When the South American flow of narcotics finds its weakest links among immigrant communities in southwestern states, the nation rancorously pays attention. That the 9/11 hijackers entered the United States legally and eleven well-behaved suburban American residents were actually Russian spies should give pause to even the most ardent immigration advocate.[20] The ugly truth is that not everyone who seeks shelter here is simply trying to start anew.

That too makes the pledging of one's life, fortune, and sacred honor a complicated matter. We who come to America seeking life and liberty have to navigate treacherous waters to confront the dark side of immigration and remain ever attuned to the changing moods of our adopted country regarding its declared "enemies." The *enemy du jour* may determine how well immigrants from a given region of the world are treated. When I arrived in the United States in 1981, Ronald Reagan was president and the bad guys were the Evil Empire and their puppets fighting proxy wars in Central America. It was not easy being a Central American immigrant then. Under President George H. W. Bush, Saddam Hussein and the Iraqis were the enemies to watch, so Middle Eastern immigrants were under a lot of pressure. President Clinton shifted our gaze to Bosnian Serbs. President George W. Bush took us back to the Middle East after 9/11.

Each shift in foreign policy brought consequences for the respective American ethnic communities already settled in the United Sates. In fact, in every way that matters, American foreign policy has a constant and deep ripple effect on the ebb and flow of American immigration. Depending on which enemy we are fighting abroad, certain immigrant communities in the United States might grow, while others may barely survive under the constant suspicion of aiding and abetting our enemies.

After the Cuban revolution, the U.S. government spent a great deal of resources monitoring Latin American nations. American universities received State Department funds to further develop the field of Latin

American Studies and to train government workers and U.S. military officers who were deployed to fight communism in our hemisphere. And since fighting Cuba meant welcoming its enemies, America became a favorite destination for upper-class Cuban exiles, along with other Latin American elites who were seeking political asylum. There was a great deal of pain involved in that migratory process, but greater still to those whose profile did not match the tired, poor, and oppressed of the moment.

The Cold War brought us immigrants from behind the Iron Curtain. American aid to independent political movements in Poland and Czechoslovakia generated waves of exiles. As American attention shifted eastward, so did the waves of Asian immigrants who were America-bound. The Korean and Vietnam wars brought new immigrant communities to the United States, including Laotians, Hmong, and Cambodians. Just as the Filipino, Japanese, and Chinese communities who arrived at the end of the nineteenth century, these groups had to re-create their identities within the broader contours of American culture.

Our current military presence in the Middle East will generate its own set of immigrants from the region. I foresee the time when Shiites, Sunnis, and Kurds from Iraq and Pashtuns, Tajiks, Hazaras, Uzbeks, Aimak, Turkmen, and Baluch from Afghanistan will be added to the American ethnic palette. Once these immigrants settle upon our soil, they will go about rebuilding their lives in the fashion that most American immigrants do. They will seek jobs, find housing, secure education for their children, and learn—as best as they can—to live by the prevailing rules of American society. They will still be caught between two worlds, as am I. But the fascination with things American will transplant their souls to the adopted country.

Here they will create their own brand of American ethnicity by continuing to treasure food from home and to enjoy their native literature, music, theater, and dance. Slowly their proud nationality will become another form of American ethnicity, as the ways of the old country mix with the cultural traits of their new world. Eventually they and their children will learn about America's beginnings, and they will start to celebrate its holidays. They will visit our country's historical sites and make U.S. history their own (remember my Brazilian American son playing Ulysses S. Grant in a school performance).

Look for their tour groups at the Lincoln and Jefferson monuments in Washington, DC. Watch them pause somberly at Gettysburg. Witness their visits to Philadelphia's hallowed civic grounds. Watch them retrace the American revolutionaries' steps in New York and Massachusetts. They will come silently, pledging their own lives to the cause. They too will understand the vision of our Founders. And their children will further pledge their lives to this country as they partake in its educational system and find opportunities that will seem extraordinary to their parents. And *that* is the virtue of our nation, most of all.

These are folks who will spend the rest of their working days adding to the progress of their adopted country. They will run the everyday businesses—the restaurants, the grocery stores, the motels, the cleaners—that are the lifeline of their local communities. They or their children will serve in local police forces and firefighting squads. They will teach in local schools and colleges. They will work in the construction, extraction, and transportation industries. They will be involved in manufacturing, installation, and repair. And they will have their fair share of workers in all forms of service occupations.[21] They will learn about the American dream and create their own versions of it.

In some cases, their entrepreneurial activities will help attract capital investment to the United States. Between 1995 and 2005, immigrant entrepreneurs helped launch one-quarter of all engineering and technology companies in America, adding 450,000 new jobs to our economy.[22]

American-born citizens have benefited an estimated $37 billion a year from immigrant participation in the U.S. economy. And since immigrants pay more taxes than they use in government services, they will help fund Social Security (undocumented immigrants alone contribute an estimated $7 billion a year in Social Security taxes), Medicaid, and Medicare, along with local state programs.

Finally, those immigrants will also expand ethnic markets in the United States. The older ethnic markets alone—the Hispanic and Asian American consumer markets—totaled an estimated 14 percent of the nation's 2008 purchasing power. Think of what all the other ethnic markets add to this country's GDP. Cable companies already provide programming in international languages for almost every cable market in this nation. Their ads sustain an enormous amount of local business. Ethnic newspapers, savings and loans, cultural associations, restaurants, and grocery stores also add to the larger pool.[23] If that is not pledging one's life, fortune, and sacred honor to America, I don't know what is.

For many immigrants, middle-class status is a source of loyalty to the United States. In 2007, 4.1 million immigrant households could be classified as middle class. They represented a quarter of the 17.5 million immigrant households in America. The percentage of middle-class households among immigrants was almost the same as native-born households in middle-class America (respectively 23.6 and 24 percent). Those middle-class immigrants shared the American suburbs with everybody else. Some 15 million of them, in fact, lived in middle-class households in 2007. Put it another way, one in every five middle-class U.S. residents lived in an immigrant household.[24]

The American-born children of immigrants intensify their loyalty to the adopted country. Nearly two out of every five residents in middle-class immigrant households were native-born U.S. citizens. Of the 5.5 million children living in immigrant middle-class households in 2007, 77 percent were native born.[25] Immigrants know that as they contribute to the welfare of this country, they are contributing to their own children's welfare. The future opportunities of their offspring only drive them to work harder, to save, to invest, and to add to our GDP. For any parent I know, their children's well-being is reason enough to pledge one's life and fortune to a nation.

More importantly, native-born middle-class Americans understand their immigrant neighbors' reasons for coming to the United States, and they actually respect their motives. In a national study of American middle-class communities, Alan Wolfe reports a great deal of tolerance toward immigrants among survey respondents. They see in "the good immigrant" someone who experienced violence and disruption back home, and whose drive to succeed led him to the United States. The "good immigrant" reminds native-born middle-class Americans of their ancestors' hardships in coming to America. As long as the immigrant is willing to learn English, work hard, and be a good citizen, they were willing to support him.[26]

On Taking Roots and Making Lasting Pledges

In order for all of this to happen, for immigrant nationalities to turn into American ethnicities, for their dreams of middle-class life to come to fruition, they have to show a disposition to pledge their lives and fortunes to the host nation. As long as immigrants see themselves as sojourners, people who are here only for a while, making money here to enjoy it in their countries of origin, that pledge will not be forthcoming. This is why it is not enough for someone to get a visa to come to the United States. It is not enough for that person to get a green card.

It is not even enough for her to become naturalized. Those are necessary legal steps, of course, the means by which one is allowed to remain in the host nation.

Pledging one's life must be the next logical thing. Until such a time, one cannot speak of a new citizen per se, or even a new ethnic community. That is one of the startling findings in Maxine Margolis's study of Brazilian immigrants in New York. Despite many of them residing here for a decade or more, they lacked an ethnic community; they lacked the ethnic solidarity we find among other American immigrants. Some 80,000 strong back in the early 1990s in New York, the Brazilians could not muster the creation of a single united cultural association to protect their interests and work on their behalf. After a year of serious fundraising, a small Brazilian cultural center on the Lower East Side had garnered $2,000 for the effort.[27]

Margolis's conclusion would be the same one I might reach. She saw the majority of Brazilian immigrants in New York as realists in their lack of esprit de corps. They never thought of themselves as a permanent community. They saw the individuals in their ethnic group striving for the same thing—to make as much money as quickly as possible prior to returning to Brazil. Involvement in clubs, organizations, or any other form of community-building effort would simply take time away from their single-minded pursuit. They were not here to pledge their lives; they were here only temporarily. As one Brazilian so aptly put it, "We don't have an immigrant spirit because we are not immigrants."[28]

Nevertheless, even those who are here for a while can make a lasting pledge or offer a permanent contribution. Perhaps the most tentative of American immigrants was also someone who made an enduring pledge to this country. Born in the village of Nelahozeves near Prague in 1841, Antonín Dvořák never imagined that he would make a home for himself in America one day. His early life unfolded like that of many classical musicians of the age. He studied music in Prague from 1857 to 1859, and played the viola in the Bohemian Provisional Theater Orchestra until he got married. Seeking greater financial security, he accepted the position of organist of Saint Adalbert's Church in Prague.

Throughout his early musical career, Dvořák composed regularly. In fact, his first String Quartet was penned at the age of twenty, barely two years after his graduation from music school.[29] Johannes Brahms, recognizing Dvořák's talent, helped his music find a larger audience. Brahms convinced the well-known European musical publishing house Simrock to distribute Dvořák's works. The maestro's fame led to nine

Antonín Dvořák (Museum of Dvořák)

visits to England, starting in 1884, and a trip to Russia, where he conducted the Moscow and Saint Petersburg orchestras. Eventually, his
success led to a prestigious appointment with the Prague Conservatory,
as professor of composition and instrumentation.

That is when fate intervened, and his American adventure began.
At the Prague Conservatory, Dvořák caught the eye of Mrs. Jeanette
Thurber, the wealthy New York philanthropist who had founded a
music conservatory in the city in 1884. She decided that she wanted
Dvořák for director of her institution. Modeled after the Paris Conservatory, Thurber's New York National Conservatory of Music (NYNCM)
was no ordinary music school. A progressive place where no tuition
was charged, the school was created to train the vanguard of American
classical musical performers, with the goal of attracting and educating
the most musically talented American students, regardless of race,
gender, or class.

The NYNCM had a demanding three-year curriculum, supported by
high-caliber instructors like the soprano Emma Fursh-Madi, the pianists
Adele Margolies and Rafael Joseffy, the violinist Leopold Lichtenberg,
the cellist and composer Victor Herbert, and the composer Rubin
Goldmark. And to direct such a roster of stars, from 1892 to 1895 Mrs.
Thurber hired the famous Antonín Dvořák. He was to teach composition and instrumentation, conduct the school's orchestra, to compose. As
part of his contract, Dvořák was required to premiere six new compositions per year. His hiring was the talk of town. Local papers asked for
interviews; one even published a series of articles by the maestro.

Somewhat reluctantly, the ever-so-European musician boarded a
ship to the New World. In his newspaper articles, he indicated the
direction he wished to give to the NYNCM. In them, Dvořák argued
that true classical American music ought to be imbued by or founded
upon the rhythms and melodies of Native American and African
American music. Already fascinated by Native American melodic
structures, at the NYNCM Dvořák was introduced to Negro spirituals
by one of his African American students, Harry Burleigh, who was
already a well-known composer of spirituals and "American-style"
music. Much of Dvořák's time in America was spent exploring the
riches of the country's sounds.

True to his word, Dvořák would incorporate those Native and
African American themes into the first symphony he wrote on American
soil. Between the winter and spring of 1893, at a house on East Seventeenth Street, Dvořák composed most of his Ninth Symphony, the one
that would become known as "From the New World." There he finished

the first three movements, the Adagio, Largo, and Scherzo, by the end of that spring. The fourth movement, however, the Allegro con fuoco, was completed at a Czech-speaking colony in Spillville, Iowa, where the homesick maestro was visiting cousins. In Spillville, surrounded by compatriots who came to America seeking a new life, he put the final touches to his symphony.

And what a symphony it was! Dvořák's Ninth Symphony became his lasting pledge to his temporary homeland. Without a doubt "From the New World" is the best musical description I know of the American immigrant condition, of someone intensely caught between two worlds. No bicultural person can listen to this symphony without immediately understanding its powerful melancholy, its nostalgia for home. There is a direct identification with the music, with the fragile balance between the Bohemian folk dances of the maestro's childhood and the powerful new American motifs he discovered in this hemisphere. You hear the fascination with the New World as strongly as his deep longing for home.

"From the New World" was first performed by the New York Philharmonic at Carnegie Hall on December 16, 1893. One of Dvořák's pupils, William Arms Fisher, would later adapt and arrange the symphony's Largo movement into the beloved African American spiritual "Goin' Home":

Goin' home, goin' home, I'm a goin' home;
Quiet-like, some still day, I'm jes' goin' home.
It's not far, jes' close by,
Through an open door;
Work all done, care laid by,
Goin' to fear no more.
Mother's there 'spectin' me,
Father's waitin' too;
Lots o' folks gather'd there,
All the friends I knew,
All the friends I knew.
Home, I'm goin' home!

In the song's music sheet, Fisher explained that the haunting English horn solo in Dvořák's Largo symbolized the maestro's own home-longing, but it was woven with "the loneliness of far-off prairie horizons, the faint memory of the red-man's bygone days, and a sense of the tragedy of the black-man as it sings in his 'spirituals.'" Fisher equates the melody with a universal nostalgia. To him the lyric opening theme automatically suggested the words of the Negro spiritual: "Goin' home, goin' home." And he thought that the largo's musical phrasing followed the form of a Negro spiritual, which suffused the whole symphony.[30]

Dvořák's Largo, in the form of the spiritual "Goin' Home," became part of America's civil religion when it was performed at President Franklin Delano Roosevelt's funeral. The initial Czech expression of homesickness became a funereal homage for a fallen American head of state, and it comforted a mourning nation on the loss of its towering political leader. As a spiritual, the Americanness of Dvořák's theme continues to be expressed by its use in African American churches throughout the United States. Every time I play Dvořák's Ninth Symphony to my college students, there are always African American pupils who tell me they grew up singing it. It rings as true a spiritual to them as those composed by their own ancestors.

The first time I heard Dvořák's Ninth Symphony, I was completely taken aback by his creation. Back in those graduate school days, all that was dear to me still lay in Brazil; the United States, despite its attractions, was not yet my home. The second movement hit me hard. Its nostalgia was so potent that I was completely enraptured by the music, caught between two worlds. I could sense the beauty and tenderness of Dvořák's homeland just as much as I understood the seductive attraction he felt for his adoptive home. There was no way to miss them—both were equally compelling as they were powerful. You could not take them apart. The music gave me, perhaps, my first inklings of a future pledge to this nation.

Dvořák would compose other works that year. In fact, he had a prolific year, with beautiful pieces like the String Quartet No. 12 in F ("The American"), the String Quintet in E flat, and the Sonatina for violin and piano. He would go on to conduct his Eighth Symphony at Chicago's Columbian Exposition, and he clearly provided steady leadership at the helm of the NYNCM. But both his Ninth Symphony and the String Quartet No. 12 would leave an indelible mark on his adopted culture. The pieces would be performed over and over by American orchestras and music ensembles around the world as Americans fell in love with Dvořák's music, and rightfully so. As far as I'm concerned, the Ninth "From the New World" Symphony was Dvořák's love letter to his accidental homeland.

The maestro returned to Europe in 1895, the homesickness having prevailed over his fascination with the New World. Other important professional European opportunities awaited him. He enjoyed a long career, writing impressive works after his American sojourn. The New York National Conservatory of Music survived a little longer as well. By the turn of the century, the school had graduated some three thousand students, but by the mid to late 1920s, as other music schools were founded in New York, such as the Institute of Musical Art (which eventually became the Juilliard School), the NNCM needed more students and money to keep running. Eventually, the Great Depression cut off the NYNCM's philanthropic support and the school closed.[31]

For me, "From the New World" hid a delicious surprise. As I got to the fourth movement, I was positive I had heard its musical phrasing before. But where? My parochial Recife did not have an orchestra during my childhood. My family did not take me to concerts as a child. Nevertheless, I was quite sure that Dvořák's fourth movement had been a part of my early years. The more I listened, the more convinced I became. I could associate that music to tender childhood memories. Then it dawned on me—when television first arrived in Recife, TV stations used a musical signature prior to their regular programming. The Jornal do Commércio station adopted Dvořák's fourth movement as its musical introit!

That awareness produced a moment of sheer transcendence. As I listened to the last bars of the fourth movement, I realized that a Czech composer, who spent a few years in the United States a hundred years before I arrived, had created a musical gem that through the mysteries of globalization ended up enchanting my own childhood. Without my being fully aware of it, Dvořák's homesickness had become my homesickness when I was growing up. All my memories of early American TV programs (dubbed in Portuguese, of course) came flooding back. Here I was in his New World, which happened to also be a place of importance in my childhood. Listening to him took me back to the sweet time when I spoke my first words and sang my first lullabies.

At that moment, Dvořák's Largo blended with William Arms Fisher's song. The melancholy turned personal for me. My nostalgia for Recife mixed with the sorrow of the lost Native American prairies, the African American suffering, and the hills of Bohemia where a young Dvořák once had found a home. The music made me deeply aware of my temporary condition as a foreign graduate student in the United States. Dvořák's loneliness pervaded my following days. No wonder "From the New World" became so universally acclaimed. No wonder it remains an important patriotic piece in this land. It is American, but it carries an oh-so-universal human cry.

6

Almost Home

An arbitrary set of boundaries determines your rights and contributes enormously to your success or failure. To be born in Bar Harbor, Maine . . . leads to a vastly different life than to be born in Burkina Faso.

John Yemma, *Christian Science Monitor*, July 5, 2010

Born near a small town in eastern Oregon (population 900), a high, dry place of deep canyons, Mark's childhood was filled by county fairs, rodeos, 4-H clubs, and FFA meetings.[1] Situated in one of the least populated areas of the United States, Mark's school was the only one for miles on end. Twenty-seven seniors graduated with him that year. Most of them remained in the area, doing farm work, running small shops, operating the co-op. They liked the lifestyle, the pace of living. Their plan after high school was simple—to get married, have kids, and settle down where they came into the world. Decades later, most of them are still there, quite content in repeating their parents' seasons, if only at a more high-tech rate.

Not Mark. For some reason, he grew up dreaming of other worlds. Small-town life was not in the cards for him. Mark loved music, especially church singing, but had no idea of what to do with the rest of his life. One of the few in his graduating class to go on to college, after high school Mark attended Oregon's land-grant university, a natural choice, since it is known for its agricultural programs. The school choir caught his attention during freshman year. After discovering that the university had an exchange program with a German school, he decided to study abroad . . . and never came back. German university life was inebriating, the students so cosmopolitan, and German cities were simply too much of a feast for his artistic taste.

So the kid from the American Northwest found his home in Germany. The food, the music, the theater, the museums all made sense to him, all seemed familiar. Despite being so removed from everything he'd known, Mark was home at last. There he found his *beruf*, his calling. After studying voice, he has spent a lifetime singing opera in one of Germany's most important companies. In Germany, he also finally found love. He has set up a wonderful life with his partner, who is an actor, in a tastefully appointed flat in one of the nation's most cultured urban centers. This year he started his German naturalization process. Mark's life is as removed from that of his high school friends as it could possibly be. But it is home to him.

Suzanne hails from a small town in Michigan (population 11,000). She too dreamed of living abroad while she was in college. Her plans were a bit different from Mark's—she wanted to visit and live in several countries. The first one she chose was Japan. She enrolled in the JET Program, an initiative of the Japanese government that places American college graduates in assistant teaching positions in local Japanese public schools. Japan was supposed to be Suzanne's springboard, but once there life took a different turn. On her second year in the country, she met the man she would marry. Twenty years later, Suzanne is happily settled in Aizumi, with a Japanese husband, her nine-year-old twins, and a doting mother-in-law. From holiday celebrations, to food, to home culture, her life is fully Japanese.

Suzanne spent her first decade in Japan teaching in public schools. Now she offers English conversation classes at a local university and at a nearby language school. As a freelance writer, Suzanne has authored two books about life in Japan. She is fluent in Japanese and for all intents and purposes seems to be well adapted to her new homeland. Sometimes, when she gets a little homesick, she wishes the Japanese were more tolerant of cultural differences. That is when she misses celebrating American traditions at home. But Suzanne has no plans to return to America. Japan is definitely home now. In fact, at the time she gave her interview, her family had just bought a house in Tokushima.[2]

Casey was born in a small town in Pennsylvania (population 2,500). Like Mark and Suzanne, he wanted to live abroad during his college days. It was while he was studying abroad in Spain that Casey got interested in Central America, more specifically Costa Rica. So, after graduating from college, with a marketing background, and one year of experience working at a dot-com, Casey landed in Costa Rica in 1998, on a tourist visa. Like other immigrants to his own homeland, it took Casey a while to get legalized in his adopted country. Now, despite the lack of the usual American job benefits (like health insurance), he thinks he is doing quite well for an outsider. His online travel agency grew so much, it branched out into Panama, and eventually Casey spun off a real estate company. Suffice it to say, after two years in Costa Rica, Casey is living abroad quite comfortably.

As a fluent Spanish speaker, he thinks that language is essential for the successful American expat experience. And Costa Rica's proximity to the United States is a plus, since he gets to visit his family at least once a year. These days Casey rents an apartment in Costa Rica and owns a condo in Panama. As an international hub for shipping, trade, and business, Panama attracts quite a diverse community of expats. So Casey likes the cosmopolitan feel of the place, and its affordable lifestyle; but most of all, he loves the Panamanians' wit, affection for their culture, and acceptance of outsiders. Obviously Casey has plenty of friends in both countries ("connections are everything," he says) and no plans to return to the United States any time soon.[3]

In case you're wondering, Mark, Suzanne, and Casey are not really exceptions. Every year millions leave their country of birth to settle elsewhere, for a variety of reasons. By one estimate, about five million Americans have resettled abroad, at least one million in Mexico.[4] According to the *New York Times*, nearly 190 million people—about 3 percent of the world's population—lived outside their country of birth in 2005.[5] The United Nations put that number at 214 million these days. That number has increased 37 percent over the last two decades. The ranks of immigrants moving to Europe increased by 41 percent during the period; the number relocating to North America grew by 80 percent.

Those are impressive numbers. It should surprise no one that immigration is a hot topic in those countries. At no other time in world history have we witnessed similar mobility.[6] All these immigrants who are moving around the globe are trailblazing other ways to be home, other means to find oneself. Some may be driven by tragedy, by wars, political persecution, or natural disasters. But others have moved of their own volition, simply seeking a new life in their adopted homelands. For migration scholars these immigrants represent the third wave of globalization. The first wave was set up by goods in the form of trade. The second pertained to capital, in the form of financial investment. The third is made up of human beings, seeking a better future in other lands.

Casting their lot with their new nations, these immigrants might play important roles in their adopted countries. For the first time in history, it is perfectly possible to find a Moroccan-born alderman in the Netherlands or a Nigerian-born mayor in Ireland.[7] This globalized world creates all kinds of possibilities for the likes of people such as Pico Iyer:

> By the time I was 9, I was already used to going to school by plane, to sleeping in airports, to shuttling back and forth, three times a year, between my home in California and my boarding school in England. While I was growing up, I was never within 6,000 miles of the nearest relative—and came, therefore, to learn how to define relations in non-familial ways. From the time I was a teenager, I took it for granted that I could take my budget vacations (as I did) in Bolivia and Tibet, China and Morocco. It never seemed strange to me that a girlfriend might be half a world (or 10 hours flying time) away, that my closest friends might be on the other side of a continent or sea.[8]

Perhaps the most surprising thing about this global movement is how recent it is. I have to remind my students that as late as 1970 the U.S. Census had stopped asking people where their parents were born, because the question was deemed insignificant. Forty-some years later, a quarter of all American residents under eighteen are children of immigrants. And the numbers migrating changed relatively fast for both Europe and the United States. In fact, I am part of this late wave, part of the cohort who resettled in the last three decades. Not until the early 1980s did real opportunities arise for worldwide migration. By then, the cost of relocation was easily offset by scholarship funds to study abroad or job opportunities in other lands.

Studying abroad opened many doors for global migrants. By 1980, partly fueled by the Cold War, the competition for international students had reached a peak as top research universities around the world fought to attract the most talented scholars from the Southern Hemisphere. Between the United States and the Soviet Union, quite a few generations of Latin Americans, Africans, and Asians gained access to higher education. But even as late as 2008–9, there were 671,616 international students enrolled in American universities, an 8 percent increase from the previous year. International students represented almost 4 percent of total U.S. college enrollment that year. And the flow now works both ways. More American students, 262,416 of them, were studying abroad in 2007-8, though for only a semester or a year. They represented a 9 percent increase in a single year, but a 150 percent increase over the whole decade.[9]

It is quite impressive to find such large numbers of international students attending American universities, some two decades after the end of the Cold War. Especially considering that most Southern Hemisphere countries have solid higher education institutions now, with far more affordable tuitions. Take Latin America, for instance. According to the UNESCO there were almost 2,500 universities in the region, 15 percent of them capable of carrying out research and development programs at internationally competitive standards in 2005. Some 13 million Latin American students were enrolled in those universities that year.[10] That is quite an infrastructure. Nevertheless, in 2008-9 there were still 67,731 Latin American students who chose to attend American universities instead, a 5 percent increase over the previous year.

While most of us came here for graduate degrees in the 1970s and 1980s, by 2008-9 most Latin American students were here for their undergraduate education.[11] There were 1,067 Bolivians in American colleges in 2008-9, an 11 percent increase from the previous year. Of those, 62 percent enrolled in undergraduate programs. Some 8,767 Brazilians chose to attend college in the United States that year, an increase of 16 percent from 2007-8. Half of the Brazilians were attending undergraduate programs. Almost two thousand Chileans (1,953) were here, 16 percent more than the previous year, with 27 percent of them in undergraduate studies. More than seven thousand Colombians came here for higher education (7,013), 5 percent more than the year before, and 42 percent of them were undergraduates. Some 14,850 Mexicans attended American universities in 2008-9, the same number as the previous year, with 60 percent of them pursuing undergraduate studies.[12]

But international education is by no means limited to American universities. Since Europe launched its Erasmus Program in 1987, students from all member states of the European Union have been able to spend a significant part of their college careers abroad. Erasmus was created to develop a single European "higher education area." With a budget of over 450 million euros, it links more than 4,000 European universities in thirty-three countries, enabling 200,000 European students to go abroad every year. Since its creation, more than 2.2 million students have taken part in it. Since 1997, the program also promotes faculty exchanges. To date 250,000 college professors and staff have participated in Erasmus.[13]

While studying abroad has contributed to the global migration movement since the 1980s, job prospects have also contributed to its volume. The expansion of truly worldwide corporations has made it possible for personnel to diversify and scatter across all continents. The economic growth during the last two decades of the twentieth century only expanded the global job market. As a result, people like the Austrian-born Herber Demel could become the first non-Italian head of Fiat in 2003, after long stints at Audi in Germany and Volkswagen in Brazil.[14] And the Brazilian-born Frenchman Carlos Ghosn could lead Nissan, a post usually reserved for Japanese CEOs. These days, Ghosn doubles as CEO for Nissan and the French Renault, splitting his time between France and Japan.[15]

International job options now cover a wide range of occupations. Most of the 4 million Turks who resettled in Germany between 1960 and 1985 came seeking unskilled, working-class employment. By 1997, Great Britain was issuing 54,000 work permits a year, most of them to Americans and Japanese, in highly skilled jobs.[16] It is not just a matter of the range of occupations either. Many countries are struggling with unfavorable demographic trends. European countries, for instance, know that immigration is critical to offset low-fertility rates.[17] If a country like Austria fails to attract enough immigrant workers, its workforce could shrink from 3.7 million in 2007 to 3.2 million by 2021. In less than two decades, the Austrian workforce could decline by 500,000, losing on average 25,000 workers per year.[18]

Conditions in sending countries also play a role in the migration of skilled workers. The literacy rate in the Philippines is over 90 percent. The country graduates some 350,000 college students a year, 50,000 in engineering alone. But the Philippines' domestic labor market cannot absorb that level of college output. Its economy cannot create those many jobs. As a result, college graduates face the daunting prospects of starting a career burdened by heavily depressed wages. In fact, despite a sizable middle class, the Philippines' average household income in 2000 was only $2,600. A third of its households earned less than $1,000 a year.[19] Talented and fluent in English, the Filipino graduates have few job prospects at home. No wonder more than 1.4 million were working overseas by 2010.[20]

As Maxine Margolis argues, the departure of well-educated migrants alleviates the "dilemma of the overqualified" in the labor markets of sending nations. Those countries invest heavily in training a professional class, and the skills of those college graduates are much needed at home, but native labor markets cannot create enough jobs at adequate wages to retain the graduates. For them, the dream of a middle-class life at home proves illusive in the long run. Their expectations of social mobility stymied, a segment of the well-educated citizens eventually make their way abroad. Only there will they find the eventual rewards for their many years of schooling.[21]

Another key factor aiding the global migratory wave is technology. Swift transportation has extended the global reach of immigrant populations. The nineteenth-century migration was transatlantic as Europeans moved to the New World. Today immigrants move in every direction around the globe. There are Bolivians going to college in Brazil, while Brazilians of Japanese descent run coffee shops in Japan. Nepalese workers are staffing Korean factories as Koreans manage car companies in the United States. The Chinese are overseeing mining operations in Africa and South America, while Mongolians do scut work in the Czech Republic.[22] The relatively low costs of relocation have opened up new areas of the globe for migration while the jobs provide the final inducement.

Technology has also delivered instant communication, another enticing feature of the global age. It is now possible to migrate without giving up family ties or one's native culture. Satellite TV, cell phones, and webcams keep immigrants connected with life back home. From the comfort of my living room in rural Virginia I can follow the matches of my Brazilian hometown soccer team, send photos to siblings, and catch the same Brazilian evening newscast that my mother assiduously watches (in fact, Brazilian immigrants tend to know more about what is going on back home than in the United States[23]). Moreover, instant communication knows no class boundaries. A nanny in Manhattan can chat with her child in Zacatecas, vote in Mexican elections, and watch Mexican soap operas from the Big Apple.[24]

Instant communication allows immigrants to truly live in multiple worlds. More than just keeping track of relatives, those who leave can contribute to their well-being as well. Internet money remittances preserve family ties and fulfill filial duties. In 2009, immigrants remitted $317 billion back home, a sum three times the amount of the world's total foreign aid. For at least seven nations the remittances received amounted to more than a quarter of their GDP.[25] Instant communications also mean investing abroad. For instance, by 2005 Vietnamese Americans had invested $200 million in businesses across Vietnam.[26]

Constant communication even allows people to retire abroad, without missing their favorite shows. Many Americans have taken advantage of the cheaper costs of foreign real estate and health care to relocate. They now live abroad without sacrificing their ties to America. Satellite TV and the Internet keep them connected, as they enjoy the extra amenities of places like Mexico or Central America, along with their low cost of living. For instance, of the 40,000 Americans resettled in Costa Rica in 2005, 11,000 were on Social Security.[27] Some 80,000 Americans retired in Mexico, in enclaves such as San Miguel de Allende and the Chapala region.[28] Another 25,000 have transferred permanently to Panama.[29] Places like Honduras, the Philippines, and Thailand compete intensely for American expats.

Choice and Contingency

So what does all of this have to do with a shy kid from the northeast of Brazil ending up in Harrisonburg, Virginia, by way of Louisville, Kentucky, and Nashville, Tennessee? A lot, as it turns out. Life for those like me is defined by a series of international choices and contingencies. Immigrants throughout the globe respond to conditions they cannot change at home by choosing to pursue a better life elsewhere. Since all countries are not equally open to newcomers, the immigrant's choice has to be made within a certain set of parameters. Obviously all human beings are subject to choices and contingencies, even those who never relocate. But immigrants navigate two sets of choices and contingencies—one in their homeland, one abroad.

The question becomes, which set will maximize one's ability to pursue life as she or he sees fit? Dealing with two sets of choices and contingencies means living constantly in comparative mode—"Now, how do we handle this back home? Why do they do it differently here? Where is the best place to buy a house? Which country will maximize my investments? Why are the health care systems so different? Under which am I better served?" You keep making judgment calls in hopes they might enhance your freedom, given the cultural and social parameters you face. Casey's search for a career led him to Costa Rica, but he still had to figure out how to work with that system to become a successful business owner. Love kept Suzanne on the other side of the globe, but she had to do so within her host country's constraints. So did Mark.

There are double sets of choices and contingencies whether you move for love, money, or art. The double set of choices and contingencies affect even those who leave their homelands to escape religious intoler-ance, tribal conflict, or ethnic wars. Choice and contingency implies that at the individual level, immigration is defined by a series of circuitous decisions, which are made within a given set of structural limitations. Say you have to choose between getting a college education at home or abroad. You're still faced with how to pay for it, with your odds of getting accepted into your school of choice in either place. You still have to choose a profitable major. And after graduation you have to find a career in one of two different places, with disparate results. Navigating those two sets of choices and contingencies successfully takes a lifetime.

By the time I finished college in Brazil, there were very few doctoral programs in the country, none in my areas of interest or my home region. The few existing programs in Rio de Janeiro and São Paulo offered little to no scholarship money. Those were the contingencies I faced. Obviously, I could have given up on a graduate education. I could have simply practiced a career with the degrees I already had. Or I could look for graduate studies elsewhere. Moreover, migrating did not solve the problem, since it took me three years and a master's degree to realize I had landed in the wrong educational institution and pursued the wrong degree, given my goals of becoming a college professor.

As I prepared to transfer, I realized that there were literally hundreds of graduate schools in the United States! How to sort them out? Which offered the best programs in my field of interest? That led me to care-fully explore the American university ranking system. Then I had to learn that state universities usually did not have funds for international students. And I had to identify the best private schools on the basis of ranking and financial aid before I could start applying for programs. Of course, none of this guaranteed that I would land in one before my student visa expired, or that those I chose would be interested in me, or that I would be able to successfully complete the path of graduate studies I wanted. Some of it was my choice; most of it was not.

The whole process of migration for me was this long sequence of choices and contingencies repeated over and over, sometimes with little time to spare. Of the three schools I chose, two accepted me, but Vanderbilt offered the best combination of quality instruction and financial aid. I still had to write to all the directors of the programs that interested me; I had to apply to each school, visit as many campuses as I could, and all of that in less than the three months prior to the expiration of my student visa. Fortunately my application was successful, I was accepted into a well-respected graduate program, and the transition went smoothly. But nothing was certain; nothing was sure, until it got done.

What many do not realize as they consider migration is that personal choices mean little if the structural conditions are not there to facilitate the process. Not all migrants find a home in other countries. Many, in fact, get shipped back at the point of entry. Not all those who do enter other nations find successful lives abroad. Many return after failing to prosper. Not all immigrants eventually find life satisfactory among people of other faiths, ethnicity, or cultures. The glitter of the new can fade rather quickly. Many who migrate become victims of racism, prejudice, and discrimination in their adopted lands, so much so that in the first decade of the twenty-first century there has been a reverse migration of Latin Americans from Europe, North America, and Asia to their countries of origin.[30]

This book is nothing if not a review of my choices and contingencies. Growing up middle-class and Protestant in Brazil gave me significant resources, among them an affluent lifestyle (compared to the average Brazilian), private education, opportunities to travel, and access to foreign languages at a very early age. Moreover, my middle-class values prepared me for life in a nation of laws. That Brazil was under military rule during my childhood only added to my desire to leave the country. But without finding optimum conditions abroad, I might not have been able to succeed. I still needed access to graduate schools, substantial scholarships, reasonable relocation costs, and campus jobs that allowed me to survive on a student budget.

Clearly, I had to make some critical choices as well. I had to give up my hometown and my lifestyle. I sacrificed growing old around my parents, siblings, relatives, and friends. I missed all the important hallmarks of my family's life cycle. Migrating meant a life away from everything that was dear and familiar to me. Life in the United States led to career struggles, divorce, and bicultural parenting. Not all the choices I made here made sense to my Brazilian family or friends. There are Brazilians whom I met in graduate school who are now college professors back home making almost twice as much as I do while enjoying the perks of a cosmopolitan life in places like Rio de Janeiro, Belo

Horizonte, and Florianópolis. As I get closer to retirement, I have to wonder how I'll grow old in a nation where friendships are highly utilitarian.

The Push and Pull of Migration

But individual choices and contingencies are not the whole picture when it comes to immigration. There are larger forces at play, of course–opportunities that affect not just the individual migrant but entire categories of people like her. The British geographer Ernest George Ravenstein was the first scholar to explore these larger forces, to study the empirical reasons for migrating. Where I speak of choices and contingencies, Ravenstein proposed pushes and pulls instead. He set a list of laws concerning migration in an 1885 article he published in the *Journal of the Royal Statistical Society*. His "laws" were supposed to predict migratory movement across entire regions and countries.[31]

Using census data from England and Wales, Ravenstein argued that unfavorable conditions in one's birthplace pushed people out, while favorable conditions elsewhere pulled on them toward relocating. But he said that only when things were bad enough at home and attractive enough in another area would people actually move. He then described the push-and-pull factors that contributed to the relocation. For example, in those preflight days, distance was a factor, since it increased the costs of relocation. Ravenstein theorized that migration decreased to the extent that distance increased. He saw migration differentials that could complicate the relocation for certain individuals. Certain traits—gender, age, class, etc.—led people to experience the pushes and pulls of migration differently.[32] Distance might be less of a problem for an upper-class male migrant who is still young and unattached. The point was simple: differentials created distinct results.

Since Ravenstein's insightful work, other theorists have built upon his model. In mid-twentieth-century America, the demographer Everett S. Lee refined Ravenstein's laws by highlighting the importance of intervening obstacles. Differentials affected migration, but so did things like physical and political barriers or having dependents. To Lee, the intervening obstacles interacted with the migration differentials to facilitate or negate an individual's migratory efforts. Furthermore, he argued that personal traits like level of education, familiarity with the host culture, or existing family ties could enhance or slow down the flow of immigrants. Lee developed quite an extensive list of pushes and pulls to explain migratory patterns.[33] Put simply, there were as many good reasons for leaving home as there were attractive options elsewhere.

The Larger Picture

Since Ravenstein's classic model of migration, other theories have been proposed to explain the effect of larger, structural forces on the international migratory movement.[34] Neoclassical economists, for instance, argue that migration is the result of an economic imbalance between the size of the labor supply and wages in two different countries. Say the size of the labor force increases in Brazil, creating a surplus of workers. Given the nature of supply and demand, that surplus will depress wages in the Brazilian economy. It is only natural then for some of the surplus workers to look for jobs in countries where there is (1) a labor shortage, and (2) more attractive wages.[35] The point is, when the differences between labor supply and wages are great between two countries, the flow of immigration is quite large between them. When they are low, the volume trickles down.

This elegant and parsimonious theory could explain, for example, the small volume of migration between Brazil and Colombia, Venezuela, or Argentina versus the high volume of migration between Brazil and the United States. People go where the labor shortages are and the wages are suitable. One could argue that my own migration fits the neoclassical theory. Brazil was graduating more people from college than its economy could retain. The fact that I chose to stay in the United States after graduate school indicates that wages for college professors at the time were more attractive here. Eventually wages in higher education became more competitive in Brazil. But by then I had an established career in the States and a U.S.-born son. There were other variables to factor into the equation.

The truth is, when I left Brazil I knew little of this. I was not even remotely the informed or rational actor that is assumed in the neoclassical theory model. In 1981, the Brazilian economy was still viable for certain middle-class careers. Things got worse after I left the country and got better again by the time I finished my PhD. When I came to the United States in 1981 the wages of a college professor in Brazil still allowed a reasonable middle-class lifestyle. Given the small number of people with doctorates in Brazil in 1990 (even by the late 1990s, only 12 percent of the Brazilian population had a college degree[36]), I am sure I could have found a rewarding career back home. So, perhaps structural conditions may create the initial impetus, but other factors become equally important over time.

Most Brazilian immigrants who came to the United States in the 1980s and 1990s actually do fit the neoclassical argument. A large number of them were professionals for whom the interplay of labor supply and wages between Brazil and the United States did create the stimulus for an international migration. In their case, my main caveat to the neoclassical theory is that skills in a particular field are not necessarily easily transferrable between countries. As a result, Maxine Margolis found Brazilian psychologists, agronomists, engineers, journalists, lawyers, and social workers cleaning houses, waiting tables, doing construction work, and performing all sorts of menial labor in the Big Apple.[37]

The irony is that compared to wages back home, the salaries for menial labor in America are still very attractive to professional Brazilian immigrants. One researcher found a Brazilian woman whose salary as a head nurse in a big city hospital in Brazil had been about $200 a month in the early 1990s. In New York, she was making almost five times more as a baby sitter. A Brazilian mechanical engineer who made $500 a month in his homeland got paid $400 a week in New York to work as a private chauffeur. Similar to those two examples, one finds story after story of professional Brazilians paid much more in the United States for a far less-skilled job. The lesson here is that those who come to American simply for the wages must be willing to sacrifice their professional status along the way.[38]

Nevertheless, there are plenty of menial jobs for those willing to work. Franklin Goza, studying Brazilian migration to Canada and the United States, found that half of his sample had gotten a job in the United States within thirteen days of their arrival. Almost 30 percent of the Brazilians he studied were working within six days of their landing in America. After twenty days, 67 percent of Brazilian immigrant women had found jobs (and here, the gender differential favors males). All in all, Brazilians averaged more than five jobs per person during their North American sojourn, at a rate of six full-time jobs for every part-time position held.[39] Many critics of immigration fail to see the serious labor shortages that attract newcomers to this country.

The rate of success of Brazilian immigrants is even more astonishing when one considers that over 80 percent of the men and 86 percent of the women arrived in the United States with absolutely no practical knowledge of English. In the entire sample, only 3 percent could be considered fluent in the language. And the level of full employment of those Brazilians took place while many faced strong nativist feelings among their coworkers, and full-fledged discrimination. In fact, almost 50 percent of Goza's sample reported experiencing discrimination in a variety of forms. He compiled a list of more than thirty different types of discriminatory actions experienced by his respondents. And yet, when asked whether they would have immigrated given what they now knew, over 90 percent of the respondents said yes.[40]

Another structural explanation for international migration is called network theory, also known as the "new economics of migration."[41] Network theorists suggest that immigrants do not simply exit their countries individually. They argue that certain conditions must exist to facilitate their exodus, most of all connections along the way. Once an early, small group of immigrants from a given nation sets up a beach-head in another country, their connections to family, friends, and geographical area back home facilitate a larger transfer of immigrants in their wake. It is the presence of this small group that lowers the costs and raises the benefits of migration for the consecutive waves. The small group also provides the incoming waves of compatriots with important social capital regarding housing, language classes, local customs, job opportunities, and related resources. Once the network is set up, it becomes self-perpetuating.

Given the Brazilian experience in the United States, one could make the case that network theory explains a lot of the migration between the two countries during the 1980s and 1990s. For example, a single Brazilian town, Governador Valadares, in the state of Minas Gerais, has created one of the strongest immigrant networks in the whole of Latin America. To date, an estimated 40,000 Valadarenses have resettled in places like Danbury, Connecticut; Framingham, Massachusetts; Newark, New Jersey; and Pompano Beach, Florida. For a town of about 260,000 inhabitants, this represents a considerable exodus.[42] One finds a similar pattern occurring at the individual level as well. A Brazilian immigrant in New York helped relocate twelve relatives and friends over a five-year period.[43]

Mine, however, would be an atypical case when it comes to network theory. None of my extended family migrated to America first. And my being here has not translated into a flow of family members or friends into this country. Moreover, once in the United States, I have never lived close to a large group of other Brazilian immigrants.[44] Offered the opportunity to do graduate work in the United States, I took advantage of that opportunity—simple as that. Once here, those back home expected me to return. None ever showed any interest in joining me abroad, even after I became an American citizen and therefore capable of sponsoring my relatives into the United States.

Finally, the third structural theory of international migration is the segmented labor markets (SLM) approach.[45] Mostly, SLM explains why immigration prior to the 1970s allowed immigrants to experience real social mobility as they relocated, while immigration since the 1970s has created differentiated pathways for integration into the receiving societies. Simply put, the nature of capitalism in the receiving countries has changed. The demands for the early waves of immigrants in the twentieth century came from manufacturing and extractive industries, with lucrative rewards for those who chose to migrate. In fact, the industrial push of the first half of the century greatly contributed to the creation of the large American middle class. As the United States transitioned from the industrial to the informational age, the mid-1970s economy created a tiered labor market instead, with lots of low-wage jobs in the service sector and far fewer opportunities in the high-skilled sector.

According to SLM, both sectors continue to recruit, but they attract very distinct sets of immigrants. Those who migrate into the high-skilled sector of the host nation continue to enjoy the same benefits that the early waves of migrants enjoyed—high salaries, career tracks, substantial benefits, and job security. The service sector, on the other hand, has low wages, minimal benefits (if any), and little room for advancement or job security. The only exception to these two segments is the ethnic enclave, the sector created by immigrant communities (Cubans in Miami or the Chinese in New York, for instance). In the ethnic enclave, ethnic enterprises hire large numbers of co-ethnic immigrants, and those immigrants tend to do better than the ones who end up in the larger service sector.

The segmented labor markets approach would certainly explain much of Brazilian migration to America, too. Once here, most Brazilian immigrants quickly find a job in the service sector. Whether in New York, New Jersey, Massachusetts, California, or Florida, the draw for Brazilians who migrate to America is the service sector opportunities. As bad as those jobs are, they are better than what the Brazilians got paid in the high-skilled sector back home. In 1994, a Brazilian woman with a college degree was making $600 a month as an executive in an

American-owned advertising agency in Brazil. That same year, a Brazilian attorney working at a prestigious bank in Porto Alegre earned $300 a month. A mechanical engineer got $500 a month for his professional expertise. *All* doubled or tripled their pay in New York.[46]

Their experience is supported by census data (though I'm sure the self-selected bunch of us who filled out the questionnaires certainly helped improve the numbers for Brazilians). In 2007, Brazilians between the ages of sixteen and sixty had lower unemployment and higher workforce participation rates than all the major racial/ethnic groups in the United States. Brazilian males enjoyed an 84 percent rate of employment and a 3 percent rate of unemployment; females a 75 percent rate of employment and a 3.3 percent rate of unemployment. That year, the median household income for Brazilians in this country was higher than for whites, blacks, and other Latinos.[47]

I suppose my own immigrant experience would fit the SLM hypothesis as well. When I graduated from Vanderbilt with a PhD in sociology back in 1990, the job market for sociologists was still wide open both in Brazil and the United States. While my degree gave me professional opportunities in both countries, and I did explore the possibilities of working in both, the segmented labor market in this country allowed me to fully integrate into the high-skilled American workforce right away. Were it not for the better wages, the possibility of promotions, the employment benefits, and the job security, I might not be here today.

Figuring It Out as You Go Along

In a perfect world we immigrants would be the ultimate rational actors. Armed with the needed data, aware of the pushes and pulls of migration, we would make the most informed of decisions about our relocation. Migrating would be a matter of carefully sifting through the available information and evaluating the possible strategies and alternatives to be deployed as we charted our migration route with the greatest efficiency and care. Then, after weighing the pros and cons of relocation, we would optimize our life chances by figuring out the most effective pathway for migrating. The problem with that picture is that no one lives in that perfect world.

Reliable immigration data is extremely hard to get prior to relocation. If anything, the hearsay from other immigrants can be quite misleading.

Nineteenth-century Europeans who migrated to America wrote bright letters home painting the rosiest of scenarios about their own experiences. Desirous of attracting relatives to the New World, they tended to exaggerate the benefits of life in the host country and to minimize the costs of moving. Only after a hard trans-Atlantic crossing and the arrival at Ellis Island would relatives become well acquainted with the hardships. By then, they had to search for jobs in overcrowded New York streets, as the rosy scenarios quickly faded away.[48]

Most immigrants have quite limited knowledge of what relocation will entail or what awaits them once they arrive in their adoptive homelands; whether entrepreneurs, students, political refugees, or day laborers, all immigrants face a serious learning curve as they decide to go abroad. No matter how prepared you think you are, you're still envisioning the whole experience from your culture's point of view. A $900-a-month job in 1990s Brazil was an attractive proposition; but the same $900-a-month job in New York bought a whole lot less. Things can be frightfully different in another country. My law degree from Brazil and the rigorous training on substantive and procedural law left me ill prepared to deal with the arcane and convoluted regulations of the U.S. Immigration and Naturalization Services.

Then, there is the real issue of struggling with previous commitments, with loyalties that never fully fade from a person's mind after the relocation is done. No matter how long you live in your host country, you never forget the delights of your birthplace or the bonds that tie you to your loved ones. No matter how settled you are in your new nation, there is always that dreamy and unrealistic scenario of going home "someday." Even well-established Brazilians in New York— people who were legal residents, home owners, who had good jobs or owned their own business—still dreamed of going home, in many cases "after they retired" or "when their children were fully grown."[49] The dream never fades.

There is also the matter of figuring out what is customary in a new society. What are the proper guidelines and legal steps for renting or buying a home, for instance? What are the advantages of renting versus buying? In some countries, that question makes all the difference in the world. Some people are not allowed to acquire property right away. How does one go about purchasing a car? What car would best fit your current needs? Car companies may be the same across the world, but they market very different brands in different nations. Moreover, cars in tropical weather are different from those in northern climates. Cars in Brazil did not have heating or air-conditioning. More importantly, how are contracts honored in your host nation? What legal assurances do aliens have in business transactions? To what extent do they enjoy the same legal protections as the natives?

This is why in most cases the immigration process is figured out in hindsight or at very deliberate stages. Coming to the United States on a student visa (F-1 visa) for my master's degree was extremely limiting. Neither my wife nor I were allowed to work. There were restrictions on our international travel as well. Getting a different visa (H-1 visa) as I started my PhD changed the situation immediately. The H-1 allowed me to work at least twenty hours a week on campus. Traveling became easier. Picking a southern university for my graduate studies set up a chain of events that affected the rest of my life, such as which job markets would be available for me and my spouse upon conclusion of the degree, what transportation needs we would face in a southern city, what type of schooling was available for our kid, and so on.

In my opinion, immigrant life is a constant process of figuring things out as you go along. Once I accepted Vanderbilt's offer, I could not turn around and move to Boston instead (I was accepted at Harvard, too) simply because Nashville did not have a good public transportation system. I had to figure out how to get a second-hand car instead and hope it would last my entire period of studies. My son was born as I was finishing my coursework. I could not very well move to another town simply to give him better odds of getting a top-notch K-12 public education. You handle the situation as best as you can given the parameters that you face.

At best, immigration is a complicated process. And that's assuming everything works as it should. Your initial optimistic expectations never take into account your own mistakes and biases, or other people's ignorance, hostility, or discrimination. My lack of know-how regarding car purchases in the States cost me dearly. The people who sell used cars make a lot of money off minorities and immigrants. Most of the cars I owned prior to my first professional job were real lemons. My first car drained every battery I installed in it, and the heater worked only intermittently. My second car lost the transmission during our move from Louisville to Nashville.

As corny and clichéd as this may sound, when it comes to international migration nothing compares to the value of personal experience. You have to learn by doing. The most effective way to figure out how to live in a foreign country is to jump in. You get there, get up in the morning, interact with other people, learn from your mistakes, and try to minimize your ignorance of local ways. If you're smart, you build a repertoire of scripts that help you navigate your days relatively unscathed. In many ways it is like a process of resocialization, relearning a culture. The main difference is that you were a kid the first time around. This time you are adding an alien culture to the one you already have.

Making Friends

Given the importance of interaction in learning a new culture, making friends is a critical component of a successful migration. It may determine whether you settle permanently in your host country or go back home. Friends are the most human of connections in a foreign land, perhaps the best way to adjust to life in another society. Nothing is more haunting when you first relocate than being lonely, feeling like an outsider. Unfamiliar with the ways of the people you interact with daily, you struggle to make sense of the whole place. Their goals seem different from yours, their dreams a bit strange to you. Living among them is a constant reminder that you do not belong.

Granted, friendship is risky for both sides. I imagine that for the native, trusting an immigrant does not come easily since the person is unlike you. Given the cultural tools you have available, he is not as easy to "decode." What works with everyone else might not work with him. For the immigrant, the friendship demands a level of vulnerability that is scary. If there is one thing I've learned it's that trust is hard to translate. When you are an immigrant you do not immediately know who could be a reliable confidant. Moreover, attractive traits in your own culture might not be so endearing in a foreign land. To Americans, Brazilians come across at first as nosy and talkative, while we see them as extremely shy and diffident, for example.

Despite the fact that everyone thinks friendship has a universal definition, different societies approach the institution of friendship quite differently. If you live in a more task-oriented society, a friend is someone you do things with. In a more people-oriented culture, friendship is measured by the depth of intimacy you enjoy with that person, not her utility to you. In some societies, a friend is someone who helps you in hard times. In others, a friend is someone who pushes you to lift yourself up by your own strength. So, there is an interesting process of mutual discovery in international friendships, a process of mutual adjustment when people befriend each other across cultures. It is nothing like befriending someone in your own culture.

Friendship can be sublime or practical, depending on the culture and the times that define it. In ancient Greece a true friend was someone who encouraged you to be virtuous, to reach your full potential as a human being. That person was not necessarily afraid to confront you when you fell short of the mark, or to expect the best of you. In fact, friendship was the basis for Greek political life.[50] At the other end of the spectrum, Thailand's notion of friendship is somewhat less demanding. For Thais, friends are people you go "pai teo-ing" with. "Pai teo" in English means "to fun," and in Thai culture, "to fun" is perfectly correct grammatically and emotionally.[51]

While I have had many acquaintances in my three decades in the United States, very few people have become real lifetime friends. Part of it is cultural. Brazilians prefer more serious friendships, and we tend to have more close friends than Americans do, since we are a more kin-oriented society.[52] But part of it is living in a highly mobile American culture. Here, you have to be prepared to constantly say goodbye to friends as they move or you do. Once we finish school, take other jobs, and change towns, the connections wither—even in the Internet age. Middle-class Americans have to maintain a "fluid" level of friendship with their neighbors and coworkers, so as to minimize loss when the next promotion or uprooting comes along.

Brazilians are encouraged to be communal when they are growing up, to be steadfastly loyal to relatives, neighbors, and peers.[53] There is a premium in Brazil on being relational, on cultivating deep connections with others. I still have a few close friends who have known me deeply since middle school. Brazilian culture values these kinds of interpersonal relationships more than American culture does. From early on, we are encouraged to develop a strong sense of intimacy not only with family members but with close friends, and sometimes even acquaintances. Being alone is definitely not the cultural norm for Brazilians. They tend to rely on a large web of emotional connections that go beyond the usual size or depth one finds among friends in the United States.[54]

Brazilian immigrants find utilitarian friendships in the United States abhorrent. It is a bit alien to our culture to befriend someone solely on the basis of that person's "usefulness." In certain areas of American life, that seems to be the norm. Talking to a Capitol Hill lobbyist, I was shocked to hear her say that "in politics, there are no permanent friends and no permanent enemies." To be effective in her business, she has to avoid permanent entanglements of either the positive or negative kind. That to a Brazilian would be extremely frustrating, extremely puzzling. But here, the few long-term friends one has are indeed the rare exceptions, not the rule. Otherwise, most middle-class Americans operate with that "middling" approach to emotional attachment that so scared C. Wright Mills.

A mid-twentieth-century American sociologist, Mills was frightened by the corporate America that grew out of World War II. He thought that the transition from small-town society to large-scale bureaucratic America had created a politically powerless and emotionally unfulfilled middle class (those were the days of *The Man in the Gray Flannel Suit*, the 1955 Sloan Wilson novel that portrayed middle-class corporate work as soulless and middle-class workers as people in search of meaning, aching for deeper emotional connections). White-collar workers, in Mills's expert opinion, were skilled in executing the marching orders from the top echelons, but spent their lives wondering whether there was more to life than that.

In contrast to the American society that existed prior to World War II, nothing that drove the 1950s white-collar workers had ultimate consequences. Nothing demanded ultimate sacrifices of them. Mills described suburban life as quiet and tepid, and thought that this applied to middle-class emotional lives as well. The idea was to avoid rocking the boat, making waves. In order not to be deeply hurt if a relationship went awry, middle-class Americans tended to minimize deep connections to anything or anybody. Mills thought that the absence of those connections left middle-class workers "morally defenseless as individuals and politically impotent as a group."[55] To him, advertising had replaced the middle-class workers' quest for meaning with a life of consumerism, where having trumped being.

Mills was afraid that in their preoccupation with the private pursuit of self-fulfillment, white-collar individuals would mistake freedom to consume with genuine autonomy. To him social mobility did not translate into freedom but into becoming a cog in a highly bureaucratic machine. The need to keep emotionally aloof from current friends was simply a symptom of the larger malaise. Middle-class workers took their fluid suburban connections for the kind of true friendship that previous generations of Americans had enjoyed, the kind where people probed deeply into each other's souls; the kind we find, for instance, in the correspondence between Thomas Jefferson and John Adams.

Mills, incidentally, was not alone in his fears. Other mid-twentieth-century American social scientists were equally concerned with the lack of emotional depth in the relationships of the American middle class. In a prescient book, Erich Fromm explored the consequences of organizing a society around *having* instead of *being*.[56] In his view, the need to consume precluded Americans from fulfilling key psychological needs like mutual security, solidarity, or even forgiveness. To him, consumerism distorted the social character of the average American. Christopher Lasch, in the 1970s, would add his own critique to Mills's and Fromm's, with a searing analysis of the excessive Narcissism he perceived in his own era.[57]

Perhaps, in an age where most of my students find friends in cyber-space, I should not expect deeply held face-to-face connections. My own son has more than 900 friends on Facebook, something that as a Brazilian and a sociologist I find incomprehensible. I guess it was only a matter of time before the fluid friendships of the 1950s and 1970s would become the electronic byte-size connections of today. To me, Twitter is the epitome of this shallowness. That people would deem important to alert others—in real time—to their most menial or mundane tasks is quite absurd.[58] Perhaps friendships like Jefferson's and Adams's are fated to dim into our collective past after all.[59]

In all honesty, the few people who truly befriended me at different times of my stay in the United States were quite indispensable to my emotional well-being during this American journey. I mentioned quite a few friends in chapter 3. But it is hard to do justice to all of those who lent a hand or a friendly shoulder along the way. Two things stand out as I review my efforts to make lifelong friendships in this country. The first one is social distance. Tamotsu Shibutani and Kian Kwan were the sociologists who introduced me to this concept as a critical variable in immigrant assimilation. They defined it as the subjective state of proximity experienced among individuals of different groups. They assumed that greater social contact with Anglos rather than one's own ethnic group could lead to greater assimilation into the dominant culture. As social distance was reduced, greater assimilation took place.[60]

I take social distance a bit farther, defining it as the level of access an immigrant gains into another's soul. Rarely, even with my closest American friends, have I felt as close or trusted as I did with folks back home. In Brazil, access to a friend's private life is immediate, unfiltered. You can figure him or her out right away. By comparison, Americans seem more emotionally multilayered. Their greater sense of privacy (one I am now fond of) allows them to reserve certain layers of the soul for only their truly trusted friends. For someone from a culture of immediate emotional access, this is a hard dance to undertake. It takes a while for a Brazilian to figure out when he or she has reached a certain level of trust with American friends.

The second aspect about American friendship has to do with social rank. Despite America's egalitarian ethos—and more so than in the ranked Latin American societies I come from—there is a tacit expectation in the United States that like will associate with like. Perhaps because the notion of class is so fluid in this country, there are quite subtle barriers against associating with folks who may occupy a lower or higher stratum. This ranking does not have the same clear-cut feel that one would find in a caste society, but its effects can be insidious. In many cases, being seen with someone of your own status is an endorsement of your rank. It strengthens your social standing in the local community. This is one of those unwritten cultural rules that take a lifetime to decipher.

American social ranking can be puzzling for an immigrant who is looking for friends. You have to reside here for a while prior to understanding these nuances. One immigrant I know who would be seen as white in Brazil struggles with her reclassification as black in the United States. She had the unfortunate experience of having a coworker tell her that she lacked the right "pedigree" to associate with her coworkers outside of the workplace. That immigrant was using her own culture's criteria for making friends. I probably broke all kinds of unwritten social rules in grad school by befriending secretaries, janitors, and cafeteria workers. This is an area of my life where I prefer to remain Brazilian.

Being True to Yourself

While friends are important, people do not move to other lands to find them. To me the bottom line regarding migration is that you relocate because certain conditions back home kept you from fulfilling your full potential. You realized, at some point, that life abroad could be more satisfying, more generous, more liberating in terms of personal freedoms. That, and a bit of wanderlust, always does the trick. This is why I am still puzzled that of my immediate family I alone chose to migrate. It is hard for me to believe that I was the only one who felt this way.

What was it about Brazil in the 1950s and 1960s, or about growing up in Recife, that triggered this reaction in me? Clearly, my brothers and sister never felt it, whatever it was; for they have remained, quite contentedly, back home.

My suspicions regarding the motivation behind non-coerced migratory patterns are confirmed by studies of other immigrants. For instance, Ana Cristina Braga Martes, the São Paulo political scientist who studies Brazilian expatriates, argues that the typical immigrant is similar to the average entrepreneur.[61] That person is compelled by a greater degree of risk-taking and sense of adventure than his or her counterparts who never leave their homelands. Immigrants, she argues, are more compelled to break with established routines, to take on new challenges. Similar to entrepreneurs, they are more willing to pursue new endeavors, making the process of migration a highly self-selected enterprise.

Those of us who migrate know quite well the journeys that Mark, Suzanne, and Casey undertook. We who left home seeking our fortune elsewhere understand them completely. We have been in their shoes. If not as fortunate as they are in triumph or love, we are well acquainted with their migrating experiences. We too made similar choices, much to the dismay or puzzlement of families, relatives, and classmates. We too faced similar risks. We have led lives that paralleled their own in our ongoing search for personal meaning. I doubt Mark, Suzanne, and Casey would be able to fully explain why they left the United States, or why Germany, Japan, or Costa Rica feel so familiar now. And yet, they are home.

It seems that it is only gradually that we come to discover, once we leave, why we had to search for home elsewhere. The answer is never immediate. It is found over a lifetime, after seasoned, weighed, careful consideration, and multiple revisions along the way. Only then are we reasonably satisfied by the logic of our decision. The rationale for relocation evolves as we add more life experience to our journey. We acquire other tastes, discover other ways to enjoy life. And as we change, we get further removed from our original culture. Its customs no longer hold us in their grip; its daily rituals no longer entice us. We still treasure our memories, but are more committed to our current lives.

The best way I can explain such a journey is to describe it as a pilgrimage toward one's true self. Moving is simply the way many of us found to get closer to what rings true within us. As we move, we keep shedding the nonessentials until what remains is mostly true, a more authentic version of ourselves, perhaps. I know I am certainly more reserved and private than all my siblings or cousins in Brazil. That reserve, that individualism, puzzles them. They have built their interdependence over multiple crises they faced. They know they have each other for whatever life throws their way, be it the loss of a relative or friend, a divorce, someone getting fired, or a parent's untimely death. I tend to face my own crises alone. I did so even prior to migrating to America.

It may sound as a truism to say that immigrants who move to another country change. But I hasten to explain that our changing is not simply a function of our moving. I suspect we change because in the new country we find the space to let our inner life and our most treasured interests match our everyday reality. When we migrate, we are seeking a more adequate setting for the living out of our wishes and dreams. Life makes more sense after we move. Change, mercifully, comes more easily, less painfully. We become more flexible, more resourceful, but our new habits also represent a truer reflection of our tastes. Obviously, we cannot avoid pondering whether those changes were needed, but for the most part we are pleased with the results, with the life we made for ourselves.

Almost Home

Even though a new country frees you to become more yourself, it does not necessarily turn you into a full-fledged native. No matter how comfortable you may become in your new culture, or how adapted you are to its language, conventions, and social expectations; there is no guarantee of full inclusion. People will respect you. They will respect your contributions, of course. And they will appreciate your competence and skills. But there are small things that keep drawing that ever-so-subtle line of demarcation—you are with them but not of them. Even after three decades in the United States, there has seldom been a time when I have not been aware of my outsideness. That line of demarcation puzzles my American friends, but it is quite real to me.

To be sure, it is not a line of exclusion. In thirty years, I have never felt excluded in this country. Nor have I experienced anything close to that overwhelming sense of apartheid that I have seen in other immigrants. In fact, I count myself fortunate for the opportunities this nation has given me. In all that matters, my being born Brazilian has not impeded my success in any endeavor I have attempted in my American life. Here

I was given full access to graduate education; I was allowed to become a citizen and participate in the body politic; I have been free to reside wherever I wished. And here I was able to pursue my career without any hindrance or malicious discrimination. If anything, America's egalitarianism has made it possible for me to be where I am now.

The "almost home" feeling comes from that nagging sense that you are not quite here yet. You may have accomplished plenty, proved your worth, jumped through all the hoops needed to reach your desired goals. But something is still slanted, still slightly off, slightly fractured. And you cannot figure out what else to do to cross that final line. I think of what W. E. B. Du Bois said about the African American soul: "One ever feels his twoness—an American, a Negro; two souls, two thoughts, two unreconciled strivings; two warring ideals in one dark body, whose dogged strength alone keeps it from being torn asunder."[62] To some extent, the same could be said of us immigrants. We may not be as unreconciled in our twoness, or as bereft in our despair. But that sense of outsideness is there, and it never leaves you.

There is a powerful scene in the movie *Chariots of Fire* that clearly illustrates my feeling of being "almost home." The British track star Harold Abrahams is dining with the opera diva Sybil Gordon in an elegant London restaurant. By then, Abrahams had already gained admittance to the prestigious Caius College at Cambridge University. As an athlete he had made a name for himself in local and national competitions. And now bound for France, he is to represent England in the 1924 Olympic Games. By all practical measures, Harold should consider himself quite successful. In fact, his life is already beyond the wildest dreams of most British subjects at the time.

Yet Mr. Abrahams faces an invisible wall, an invisible line—one perhaps not as subtle as an immigrant's, but equally incisive. You see, he struggles with anti-Semitism in an imperial Anglo-Saxon society. His efforts to gain full acceptance to the upper echelons of British society betray his very sense of being deprived of his peers' natural privileges. One could dismissively argue that the struggle was of Abrahams's own making, as some of his friends suggest at different points in the film. After all, he was a Caius scholar, someone who played leading roles in his college clubs, who had broken a seven-hundred-year record by completing the Trinity Great Court Run in the time it took for a clock to strike twelve. But to Harold, the line is quite real.

So we watch as the restaurant patrons applaud Harold and Sybil as they enter the establishment. At the peak of their careers, enjoying enormous prestige in British society, they both bask in the adulation.

Once seated, they seek to learn more about each other. "So you love running?" asks Sybil. "I am an addict," answers Harold. "It's more of a weapon," he explains. "A weapon against what?" puzzles the soprano. "A weapon against being Jewish," he replies. She finds that hard to believe. "Fiddlesticks," she adds, incredulous. "You must be joking! No one cares about these things anymore." To which Harold responds, "I'm semi-deprived. They lead me to water but won't let me drink." The phrase darts out of his mouth with a power that fills the whole screen.

Chariots of Fire came out in 1981, the year I arrived in America. I was already in Louisville that October, when the film was released to American audiences. Needless to say, it was an enormous box office hit. Costing a little over $5 million to produce, it grossed more than $55 billion worldwide. Americans were riveted by the Eric Liddell character, the Scottish runner who raced for God's glory and therefore refused to run on Sunday. He would go on to become a missionary in China after the Olympics. I was taken instead with Mr. Abrahams, the lonely, temperamental, insecure but superb athlete who disciplined himself to excel at all costs.

Abrahams felt more human, more real to me. His sense of being "almost home" gave me the means to name my own condition. I was overwhelmed in the movie theater with the restaurant scene. Abrahams's deep sense of relative deprivation was palpable. Here he was, as much an Englishman as any of his Cambridge peers, having a successful financier for a father and a well-respected physician for a brother. He had a life full of victories and accomplishments. As a product of his nation, he was a proud representative of the British aristocratic spirit. Yet, this man remains haunted by the injustice of his condition, of his outsideness. When he tells Sybil he is semi-deprived, I thought to myself, "That IS what it feels like to be 'almost home'!"

The other day, reviewing Brazilian Census data for a project, I discovered that 350,000 residents of Recife are in my age bracket.[63] Boomers all, we fifty-something Recifenses have much in common. We witnessed the same things growing up in Northeast Brazil. We experienced the same stretch of Brazilian history together. All of a sudden, in my little corner office in the Shenandoah Valley, I no longer felt alone. "There are 350,000 of us," I told myself, "350,000 people in the same boat with me, 350,000 who grew up with the same songs, the same stories, the same events." I felt a strong sense of kinship with people who could very well be perfect strangers! That was a feeling I was not prepared for. But these were clearly "my folks."

If asked, they probably would remember the teenage dances back in our high school days or the crowded movie matinees at the downtown theaters every Saturday afternoon. They would recall the day when Brazilian rock and roll burst through our transistor radios, changing our lives forever. We could have debated what the best ice-cream parlor was when we were growing up, or which soccer teams filled our Sundays afternoons and Wednesday evenings with passion and cheer. Other memories flooded back—the trips to sugarcane plantations and farmers' markets, the winter vacations in the countryside, the beach picnics with bonfires and freshly roasted cashew nuts, the Friday night serenades at open-air bars by the seashore.

Part of me wondered whether many of them shared the same interests, the same habits of my childhood—the fried bananas for breakfast, the avocado milkshakes at the downtown pizza joints, the sugary coconut bars at the school cafeteria, the roasted corn on the cob sold at street fairs, the tropical fruit popsicles at the beach every weekend, and the sweetest taste of ripe mangoes or guavas straight from the trees in our backyards. So much to remember! I thought of the collegiate games that had the whole town in a buzz. I could see the crowds of loud high school students, roaming around Recife, cheering their teams on, vying for bragging rights. Nobody missed a game. The feeling now was quite tribal.

After a while, the cool-headed sociologist took over. "Odds are," I told myself, "a good number of those folks did not live through those things. They could have grown up in other parts of town. They could have moved to Recife later in life." Moreover, if we controlled for faith (schools were run by Catholic religious orders and Protestant denominations), gender, race, class, education, and a few other variables, it might turn out that my memories would be matched by those of only a small pool of Recifenses. But it was striking how powerful a sense of kinship I felt with those 350,000 folks. Perhaps it was the idea that thousands may have shared similar experiences.

What is more remarkable is that I could just as easily identify with those of my same age here in the United States. We probably grew up watching the same TV programs, going to the same movies on weekends, and eating the same kinds of fast food. In all my conversations with American boomers, our shared interests match, down to the artists and records we enjoyed in our teen years. We all remember the moon landing in 1969. Then there is the personal connection with high school life in New Mexico—running track, playing 1970s rock at talent shows, going on hikes and field trips to the Rockies. I even remember watching the Watergate hearings on our black-and-white TV.

It is precisely this "twoness" of my soul that makes it hard for me, and for folks like me, to ever go home. There is clearly a Brazilian side to my story, but there is clearly an equally strong American side. In fact, at this point, I have lived longer in the United States than in my country of birth. "Two souls, two thoughts, two unreconciled strivings," wrote the African American sage W. E. B. Du Bois about his own struggle. Growing up between two worlds certainly resonates with me. Perhaps in not as tragically a sad or difficult way as Du Bois experienced, but just as bittersweet, soulful, and lonely. Margolis argues that many factors impact the resolve of a Brazilian to eventually stay in the United States. And even after one decides to do so, it is impossible not to revisit that decision, given that condition of "twoness" in this society.

At first, Brazilians see themselves as sojourners, as people temporarily caught between two worlds.[64] But what if you are equally home in both worlds? What if you are the connecting node between the two? Only inside you do they converge. Their discrete parts find countervailing parallels in each other. They populate your life span with unique, disparate, yet harmonious experiences. Whether listening to rock and roll in English or Portuguese, the memories are just as fresh, just as enchanting. Whether remembering proms in New Mexico or Recife, the thought of the sweet company is still pervasive. Both lives are equally important to me; the stories blend into a single storyline. And I am "almost home" as I inhabit both places, perhaps doubly blessed by their equidistant veracity.

Notes

Chapter 1. A Southern Beginning

1. The early missionaries wrote hymns to the tune of Stephen Foster's songs. A few are still part of the Protestant hymnology in Brazil today.

2. Charles R. Wilson's perceptive book *Baptized in Blood: The Religion of the Lost Cause, 1865–1920* (Athens: University of Georgia Press, 1980) first brought to my attention the extent to which a southern civil religion had evolved in the aftermath of the Civil War. Many of its shrines, such as the tomb of General Robert E. Lee, the burial place of Stonewall Jackson, and important Civil War battlefields, are located in the Shenandoah Valley.

3. The early missionaries to the Brazilian field tended to come more from rural areas of the South and from the more conservative wings of their denominations. They brought a stricter version of their faith, one with more restrictive guidelines, to my homeland. For more information on their demographics and religious culture, see Ronald G. Frase, "The Subversion of Missionary Intentions by Cultural Values: The Brazilian Case," *Review of Religious Research* 23 (1981): 180–94; and Paul E. Pierson, *A Younger Church in Search of Maturity: Presbyterianism in Brazil from 1910 to 1959* (San Antonio: Trinity University Press, 1974). Pierson served as a missionary in my hometown of Recife and taught at the Seminário Presbiteriano do Norte do Brasil.

4. For a short survey of Dom João VI's Brazilian sojourn, see chap. 2 of Roderick J. Barman's *Brazil: The Forging of a Nation, 1798–1852* (Stanford: Stanford University Press, 1988). For a detailed Portuguese account, see Laurentino Gomes's *1808: Como Uma Rainha Louca, Um Príncipe Medroso e Uma Corte Corrupta Enganaram Napoleão e Mudaram A História De Portugal e Do Brasil* (São Paulo: Editora Planeta Brasil, 2007).

5. James S. Olson and Heather Olson Beal, *The Ethnic Dimension in American History* (Malden, MA: Wiley-Blackwell, 2010), 5–6.

6. Blanche H. C. Weaver's "Confederate Immigrants and Evangelical Churches in Brazil," *Journal of Southern History* 18 (1952): 446–68, offers a more thorough treatment.

7. See Daniel P. Kidder and James C. Fletcher, *Brazil and the Brazilians: Portrayed in Historical and Descriptive Sketches* (Philadelphia: Charles and Peterson, 1857).

8. See Weaver's "Confederate Immigrants and Evangelical Churches in Brazil," 447–52.

9. Blanche H. C. Weaver presents the more conservative numbers, based on journals and interviews; the larger figure comes from data on port records in Rio de Janeiro gathered by Betty de Oliveira as quoted in Alan M. Tigay's "The Deepest South: Five Thousand Miles below Mason-Dixon Line, a Brazilian Community Celebrates its Ties to Antebellum America," *American Heritage* 49 (1998): 84–95.

10. One commentator mentions a colony in Santarém, one in Bahia, and two in São Paulo. See James E. Bear's *Mission to Brazil* (Nashville: Board of World Mission, Presbyterian Church U.S., 1961), 5.

11. Two descendants of the Brazilian Confederates, Cyrus B. and James M. Dawsey, offer a detailed account of their ancestors' exploits in *The Confederados: Old South Immigrants in Brazil* (Tuscaloosa: University of Alabama Press, 1998). So does another descendant, Eugene C. Harter, in *The Lost Colony of the Confederacy* (Jackson: University Press of Mississippi, 1985). For a video of the descendants of Confederates in Brazil, uploaded May 30, 2008, see http://www.youtube.com/watch?v=L2LLM38bHDY.

12. See Dawsey and Dawsey, *Confederados*.

13. E. H. Quillin, letter from Santa Bárbara, October 18, 1879, Records Center of the International Mission Board of the Southern Baptist Convention, Richmond, Virginia.

14. See Stuart B. Schwartz, *Sugar Plantations in the Formation of Brazilian Society: Bahia, 1550–1835* (Cambridge: Cambridge University Press, 1985), 245–46.

15. Ibid., 247.

16. For more on Julião and the Peasant Leagues, see chap. 1 of Nancy Scheper-Hughes's *Death without Weeping: The Violence of Everyday Life in Brazil* (Berkeley: University of California Press, 1993); as well as Shepard Forman's "Disunity and Discontent: A Study of Peasant Political Movements in Brazil," *Journal of Latin American Studies* 3 (1971): 3–24. Anthony W. Pereira offers a broader view on the Northeast's rural labor movement in his book *The End of Peasantry: The Rural Labor Movement in Northeast Brazil, 1961–1988* (Pittsburgh: University of Pittsburgh Press, 1997).

17. For more on the Southern Tenant Farmers' Union, see Donald H. Grubbs's *Cry from the Cotton: The Southern Tenant Farmers' Union and the New Deal* (Chapel Hill: University of North Carolina Press, 1971); and Lowell K.

Dyson's "The Southern Tenant Farmers Union and Depression Politics," *Political Science Quarterly* 88 (1973): 230-52.

18. In reports back home the missionaries complained about the Roman Catholic Church's disregard for the Sabbath, of the tolerance of immorality among the Catholic clergy and laity, and of idolatry. Missionary women complained that Catholic high wedding fees contributed to "concubinage and illegitimate birth." Brazilian women's home life was seen as oppressive and harsh even among the better classes. Most could not read or write. And many husbands kept multiple households. Missionaries also blamed the Catholic faith for the state of social development in the country. They argued that the Catholic faith deprived individuals of personal accountability, keeping the faithful under the priests' control. That faith could never promote modern, scientific education, or abide the wise exercise of free choice among its members. Without a freethinking and educated citizenry, political democracy could not flourish in the country. For more on the missionary views, see Ballard S. Dunn, *Brazil, The Home for Southerners* (New Orleans: Bloomfield and Steel, 1866); and William B. Bagby, *Brazil and the Brazilians* (Baltimore: Maryland Baptist Missions Room, 1889).

19. Vivid descriptions in English of the Vargas years are found in Richard Bourne, *Getulio Vargas of Brazil, 1883-1954* (London: C. Knight, 1974); and Karl Loewenstein, *Brazil under Vargas* (New York: Russell and Russell, 1973). For a more recent treatment, see Robert M. Levine, *Father of the Poor? Vargas and His Era* (Cambridge: Cambridge University Press, 1998).

20. Bear, *Mission to Brazil*, 34.

21. Data is from the website of the First Presbyterian Church of Recife, http://www.primeiraigreja.org.br/.

22. It was so reassuring, decades later, to find one of America's prominent twentieth-century theologians making the same argument. Discussing the authority of scripture, Robert McAfee Brown said, "Let us state the modern predicament as sharply as we can: We are confronted with the historic claim that the Bible is authoritative, and yet when we read it, we find ourselves in an unbelievable world. We read about bodies being levitated up into heaven—and we know that heaven, wherever it may be, is not located 50,000 feet or so above Palestine. We read about demons leaving demented persons and taking up habitation in a herd of pigs so that the latter rush headlong over cliffs into the sea—and nothing in modern psychiatry leads us to place any credence in the tale. We discover that the whole biblical framework seems to presuppose a 'three-story universe,' with heaven up in the air, hell beneath the earth, and earth a fixed point in between—and we know that this view was exploded at least as long ago as the seventeenth century. These may not have been problems for the Reformers, but they are most certainly problems for us. We cannot accept either the Reformers' view of the universe or their sixteenth-century view of the Bible. Too much has happened in between their day and ours."

Robert McAfee Brown, *The Spirit of Protestantism* (New York: Oxford University Press, 1961), 73.

23. Noel de Medeiros Rosa (December 11, 1910–May 4, 1937) was one of Brazil's greatest composers. Singer, songwriter, guitar and mandolin player, in lyricism Noel was to Brazil what Cole Porter was to the United States (but in tragic life perhaps it might be more appropriate to compare him to Hank Williams). He re-created a popular Brazilian music genre, *samba*, by dressing it up in sophisticated urban rhymes and spicy social commentary. Despite his middle-class origins, Noel would spend most of his short adult life in the outskirts of Rio de Janeiro in the slum areas immersed in the nightlife where Rio's music came alive. A tormented man, he made it a point to spend his days among the criminal element, in bars, cabarets, and brothels. He died at the age of twenty-six, but not before composing almost three hundred songs that forever framed urban life in 1930s Brazil. Unfortunately, there is very little of Noel's poetry translated into English, and few American or British sources document his genius. For those interested in Rio's musical scene, I recommend Lisa Shaw, *The Social History of the Brazilian Samba* (London: Ashgate, 1999).

24. Fortunately, Northeastern migration has been a topic of much scholarly interest, and there is some good work that documents its costs to Brazilian society. See, for instance, Gerald Michael Greenfield, "The Great Drought and Elite Discourse in Imperial Brazil," *Hispanic American Historical Review* 72 (1992): 375–400; Naomar de Almeida Filho, "The Psychosocial Costs of Development: Labor, Migration and Stress in Bahia, Brazil," *Latin American Research Review* 17 (1982): 91–118; or Mary Lorena Kenny, "Drought, Clientalism, Fatalism and Fear in Northeast Brazil," *Ethics, Place and Environment* 5 (2002): 123–34.

25. There is a Northeastern song by Patativa do Assaré that encapsulates the whole migratory experience. In "A Triste Partida" he talks about a drought that drains all hope and wealth from a farming family. They have to sell everything they own to buy passage south. He describes what each person will miss most in the process, the anguish experienced by the parents in denying their children the same home they shared in their childhood. Life in São Paulo is cold, cruel, and demeaning. They lose their hope of returning after many years but never the homesickness for the place they left behind. You can read the lyrics and hear the song at http://letras.mus.br/patativa-do-assare/1072884/.

26. We have been wondering about that for a long while. Gerald Michael Greenfield documents how the 1878 congress of agricultural experts in my home state bemoaned even then "what they perceived as the imperial government's longstanding favoritism toward southern coffee interests. . . . Recife congress delegates emphasized the difficulties of obtaining agricultural credits and the need for more roads and railroads; [while] generally [agreeing with] their southern counterparts on the desirability of improved agricultural techniques." Greenfield, "The Great Drought and Elite Discourse in Imperial Brazil," 392.

27. Walt Whitman, *Leaves of Grass: Comprising all the Poems Written by Walt Whitman Following the Arrangement of the Edition of 1891–1892* (Philadelphia: David McKay, 1891–92), 73.

28. Ibid.

29. In my opinion no book better outlines Whitman's struggle than David S. Reynolds's *Walt Whitman's America: A Cultural Biography* (New York: Vintage Books, 1995).

30. For more on Whitman's influence, see Mary Edgar Meyer, "Walt Whitman's Popularity among Latin-American Poets," *Americas* 9 (1952): 3–15; see also Josef Raab, "El Gran Viejo: Walt Whitman in Latin America" *CLCWeb* 3, no. 2 (2001).

31. Pablo Neruda, "We Are Many," in *The Vintage Book of Contemporary World Poetry*, ed. J. D. McClatchy, trans. Alastair Reid (New York: Vintage Books, 1996), 528–29.

Chapter 2. Military Rule

1. In the United States, the federal statute known as the Posse Comitatus Act (18 U.S.C. § 1385) strictly bars the use of the army or air force for law enforcement purposes. A similar directive from the U.S. Secretary of Defense also forbids the navy and the Marine Corps from law enforcement activities. Unfortunately such key legal disposition is not part of the Latin American political heritage. For more on the legal underpinning of the Posse Comitatus Act, see Charles Doyle, *The Posse Comitatus Act and Related Matters: The Use of the Military to Execute Civilian Law* (Washington, DC: Congressional Research Service, 2000).

2. The Report of the Guatemalan Commission for Historical Clarification (http://shr.aaas.org/guatemala/ceh/report/english/toc.html) describes in vivid language, with ample documentation, the atrocities unleashed by the military and the guerrillas upon the civilian population. One of its statements is typical of the kind of military intervention we see in the region: "The CEH has noted particularly serious cruelty in many acts committed by agents of the State, especially members of the Army, in their operations against Mayan communities. The counterinsurgency strategy not only led to violations of basic human rights, but also to the fact that these crimes were committed with particular cruelty, with massacres representing their archetypal form. In the majority of massacres there is evidence of multiple acts of savagery, which preceded, accompanied or occurred after the deaths of the victims. Acts such as the killing of defenceless children, often by beating them against walls or throwing them alive into pits where the corpses of adults were later thrown; the amputation of limbs; the impaling of victims; the killing of persons by covering them in petrol and burning them alive; the extraction, in the presence of others, of the viscera of victims who were still alive; the confinement of

people who had been mortally tortured, in agony for days; the opening of the wombs of pregnant women, and other similarly atrocious acts, were not only actions of extreme cruelty against the victims, but also morally degraded the perpetrators and those who inspired, ordered or tolerated these actions." "Guatemala Memory of Silence, Tz'inil Na 'Tab' Al, Report of the Commission for Historical Clarification," Conclusions and Recommendations, Guatemalan Commission for Historical Clarification, Conclusions II, 87. For more on the specific conditions in Guatemala, see Jorge Luján Muñoz, *Historia General de Guatemala* (Guatemala: Asociación de Amigos del País, 2005).

3. The horrors the Argentine military visited upon its own population are fully documented in English-language works such as Iain Guest, *Behind the Disappearances: Argentina Dirty War Against Human Rights and the United Nations* (Philadelphia: University of Pennsylvania Press, 1990); Paul H. Lewis, *Guerrillas and Generals: The "Dirty War" in Argentina* (Westport, CT: Greenwood, 2002); and Patricia Marchak, *God's Assassins: State Terrorism in Argentina in the 1970s* (Toronto: McGill-Queen's University Press, 1999).

4. The numbers come from two official reports, The *Rettig Report* by the National Commission for Truth and Reconciliation, released in February 1991, http://www.usip.org/files/resources/collections/truth_commissions/Chile90-Report/Chile90-Report.pdf; and the *Valech Report* by the National Commission on Political Imprisonment and Torture, released in November 2004 and June 2005, http://www.comisionvalech.gov.cl/.

5. Abraham Lincoln, "Gettysburg Address," in *The Collected Works of Abraham Lincoln*, ed. Roy Basler (Springfield, IL: Abraham Lincoln Association, 1953).

6. "De Deodoro a Dilma," *Estado de São Paulo*, January 3, 2011, http://www.estadao.com.br/especiais/de-deodoro-a-dilma,128452.htm.

7. Jack Chang and Lisa Yulkowski, "Vocal Minority Praises Pinochet at His Funeral," *Bradenton Herald*, December 13, 2006.

8. "SURINAME: EX-LEADER SENTENCED—A court in The Hague convicted Suriname's former military leader, Desi Bouterse, of cocaine trafficking, sentencing him in absentia to 16 years in prison and fining him $2.18 million. The court ruled that Mr. Bouterse, who staged two military coups, in 1980 and 1990, was the lynchpin of a cartel that tried to smuggle about two tons of cocaine seized at Dutch and Belgian ports and airports between 1989 and 1997. Mr. Bouterse, 54, was chief adviser to President Jules Wijdenbosch until he was fired in April." Terence Neilan, "World Briefing," *New York Times*, July 17, 1999.

9. Guatemala was ruled by General Miguel Ydígoras Fuentes (1957–63), Colonel Enrique Peralta Azurdia (1963–66), Julio César Méndez Montenegro (1966–70), Colonel Carlos Manuel Arana Osório (1970–74), General Kjell Laugerud García (1974–78), General Romeo Lucas García (1978–82), and General Efraín Rios Montt (1982–86), who finally overthrown by General Óscar Humberto Mejía Victores.

10. "In the future days, which we seek to make secure, we look forward to a world founded upon four essential human freedoms. The first is freedom of speech and expression—everywhere in the world. The second is freedom of every person to worship God in his own way—everywhere in the world. The third is freedom from want—which, translated into world terms, means economic understandings which will secure to every nation a healthy peacetime life for its inhabitants—everywhere in the world. The fourth is freedom from fear—which, translated into world terms, means a worldwide reduction of armaments to such a point and in such a thorough fashion that no nation will be in a position to commit an act of physical aggression against any neighbor— anywhere in the world." President Franklin D. Roosevelt, "The Four Freedoms Speech," in *Congressional Record* (Washington, DC: Government Printing Office, 1941), vol. 87, pt. 1.

11. "The expansion of the press in the Americas . . . took place in the second half of the 18th century. . . . Libraries no longer had just Spanish classics. As in Spain, the influence of France was felt in the Americas. . . . The likes of Montaigne, Rousseau, Voltaire, and Montesquieu were read, as well as proto-liberal English thinkers such as Hobbes, Locke, and Hume." Carlos Alberto Montaner, *Latin Americans and the West: The Historical and Cultural Roots of Latin America* (Miami: InterAmerican Institute for Democracy, 2009), 65.

12. Lincoln's words in the Gettysburg Address remain a source of inspiration for all of us who dream of a democratic Latin America:

> Four score and seven years ago our fathers brought forth on this continent a new nation, conceived in liberty, and dedicated to the proposition that all men are created equal.
>
> Now we are engaged in a great civil war, testing whether that nation, or any nation, so conceived and so dedicated, can long endure. We are met on a great battle-field of that war. We have come to dedicate a portion of that field, as a final resting place for those who here gave their lives that that nation might live. It is altogether fitting and proper that we should do this.
>
> But, in a larger sense, we can not dedicate, we can not consecrate, we can not hallow this ground. The brave men, living and dead, who struggled here, have consecrated it, far above our poor power to add or detract. The world will little note, nor long remember what we say here, but it can never forget what they did here. It is for us the living, rather, to be dedicated here to the unfinished work which they who fought here have thus far so nobly advanced. It is rather for us to be here dedicated to the great task remaining before us—that from these honored dead we take increased devotion to that cause for which they gave the last full measure of devotion—that we here highly resolve that these dead shall not have died in vain—that this nation, under God, shall have a new birth of freedom—and that government of the people, by the people, for the people, shall not perish from the earth.

13. The Brazilian writer Jorge Amado alone was published in fifty-two countries and translated into forty-nine languages and dialects. And he is by no means alone. Personally, it was a thrill to witness Isabel Allende autographing editions of her books in Arabic, Japanese, Italian, and English during her recent visit to Washington, DC.

14. For a better sense of Latin America's rich heritage I recommend Montaner's book *Latin Americans and the West*.

15. See Ana Cristina Braga Martes, *New Immigrants, New Land: A Study of Brazilians in Massachusetts* (Gainesville: University Press of Florida, 2011), 166–76.

16. For more on Kubitschek, see Robert J. Alexander, *Juscelino Kubitschek and the Development of Brazil* (Athens: Ohio University Press, 1992). For more on the Arbénz Gúzman administration, see Stephen M. Streeter, *Managing Counterrevolution: The United States and Guatemala, 1954–1961* (Athens: Ohio University Press, 2001). For more on Belaúnde Terry's presidency, see Pedro-Pablo Kuczynski, *Peruvian Democracy under Economic Stress: An Account of the Belaúnde Administration, 1963–1968* (Princeton, NJ: Princeton University Press, 1977).

17. Much of the information for the section on President Bachelet is based on U.S. newspaper reporting. Key articles include Alexei Barrionuevo, "Chilean President Rides High as Term Ends," *New York Times*, October 28, 2009, A6; and Paula Escobar Chavarría, "In Chile, Departing President Michelle Bachelet Proved Women Can Lead," *Washington Post*, March 14, 2010. Biographical information is from Bachelet's page at the Centro de Estudios y Documentación Internacionales de Barcelona, http://www.cidob.org/es/documentacion/biografias_lideres_politicos/america_del_sur/chile/michelle_bachelet_jeria.

18. Biographical information is from the Centro Internacional Celso Furtado de Políticas para o Desenvolvimento, http://www.centrocelsofurtado.org.br/geral.php?ID_S=64. For more on Furtado's work, see Cristóbal Kay, "Celso Furtado: Pioneer of Structuralist Development Theory," *Development and Change* 36 (2005): 1201–7; and Mauro Boianovsky, "A View from the Tropics: Celso Furtado and the Theory of Economic Development in the 1950s," *History of Political Economy* 42 (2010): 221–66.

19. For more on Cardoso, see his memoir, *The Accidental President of Brazil: A Memoir* (New York: Public Affairs, 2007); or Ted G. Goertzel, *Fernando Henrique Cardoso: Reinventing Democracy in Brazil* (Boulder: Lynne Rienner, 1999).

20. For more on Óscar Arias Sanchéz, see Vicki Cox, *Oscar Arias Sanchez: Bringing Peace to Central America* (New York: Chelsea House Publications, 2007).

21. I found little in English about Aguilera. Most of the biographical information, including news on his tragic death while in office, is reported in Spanish. A good example is an article in the *Correo* of May 24, 2007, http://www.diariocorreo.com.ec/archivo/2007/05/24/jaime-roldos-aguilera (no longer accessible online).

22. For more on Sánchez Lozada, see Stanley B. Greenberg, *Dispatches from the War Room: In the Trenches with Five Extraordinary Leaders* (New York: Thomas Dunne Books, 2009).

23. For more on García Márquez, see Gene H. Bell-Villada, *Conversations with Gabriel García Márquez* (Jackson: University of Mississippi Press, 2005) or García Márquez's own memoir, *Living to Tell the Tale* (New York: Alfred A. Knopf, 2003).

24. Neruda's *Memoirs* (New York: Farrar, Straus and Giroux, 2001) is a fascinating read. I read it first in Spanish, and in my opinion, the Spanish title, *Confieso que He Vivido*, is the best I've seen for a memoir. Adam Feinstein, *Pablo Neruda: A Passion for Life* (New York: Bloomsbury, 2005), is a nice English introduction to the man and his craft.

25. Fuentes's *Buried Mirror: Reflections on Spain and the New World* (New York: Houghton Mifflin Company, 1999) is an ode to all that unites Latin Americans, a paean to our rich Old World heritage. Raymond L. Williams, *The Writings of Carlos Fuentes* (Austin: University of Texas Press, 1996), traces the strong sense of Latin American history, culture, and identity in Fuentes's works.

26. The Brazilian participation in the Mediterranean Theater alongside the Allied forces is little known outside the country. The best coverage in English, *The Brazilian Expeditionary Force* (Washington, DC: U.S. Government Printing Office, 1966), was written by Brazil's armed forces supreme commander, Marshal J. B. Mascarenhas de Moraes.

27. Stephen G. Rabe documented U.S. involvement in the region, including the money for my hometown's gear, in his book *The Most Dangerous Area in the World: John F. Kennedy Confronts Communist Revolution in Latin America* (Chapel Hill: University of North Carolina Press, 1999).

28. The Brazilian 1964 military coup has been the subject of several scholarly works in English. Among them are Joseph A. Page, *The Revolution that Never Was: Northeast Brazil, 1955–1964* (New York: Grossman, 1972); Thomas E. Skidmore, *The Politics of Military Rule in Brazil, 1964–1985* (New York: Oxford University Press, 1988); and Alfred Stepan, *Authoritarian Brazil: Origins, Policies, and Future* (New Haven, CT: Yale University Press, 1973).

29. Only forty years later would declassified CIA documents confirm the presence of the American Navy convoy off the Brazilian coast. The mission was codenamed Operation Brother Sam. The declassified transcripts of communications between Lincoln Gordon and the U.S. government indicate that President Johnson expected an all-out civil war. To support a friendly military, Johnson authorized logistical materials that could aid the military rebellion, including ammunition, motor oil, gasoline, and aviation gasoline. About 110 tons of ammunition and CS gas were made ready in New Jersey for a potential airlift to Viracopos Airport in Campinas. An aircraft carrier (USS *Forrestal*), two guided missile destroyers, and four destroyers were sent to Brazil under the guise of a

military exercise. For more on the incident, see Peter Kornbluh, "Brazil Marks 40th Anniversary of Military Coup: Declassified Documents Shed Light on U.S. Role," *National Security Archive*, March 31, 2004, http://www.gwu.edu/ ~nsarchiv/NSAEBB/NSAEBB118/index.htm#docs.

30. The military placed censors in all the major media outlets, seriously monitored professional associations, and controlled labor unions down to their funding. Among books dealing with the early phase of the military regime, see Ronald M. Schneider, *The Political System of Brazil: Emergence of a "Modernizing" Authoritarian Regime, 1964–1970* (New York: Columbia University Press, 1973); Alfred Stepan, *The Military in Politics: Changing Patterns in Brazil* (Princeton, NJ: Princeton University Press, 1974); and Wilfred A. Bacchus, *Mission in Mufti: Brazil's Military Regimes, 1964–1985* (Westport, CT: Greenwood Press, 1990).

31. Archdiocese of São Paulo, *Torture in Brazil: A Shocking Report on the Pervasive Use of Torture by Brazilian Military Governments, 1964–1974, Secretly Prepared by the Archdiocese of São Paulo* (Austin: University of Texas Press, 1998). Related narratives of Brazilian torture can be found in Leigh A. Payne, *Unsettling Accounts: Neither Truth nor Reconciliation in Confessions of State Violence* (Durham, NC: Duke University Press, 2008); and Lawrence Weschler, *A Miracle, A Universe: Settling Accounts with Torturers* (Chicago: University of Chicago Press, 1990).

32. Among college leaders apprehended were Aécio Matos, José Carlos Nogueira de Melo, and Dirceu Carlos Brasileiro. Among high school students, Daniel Miranda Monteiro, Fernando Santa Cruz, and Raniere Maranhão.

33. Unfortunately, documentation of the military repression in Pernambuco is still mostly available only in Portuguese. One of the most detailed articles I found was Simone Rocha, "Articulações e Confrontos: A Consolidação do Discurso de Esquerda no Movimento Estudantil Pernambucano (1964–1967)," *Saeculum: Revista de História* 13 (2005): 90–104.

34. The memory of Father Henrique has not been forgotten. There is a public school in my hometown named after him. And a local professor has published a detailed book on his life and death: Diogo Cunha, *Estado de Exceção, A Igreja Católica e a Repressão: O Assassinato do Padre Antônio Henrique Pereira da Silva Neto* (Recife: Universidade Federal de Pernambuco, 2007).

35. "Livro do Governo Culpa Ditadura por Tortura e Mortes," *Folha de São Paulo*, August 25, 2007, http://www1.folha.uol.com.br/folha/brasil/ult96u323017.shtml.

36. Eremias Delizoicov, Centro de documentação, "O Dossiê dos Mortos e Desaparecidos a partir de 1964," http://www.desaparecidospoliticos.org.br/quem_somos_dossie.php?m=2.

37. Archdiocese of São Paulo, *Torture in Brazil*, 77–80.

38. For more on this, see José M. Bello, *A History of Modern Brazil* (Stanford: Stanford University Press, 1966); and Emilia Viotti da Costa, "1870–1889," in *Brazil: Empire and Republic, 1822–1930*, ed. Leslie Bethell (Cambridge: Cambridge University Press, 1987).

39. The English lyrics to "Apesar de Você" in rough translation are: "Today you're the boss; what you command goes; without argument. So my people have to talk sideways, with downcast eyes; do you see it? You invented this condition, you created this darkness. You, who invented sinning forgot to invent forgiveness. But despite you, tomorrow will be a new day. And I ask you, as it dawns, how will you hide from the enormous euphoria? Can you keep the rooster from crowing? New water will cleanse all this and we [those of us who suffered] shall finally love endlessly. The time will come when all my suffering will be paid back with interest, I swear! All this repressed love, this censored shout, this samba played in the dark. You, who invented sadness, please have the decency to un-invent it! You shall pay double for every tear dropped in this sorrow of mine. [But] despite you, tomorrow will be a new day. And I'll pay to see it bloom even as you work hard to prevent it. You will rue the sunrise, when that day will burst forth without your permission. And I will die of laughter, watching that day arrive sooner than you imagine. [Because] despite you, tomorrow will be a new day, and you will witness the dawn of that new day, filled with poetry. How will you explain, the sudden brightening of the sky with impunity? How will you smother our chorus, which will sing in front you, despite you: Tomorrow shall be a new day; Tomorrow shall be a new day."

40. Two of my early articles come to mind here: "Political Cooperation and Religious Repression: Presbyterians under Military Rule in Brazil (1964-1974)," *Review of Religious Research* 34 (1992): 97–116; and "Unrealistic Expectations: Contesting the Usefulness of Weber's Protestant Ethic for the Study of Latin American Protestantism," *Journal of Church and State* 37 (1995): 289–308.

41. The United Presbyterian Church of Brazil (Igreja Presbiteriana Unida) is made up of the Presbyterian jurisdictions kicked out by the Presbyterian Church of Brazil: "The formation of the United Presbyterian Church of Brazil goes back to the period of military dictatorship (1964–84) in Brazil, when some pastors, churches, and even presbyteries were pursued for being critical of the regime, and for participating in ecumenical groups and movements devoted to the search for social justice. Expelled by the denomination they belonged to, these communities and pastors had a painful period of isolation and dispersion until 1978, when they founded the National Federation of Presbyterian Churches, which from 1983 on was named the United Presbyterian Church of Brazil (IPU)." Information is from the World Council of Churches website, last updated January 1, 2006, http://www.oikoumene.org/gr/member-churches/regions/latin-america/brazil/united-presbyterian-church-of-brazil.html.

Chapter 3. Naturalization

1. Martes, *New Immigrants, New Land*, 233. See the fuller quotation later in this chapter.

2. Arnold Strickon and Sidney M. Greenfield's edited collection *Structure and Process in Latin America: Patronage, Clientage, and Power Systems* (Albuquerque: University of New Mexico Press, 1972) offers an overview of the Latin American patronage system; while Sidney M. Greenfield, "The Patrimonial State and Patron-Client Relations in Iberia and Latin America: Sources of 'The System' in the Fifteenth-Century Writings of the Infante D. Pedro of Portugal," *Ethnohistory* 24 (1977): 163–78, delves deeper into the Brazilian patronage system.

3. There is research that documents this Brazilian aversion to American ways. See, for instance, Charlotte I. Miller, "The Function of Middle-Class Extended Family Networks in Brazilian Urban Society," in *Brazil: Anthropological Perspectives*, ed. Maxine L. Margolis and William E. Carter (New York: Columbia University Press, 1979), 305–16; and Maxine L. Margolis, "With New Eyes: Returned International Immigrants in Rio de Janeiro," in *Raízes e Rumos: Perspectivas Interdisciplinares em Estudos Americanos*, ed. Sonia Torres (Rio de Janeiro: Editora 7 Letras, 2001), 239–44. According to Margolis, Brazilian immigrants complain that Americans "simply do not know how to enjoy themselves. On weekends and holidays 'people go shopping instead of getting together with family and friends. . . . All the stores are open and the health clubs are full.' Americans are either working or shopping . . . not having fun." Margolis, *An Invisible Minority: Brazilians in New York City* (Gainesville: University Press of Florida, 2009), 73. On a similar note, Conrad Phillip Kottak argues that unlike Americans, Brazilians are not joiners: "The typical American belongs to dozens of non-kin based groups. These include churches, political parties, clubs, teams, occupational groups, organizations. . . . In Brazil, where home and extended family hold their own so vigorously against the external world, non-kin associations are fewer." Conrad Phillip Kottak, *Prime Time Society: An Anthropological Analysis of Television and Culture* (Belmont, CA: Wadsworth, 1990), 166.

4. Martes, *New Immigrants, New Land*, 233.

5. Ketevan Mamiseishvili and Jill Hermsen, "Employment Patterns and Job Satisfaction of Foreign-Born Science and Engineering Doctorate Recipients in the United States," *Academic Leadership Live* 7, no. 1 (2009): 1–13.

6. Alexandro Portes and Rubén G. Rumbaut, in *Immigrant America: A Portrait* (Berkeley: University of California Press, 1996), show how the first generation delays getting involved in the politics of the host country—they hold on to monitoring political issues back home. The same can be said for most immigrant groups in American history. See, for instance, Olson and Beal, *The Ethnic Dimension in American History*. People come to America hoping to return home.

7. Maxine L. Margolis, "Brazilians and the 1990 United States Census: Immigrants, Ethnicity, and the Undercount," *Human Organization* 54 (1995): 57.

8. See, for instance, Nestor P. Rodriguez and Jacqueline S. Hagan, *Investigating Census Coverage among the Undocumented: An Ethnographic Study of Latino Immigrant Tenants in Houston* (Washington, DC: Center for Survey Methods Research, Bureau of the Census, 1991).

9. Adriana Garcia, "Immigrants Hit Hard by Slowdown, Subprime Crisis," *Reuters*, January 30, 2008.

10. Nina Bernstein and Elizabeth Dwoskin, "Brazilians Giving up Their American Dream," *New York Times*, December 4, 2007. See also Taylor Barnes, "No Place Like Home: Brazilian Immigrants Leave US for Better Job Prospects," *Christian Science Monitor*, September 24, 2009; and Jared Goyette, "Back to Brazil," *Charleston City Paper*, February 20, 2008.

11. Portes and Rumbaut, *Immigrant America: A Portrait*.

12. James Brooke, "In Brazil Wild Ways to Counter Wild Inflation," *New York Times*, July 25, 1993.

13. Luciana Peluso and Simone Goldberg, "Heróis da Sobrevivência," *Isto É*, December 7, 1995, 126.

14. Based on data from Brazilian Consulates, Margolis estimates that there are currently 1.1 million Brazilians living in the United States. Starting in the mid-1980s Brazilians also migrated to Canada, Japan, and Europe. Never before had the country faced emigration in such numbers. See Margolis, *Invisible Minority*, 6.

15. See Maxine L. Margolis, *Little Brazil: An Ethnography of Brazilian Immigrants in New York City* (Princeton, NJ: Princeton University Press, 1994). In *New Immigrants, New Land*, Ana Cristina Braga Martes reports similar social class results for Brazilians in the greater Boston area. The same was found by Bernadete Beserra, in *Brazilian Immigrants in the United States: Cultural Imperialism and Social Class* (New York: LFB Scholarly Publishing, 2003), for Brazilians in Los Angeles.

16. "Between 1980 and 2000, the percentage of PhD scientists and engineers employed in the United States who were born abroad has increased from 24% to 37%. The current percentage of PhD physicists is about 45%; for engineers, the figure is over 50%. One-fourth of the engineering faculty members at U.S. universities were born abroad. Between 1990 and 2004, over one-third of Nobel Prizes in the United States were awarded to foreign-born scientists. One-third of all U.S. PhDs in science and engineering are now awarded to foreign-born graduate students. We have been skimming the best and brightest minds from across the globe and prospering because of it; we need these new Americans even more now as other countries become more technologically capable." William A. Wulf, "The Importance of Foreign-born Scientists and Engineers to the Security of The United States," testimony before the Subcommittee on Immigration, Border Security, and Claims of the Committee on the Judiciary, U.S. House of Representatives, 109th Cong., September 15, 2005, http://www7.nationalacademies.org/ocga/testimony/Importance_of_Foreign_Scientists_and_Engineers_to_US.asp.

17. Mamiseishvili and Hermsen, "Employment Patterns and Job Satisfaction of Foreign-Born Science and Engineering Doctorate Recipients in the United States."

18. Kenneth E. Foote, Wei Li, Janice Monk, and Rebecca Theobald, "Foreign-born Scholars in American Universities: Issues, Concerns and Strategies," *Symposium: Journal of Geography in Higher Education* 32 (2008): 167–78.

19. Gabriela Montell, "A Preference for Foreigners?" *Chronicle of Higher Education*, May 11, 2007.

20. Jan Vilcek and Bruce N. Cronstein, "A Prize for the Foreign-Born," *FASEB Journal* 20 (2006): 1281–83.

21. For the mid-1970s figure, see Portes and Rumbaut, *Immigrant America*. For today's figure, see Carl Shusterman, "Immigration Knowledge Essential to Recruiting IMGs," *New England Journal of Medicine Career Center*, July–August 2000.

22. Jill Laster, "Onetime Foreign Student Leads Lehigh U.'s Globalization Project," *Chronicle of Higher Education*, June 18, 2010, A4.

23. "AILA Backgrounder: Myths and Facts in the Immigration Debate," August 3, 2003, http://www.visalaw.com/03aug3/ailabackgrounder.pdf.

24. "Hispanics: A People in Motion" (Pew Hispanic Center, Washington, DC, January 2005), http://pewhispanic.org/files/reports/40.pdf.

25. Robert W. Fairlie, "Estimating the Contribution of Immigrant Business Owners to the U.S. Economy" (Small Business Research Summary no. 334, SBA Office of Advocacy, November 2008), http://www.sba.gov/advo/research/rs334tot.pdf.

26. Ana Cristina Braga Martes, *Brasileiros nos Estados Unidos* (São Paulo: Editora Paz e Terra, 2000).

27. Margolis, *Invisible Minority*, 23–25.

28. Ibid., 45–46.

29. Sergio Bustos, "Backlog Keeps Immigrants Waiting Years for Green Cards," *USA Today*, January 26, 2005.

30. S. Mitra Kalita, "For Green Card Applicants, Waiting Is the Hardest Part," *Washington Post*, July 23, 2005.

31. Bustos, "Backlog Keeps Immigrants Waiting Years for Green Cards."

32. Julia Preston, "Surge Brings New Immigration Backlog," *New York Times*, November 23, 2007.

33. "The High Cost of Immigration," Editorial, *New York Times*, June 22, 2010, A26.

34. "For Many in the US, the Green Card Wait Is Long," WorkPermit.Com (a service of the *Washington Post*), July 25, 2005.

35. Stuart Anderson, "Family Immigration: The Long Wait to Immigrate" (NFAP Policy Brief, National Foundation of American Policy, Arlington, VA, May 2010), 1.

36. Bustos, "Backlog Keeps Immigrants Waiting Years for Green Cards."

37. My discussion of cultural identity and ethnocentrism is heavily influenced by the work of Joel M. Charon, especially *Ten Questions*, 6th ed. (Belmont, CA: Wadsworth, 2007).

38. Francis Bellamy, "The Story of the Pledge of Allegiance to the Flag," *University of Rochester Library Bulletin* 8, no. 2 (1953).

39. W. C. Costin and J. Steven Watson, *The Law & Working of the Constitution*, vol. 1 (London: A&C Black, 1952), 57-59.

40. "The Act of Supremacy, 1559," in *English History in the Making*, vol. 1, ed. William Sachse (New York: John Wiley and Sons, 1967), 198-99.

41. *The Constitution of the Vermont Republic*, 1777, http://vermont-archives. org/govhistory/constitut/con77.htm.

42. U.S. Citizenship and Immigration Services, "Naturalization Oath of Allegiance to the United States of America," http://www.uscis.gov/portal/site/uscis/menuitem.5af9bb95919f35e66f614176543f6d1a/?vgnextoid=facd6db8d7e37210VgnVCM100000082ca60aRCRD&vgnextchannel=dd7ffe9dd4aa3210VgnVCM100000b92ca60aRCRD.

43. The research eventually resulted in a book I coauthored with Debra Schleef, *Latinos in Dixie: Class and Assimilation in Richmond, Virginia* (Albany: State University of New York Press, 2009).

44. In a book focused on family therapy, Nydia Garcia-Preto put it best—when it came to lumping all Latinos into a single category in the United States: "For many of us, the label, whether Latino/Latina or Hispanic, takes away our nationality and symbolizes a loss of identity. However, the benefit is that it provides a way for the Latinos of various nationalities to have some unity in order to gain political power." Nydia Garcia-Preto, "Latino Families: An Overview," in *Ethnicity and Family Therapy*, ed. Monica McGoldrick, Joseph Giordano, and Nydia Garcia-Preto (New York: Guilford Press, 2005), 153-65.

45. For more on the fascinating world of the Gabra, see Toru Soga, "System and Reality: The Camel Trust System of the Gabra," *African Study Monographs* 18 (1997): 157-74.

Chapter 4. Immigrant Parenting

1. Much of the information in the following paragraphs is my own response to findings by Neil Howe and William Strauss in their book *Millennials Rising: The Next Great Generation* (New York: Vintage Books, 2005).

2. For more on the self-driven college students of today, I recommend two pertinent articles for their devastating clarity and lucid analysis: David Brooks, "The Organization Kid," *Atlantic*, April 2001, regarding college students at Princeton; and Mark Edmundson, "Dwelling in Possibilities," *Chronicle of Higher Education*, March 14, 2008, B7, about similar students at the University of Virginia. Brooks puts it well. While describing students he found at his alma mater, he could have been talking about their whole suburban generation: "The world they live in seems fundamentally just. If you work hard, behave pleasantly, explore your interests, volunteer your time, obey the codes of political correctness, and take the right pills to balance your brain chemistry, you

will be rewarded with a wonderful ascent in the social hierarchy. You will get into Princeton and have all sorts of genuinely interesting experiences open to you. You will make a lot of money—but more important, you will be able to improve yourself. You will be a good friend and parent. You will be caring and conscientious. You will learn to value the really important things in life. There is a fundamental order to the universe, and it works. If you play by its rules and defer to its requirements, you will lead a pretty fantastic life."

3. Lena H. Sun, "From Curiosity to Eureka," *Washington Post,* September 3, 2011, A1, A6.

4. Neil Howe and William Strauss, *Millennials Go to College: Strategies for a New Generation on Campus* (Washington, DC: American Association of Collegiate Registrars and Admissions Offices, 2003).

5. My discussion of family importance in this section follows closely the therapeutic findings of Garcia-Preto in "Latino Families: An Overview."

6. See Martes, *New Immigrants, New Land.*

7. For this section of the chapter I rely on the work of Eliana Catão de Korin and Sueli S. de Carvalho Petry, especially their chapter titled "Brazilian Families," in *Ethnicity and Family Therapy,* ed. Monica McGoldrick, Joseph Giordano, and Nydia Garcia-Preto (New York: Guilford Press, 2005), 166–77.

8. For more on the dilemma of Brazilian social hierarchy, see Roberto da Matta, *Carnival, Rogues, and Heroes* (Notre Dame: University of Notre Dame Press, 1991). For a detailed description of family networks in urban Brazil, see Miller, "The Function of Middle-Class Extended Family Networks in Brazilian Urban Society."

9. Calvin J. Veltman, *Language Shift in the United States* (New York: Mouton, 1983).

10. Alejandro Portes and Rubén G. Rumbaut, *Legacies: The Story of the Immigrant Second Generation* (Berkeley: University of California Press, 2001), 126.

11. This section is based on my experience and the work of Andrew Fuligni, Gwendelyn Rivera, and April Leininger, in "Family Identity and the Educational Persistence of Students with Latin American and Asian Backgrounds," in *Contesting Stereotypes and Creating Identities,* ed. Andrew J. Fuligni (New York: Russell Sage Foundation, 2007), 239–65.

12. Portes and Rumbaut, *Legacies,* 151.

13. Henri Tajfel, *Human Groups and Social Categories* (London: Cambridge University Press, 1981).

14. Portes and Rumbaut, *Legacies,* 157.

15. Studies find that students in better suburban schools are more likely to adopt a plain American identity. See Portes and Rumbaut, *Legacies,* 173.

16. Fuligni, Rivera, and Leininger, "Family Identity and the Educational Persistence of Students with Latin American and Asian Backgrounds," 241.

17. See Portes and Rumbaut, *Legacies,* 201–2.

18. The highest levels of self-esteem were Cubans and other Latin Americans (with the notable exception of Mexicans), West Indians, and European/Canadians. Those with the lowest self-esteem scores were the children of Southeast Asian refugees—Vietnamese, Lao, Hmong, and Cambodians. Portes and Rumbaut, *Legacies*, 207. Of course, higher psychological well-being is correlated with low-conflict families, good teaching, and a fair and supportive learning climate too. Ibid., 210.

19. Karina Fortuny, Randy Capps, Margaret Simms, and Ajay Chaudry, "Children of Immigrants: National and State Characteristics" (Brief 9, The Urban Institute, Washington, DC, August 2009), 1, 4–5, http://www.urban.org/uploadedpdf/411939_childrenofimmigrants.pdf.

20. Fortuny, Capps, Simms, and Chaudry, "Children of Immigrants: National and State Characteristics," 1, 6–8.

21. For more on the children of Brazilian immigrants, see Teresa Sales, "Second Generation Brazilian Immigrants in the United States," in *The Other Latinos*, ed. José Luis Falconi and José Antonio Mazzotti (Cambridge, MA: David Rockefeller Center for Latin American Studies, Harvard University, 2007), 195–211. See also Christina Scudeler, "Immigrantes Valadarenses no Mercado de Trabalho dos EUA," in *Cenas do Brasil Migrante*, ed. Rosana Rocha Reis and Teresa Sales (São Paulo: Boitempo, 1999), 193–232.

22. The main proponents of the segmented assimilation theory are Alejandro Portes and Rubén G. Rumbaut. Their work is based on the findings from the Children of Immigrants Longitudinal Study that they conducted in three waves—in 1992–93, in 1995–96, and in 2002–3. For more on the theory, see Portes and Rumbaut, *Legacies*.

23. The consistency of those results is pretty strong. As Alejandro Portes and Alejandro Rivas put it, "Good early school grades and positive early educational expectations significantly increase educational attainment and occupational status while preventing downward assimilation. . . . Having higher-status parents and being raised by both natural parents also raise educational levels and powerfully inhibit downward assimilation." Alejandro Portes and Alejandro Rivas, "The Adaptation of Migrant Children," *Future Child* 21 (2011): 235. See also Patricia Fernández-Kelly, "The Back Pocket Map: Social Class and Cultural Capital as Transferable Assets in the Advancement of Second Generation Immigrants," *Annals of the American Academy of Political and Social Science* 620 (November 2008): 116–37; Krista M. Perreira, Kathleen Harris, and Dohoon Lee, "Making It in America: High School Completion by Immigrant and Native Youth," *Demography* 43 (2006): 511–36; and Grace Kao and Marta Tienda, "Educational Aspirations of Minority Youth," *American Journal of Education* 106 (1998): 349–84.

24. Timothy Ferris, *The Science of Liberty: Democracy, Reason, and the Laws of Nature* (New York: Harper, 2010), 74.

25. The college Gui attended gave each student an intro web page. On his page Gui's reasons for choosing the school had everything to do with engineering and striking out on his own: "With a passion for mechanical engineering and fabrication technology, Gui claims 'there is no greater feeling than knowing you have the ability to build anything you want.' He recently worked in a machine shop and learned to program and run computer-controlled mills and lathes. 'Any mechanical engineer who creates parts for a living should know exactly how they will be made, so they can do their job more efficiently,' he says. An avid swing dancer, rock climber and robot whiz, Gui came to Olin because he disdains living with ruts and traditions. 'I knew this was one of the few places where I could single-handedly start something new and exciting and influence the school's culture. Olin will continuously evolve,' he says."

Chapter 5. Pledging One's Life

1. Timothy Ferris presents an appalling beginning for the American Revolution: "Only through daring and luck was Washington able to convey the remainder of his Brooklyn forces across the East River by night, fleeing north through Manhattan before the British could catch up. Washington had been in retreat ever since, through New Jersey and on into Pennsylvania, and was close to despair. 'I think the game is pretty near up,' he wrote to his brother John Augustine on December 18. The enlistments of three-quarters of his troops were due to expire at the end of the month; many, badly demoralized, had already declared their intention to quit fighting and go home and attend to their shops and farms." Ferris, *Science of Liberty*, 75.

2. Barack H. Obama, "Why I'm Optimistic," *Smithsonian*, July/August 2010, 59.

3. Jorge Caldeira, in *A Nação Mercantilista: Ensaio Sobre o Brasil* (São Paulo: Editora 34, 1999), provides an insightful analysis of how Brazilians lost the development race to their northern neighbor. For a similar survey in the English language, see Clodovir Vianna Moog, *Bandeirantes and Pioneers* (New York: George Braziller, 1964).

4. For more on Carnegie's life, see Peter Krass, *Carnegie* (Hoboken: John Wiley and Sons, 2002).

5. Ferris, *Science of Liberty*, 97.

6. "Another reason undocumented Brazilians are fearful is because in Brazil everyone is required to carry a national identity card that must be presented to authorities upon request. Most Brazilians are unaware that there is no equivalent document in the United States and that the New York police will not arbitrarily stop them on the street and demand to see their papers." Margolis, *An Invisible Minority*, 76.

7. Hernando de Soto, interview, *Commanding Heights*, March 30, 2001,

http://www.pbs.org/wgbh/commandingheights/shared/minitextlo/int_
hernandodesoto.html, as cited in Ferris, *Science of Liberty*, 164–65.

8. Ibid., 165. The further irony is that those who are excluded generate enormous amounts of wealth: "In every country we have examined, the entrepreneurial ingenuity of the poor has created wealth on a vast scale—wealth that also constitutes by far the largest source of potential capital development. These assets not only far exceed the holdings of the government, the local stock exchanges, and foreign direct investments; they are many times greater than all the aid from advanced nations and all the loans extended by the World Bank." Hernando de Soto, *The Mystery of Capital: Why Capitalism Triumphs in the West and Fails Everywhere Else* (New York, Basic Books, 2000), 34, as cited in Ferris, *Science of Liberty*, 166. Without legal permits, the poor cannot leverage their assets, and therefore cannot obtain loans, credit, or mortgages. Moreover their assets are "dead capital," because they are funds unavailable for investment.

9. Margolis, *Invisible Minority*, 73.

10. That is what Ana Cristina Braga Martes found among Brazilian immigrants in Boston. See Martes, *New Immigrants, New Land*, 165.

11. See Stephen C. Poulson, *Social Movements in Twentieth-Century Iran: Culture, Ideology and Mobilizing Frameworks* (Lanham, MD: Lexington Books, 2005), chap. 11.

12. See Darren Hawkins, "Democratization Theory and Nontransitions: Insights from Cuba," *Comparative Politics* 33 (2001): 441–61.

13. Tip O'Neill, *Man of the House: The Life and Political Memoirs of Speaker Tip O'Neill* (New York: Random House, 1987), 6.

14. Steven E. Finkel, "Reciprocal Effects of Participation and Political Efficacy: A Panel Analysis," *American Journal of Political Science* 29 (1985): 893. Political efficacy has influenced the politics of most developed nations. For more on its effects, see also Harold D. Clarke and Alan C. Acock, "National Elections and Political Attitudes: The Case of Political Efficacy," *British Journal of Political Science* 19 (1989): 551–62; Steven Finkel, "The Effects of Participation on Political Efficacy and Political Support: Evidence from a West German Panel," *Journal of Politics* 49 (1987): 441–64; and Alan C. Acock, Harold D. Clarke, and Marianne C. Stewart, "A New Model for Old Measures: A Covariance Structural Analysis of Political Efficacy," *Journal of Politics* 47 (1985): 1062–84. For recent research, see Jeffrey A. Karp and Susan A. Banducci, "Political Efficacy and Participation in Twenty-Seven Democracies: How Electoral Systems Shape Political Behaviour," *British Journal of Political Science* 38 (2008): 311–34; and Michele Vechionne and Gian Vittorio Caprara, "Personality Determinants of Political Participation: The Contribution of Traits and Self-Efficacy Beliefs," *Personality and Individual Differences* 46 (2009): 487–92.

15. Seymour Martin Lipset, *The First New Nation: The United States in Historical and Comparative Perspective* (New York: Basic Books, 1963).

16. Marc Kaufman, "Jefferson Changed 'Subjects' to 'Citizens' in Declaration of Independence," *Washington Post*, July 3, 2010.

17. Abigail Adams, letter to John Adams, March 31, 1776, Massachusetts Historical Society, Adams Family Papers, http://www.masshist.org/digitaladams/aea/cfm/doc.cfm?id=L17760331aa.

18. For more on those old fears and irascible beliefs, see David Harry Bennett, *The Party of Fear: The American Far Right from Nativism to the Militia Movement* (Chapel Hill: University of North Carolina Press, 1988); and Tyler Anbinder, *Nativism and Slavery: The Northern Know Nothings and the Politics of the 1850s* (Oxford: Oxford University Press, 1992). For local expression of the same fears, see John David Bladek, "'Virginia Is Middle Ground': The Know Nothing Party and the Virginia Gubernatorial Election of 1855," *Virginia Magazine of History and Biography* 106 (1998): 35–70; Dale Baum, "Know-Nothingism and the Republican Majority in Massachusetts: The Political Realignment of the 1850s," *Journal of American History* 64 (1977–78): 959–86; and William E. Gienapp, "Salmon P. Chase, Nativism, and the Formation of the Republican Party in Ohio," *Ohio History* 93 (1984): 5–39.

19. Of the signers of the Declaration of Independence, four Pennsylvania Representatives were born in the British Isles—Robert Morris in England, James Smith and George Taylor in Ireland, and James Wilson in Scotland. Matthew Thornton, Representative from New Hampshire, was born in Ireland. Francis Lewis, representing New York, was born in Wales. Button Gwinnett, representing Georgia, was born in England. And John Witherspoon, representing New Jersey, was born in Scotland. Of the signers of the Constitution, three Pennsylvania Representatives were born abroad—Robert Morris and James Wilson—already cited above; along with Thomas Fitzsimmons, who was born in Ireland. Alexander Hamilton, the Representative from New York, was born in the British West Indies. Pierce Butler, Representative of South Carolina, was born in Ireland. James McHenry, of Maryland, was born in Ireland as well, as was William Patterson, the Representative from New Jersey. U.S. National Archives and Records Administration (NARA), "Signers of the Declaration of Independence," http://www.archives.gov/exhibits/charters/declaration_signers_gallery_facts.pdf.

20. Scott Shane and Charlie Savage, "In Ordinary Lives, U.S. Sees the Work of Russian Agents," *New York Times*, June 29, 2010, A1.

21. Migration Policy Institute, "Middle-Class Immigrant Households in the United States," April 2009, http://www.migrationinformation.org/USFocus/display.cfm?id=725.

22. Vivek Wadhwa, AnnaLee Saxenian, Ben Rissing, and Gary Gereffi, "America's New Immigrant Entrepreneurs" (report by the Duke School of Engineering and the UC–Berkeley School of Information, January 4, 2007), http://people.ischool.berkeley.edu/~anno/Papers/Americas_new_immigrant_entrepreneurs_I.pdf.

23. This is not a recent phenomenon. There have been ethnic commercial communities in America since its early days. For more on the phenomenon, see Olson and Beal, *The Ethnic Dimension in American History*.

24. Migration Policy Institute, "Middle-Class Immigrant Households in the United States." Of the 74.2 million U.S. residents who were middle class in 2007, 14.7 million (19.9 percent) resided in immigrant households.

25. Ibid.

26. See chap. 4 of Alan Wolfe's *One Nation After All: What Americans Really Think About God, Country, Family, Racism, Welfare, Immigration, Homosexuality, Work, The Right, The Left and Each Other* (New York: Penguin Books, 1998).

27. Margolis, *Little Brazil*, 197.

28. Ibid., 199.

29. For more on Dvořák's life, see Kurt Honolka, *Dvořák: Life and Times*, trans. Anne Wyburd (London: Haus Publishing, 2004); for more on the spirit of his American compositions, see Michael B. Beckerman, *New Worlds of Dvořák: Searching in America for the Composer's Inner Life* (New York: W. W. Norton, 2003).

30. Roger Lee Hall, "The True Story of 'Goin' Home': From Bohemia to Boston," n.d., http://www.americanmusicpreservation.com/GoinHome.htm.

31. For more details on the history of the National Conservatory of Music, see Emanuel Rubin, "Jeannette Meyers Thurber and the National Conservatory of Music," *American Music* 8 (1990): 294–325.

Chapter 6. Almost Home

1. A pseudonym is used to protect Mark's privacy.

2. Expat Interviews, accessed December 5, 2011, http://www.expat interviews.com/japan/suzanne-kamata.html.

3. Expat Interviews, accessed December 5, 2011, http://www.expat interviews.com/Casey-Halloran.html.

4. John R. Wennersten, *Leaving America: The New Expatriate Generation* (Westport, CT: Greenwood Publishing, 2008), 26; Sheila L. Croucher, *The Other Side of the Fence: American Migrants in Mexico* (Austin: University of Texas Press, 2009), 48.

5. "Snapshot: Global Migration," *New York Times*, June 22, 2007.

6. Jason DeParle, "Global Migration: A World Ever More on the Move," *New York Times*, June 27, 2010, WK1.

7. See DeParle, "Global Migration," WK1; and Euro-Islam, "Islam in Netherlands," 2007, http://www.euro-islam.info/country-profiles/the-netherlands/.

8. Pico Iyer, "Nowhere Man: Confessions of a Perpetual Foreigner," *Utne Reader*, May–June 1997, 78.

9. Scott Jaschik, "Mixed Outlook on Foreign Students," *Inside Higher Ed*, November 16, 2009.

10. Juan Carlos Moreno-Brid and Pablo Ruiz-Nápoles, "Public Research Universities in Latin American and their Relation to Economic Development" (Working Papers on Latin America, no. 07/08-1, David Rockefeller Center for Latin American Studies, Harvard University, Cambridge, MA, 2008), 8, 10.

11. International Student Mobility by Region—Latin America 2008/2009, table in *Open Doors 2009: Report on International Educational Exchange* (New York: Institute of International Education, 2009).

12. Ibid.

13. European Commission, "The ERASMUS Programme—Studying in Europe and More," last updated June 8, 2010, http://ec.europa.eu/education/lifelong-learning-programme/doc80_en.htm.

14. Deborah Kondek, "Herbert Demel," in *Reference for Business: Encyclopedia of Business*, 2nd ed. (online publication, 2005), http://www.referenceforbusiness.com/biography/A-E/Demel-Hebert-1953.html.

15. Chang-Ran Kim, "Update 2—Nissan CEO Pay Was $9.5 million, Below Overseas Peers," *Reuters*, June 23, 2010.

16. Ben Hall, "Immigration in the European Union: Problem or Solution?" *OECD Observer*, Summer 2000, http://www.oecdobserver.org/news/fullstory.php/aid/337/.

17. For instance, the adoption of the EU Blue Card by the European Commission made it easy for skilled third-country workers to live and work in any of the participating EU member states. EU Blue Card Network, accessed December 5, 2011, http://www.apply.eu/.

18. Rainer Münz, "East-West Migration after European Union Enlargement," *Austrian Information*, February 15, 2007.

19. Hiawatha Bray, "The White Collar Migration," *Boston Globe*, November 5, 2003.

20. Philippine Overseas Employment Administration, "Overseas Employment Statistics 2010," http://www.poea.gov.ph/stats/2010_Stats.pdf.

21. Margolis, *An Invisible Minority*, 129.

22. DeParle, "Global Migration," WK1.

23. Maxine L. Margolis, "Transnationalism and Popular Culture: The Case of Brazilian Immigrants in the United States," *Journal of Popular Culture* 29 (1995): 30.

24. DeParle, "Global Migration," WK1.

25. Ibid.

26. See Nguyen Y. Duc, "Vietnamese American: The Best Outcome of Vietnam War" (lecture, Fifth Triennial Vietnam Symposium at the Viet Nam Center, Texas Tech University, March 17–20, 2005), http://www.vietamerican vets.com/Page-Diaspora-BestOutcomeofVNWar.htm. Another example of Vietnamese American business investments in Vietnam is the Vietnam Resource Group, http://www.vietgroup.net/.

27. Frank Kaiser, "A Rich Retirement in Costa Rica," *Tampa Bay Times,* September 27, 2005.

28. Chris Hawley, "Seniors Head South to Mexican Nursing Homes," *USA Today,* August 16, 2007.

29. Michelle Conlin, "Retirement: Why Panama Is the New Florida," *Bloomberg/Business Week,* Special Report, July 2, 2009.

30. See, for instance, Hiroko Tabuchi, "Japan Pays Foreign Workers to Go Home," *New York Times,* April 23, 2009, B1, describing how the Japanese government is trying to get foreign workers to leave the country permanently; or, on the tough measures the Spanish government is taking toward Latin American immigrants, see Cheryl Gallagher, "Spain Closes the Door," *New Statesman,* May 7, 2009.

31. John Corbett, "Ernest George Ravenstein: The Laws of Migration, 1885" (webpage hosted by Center for Spatially Integrated Social Science, University of California, Santa Barbara, n.d.), http://www.csiss.org/classics/content/90.

32. E. G. Ravenstein, "The Laws of Migration," *Journal of the Royal Statistical Society* 48, pt. 2 (1885): 167–235; see also E. G. Ravenstein, "The Laws of Migration," *Journal of the Royal Statistical Society* 52, no. 2 (1889): 241–305.

33. Everett S. Lee, "A Theory of Migration," *Demography* 3, no. 1 (1966): 47–57. Among push factors are not enough jobs in the country of origin, few economic prospects, "primitive" conditions, desertification, famine or drought, political persecution, poor health care, loss of wealth, natural disasters, death threats, religious persecution, pollution, poor housing, tenant issues, bullying, discrimination, and poor chances of marrying. Among pull factors are job opportunities in the host country, better living conditions, political or religious freedom, education, better health care, attractive climates, security, family links, industry, and better chances of marrying.

34. I am deeply indebted in my discussion of the structural forces of migration to Peter Kivisto and Thomas Faist's book *Beyond a Border: The Causes and Consequences of Contemporary Immigration* (Los Angeles: Pine Forge Press, 2010).

35. There are a number of neoclassical economists who have researched the imbalance between labor supply and wages and its role in migration. A short list includes George J. Borjas, "Economic Theory and International Migration," *International Migration Review* 23 (1989): 457–85 (he also has a more recent edited work, *Issues in the Economics of Immigration* [Chicago: University of Chicago Press, 2000]); and Douglas S. Massey, Joaquin Arango, Graeme Hugo, Ali Kouaouci, Adela Pellegrino, and J. Edward Taylor, "Theories of International Migration: A Review and Appraisal," *Population and Development Review* 19 (1993): 431–66. For a research that is closer to home, see Daniel Chiquiar and Gordon Hanson, "International Migration, Self-Selection, and the Distribution of Wages: Evidence from Mexico and the US," *Journal of Political Economy* 113 (2005): 239–81.

36. Margolis, *Invisible Minority*, 25.

37. One of the surprising pieces of census data on Brazilians in the United States is the level of educational attainment of my expats. In 2007 Brazilians in the United States had slightly higher college and postbaccalaureate graduation rates than white Americans. Nearly 32 percent of all Brazilians aged twenty-five and over had at least a college degree (30 percent for males, 33 percent for females). For more on the matter, see Laird W. Bergad, "Brazilians in the United States 1980–2007" (Latino Data Project, Report 33, Center for Latin American, Caribbean, and Latino Studies, City University of New York, March 2010), 9, http://web.gc.cuny.edu/lastudies/latinodataprojectreports/Brazilians%20 in%20the%20U.S.%201980%20-%202007.pdf.

38. Margolis, *Invisible Minority*, 43.

39. Franklin Goza, "Brazilian Immigration to North America," *International Migration Review* 28 (1994): 145–46.

40. Ibid., 146–49.

41. One of the dominant figures in network theory these days is the Harvard economist Odek Stark. See, for instance, his early paper with David E. Bloom, "The New Economics of Labor Migration," *American Economic Review* 75, no. 2 (May 1985): 173–78; or his more recent book *The Migration of Labor* (Cambridge: Basil Blackwell, 1991). Other resources include Monica Boyd, "Family and Personal Networks in International Migration: Recent Developments and New Agendas," *International Migration Review* 23 (1989): 638–70; Douglas T. Gurak and Fe Caces, "Migration Networks and the Shaping of Migration Systems," in *International Migration Systems*, ed. Mary Kritz, Lin Lean Lim, and Hania Zlotnik (Oxford: Clarendon Press, 1992), 150–76; and Alejandro Portes and Julia Sennsenbrenner, "Embeddedness and Immigration: Notes on Social Determinants of Economic Action," *American Journal of Sociology* 98 (1993): 1320–50.

42. Larry Rother, "Brazilians Streaming into U.S. Through Mexican Border," *New York Times*. See also Sueli Siqueira, "Projeto de Retorno e Investimento dos Imigrantes Valadarenses nos EUA" (paper presented at the National Congress on Brazilian Immigration to the United States, David Rockefeller Center for Latin American Studies, Harvard University, Cambridge, MA, March 18–19, 2005).

43. Margolis, *Little Brazil*, 103.

44. According to the U.S. Census, Florida and Massachusetts now hold the largest contingent of Brazilians in the United States (40 percent combined), while California and New York together are home to 17 percent of the Brazilian population. New Jersey houses another 10 percent of Brazilians as well. When I got here in 1981, California and New York were the preferred destinations. In thirty years I have lived in Kentucky, Tennessee, and Virginia instead. These places could not have been farther from Brazilian population centers in the United States. Bergad, "Brazilians in the United States 1980–2007," 7.

45. The MIT economist Michael J. Piore was the pioneer of segmented labor markets theory. His book *Birds of Passage: Migrant Labor in Industrial Societies* (Cambridge: Cambridge University Press, 1979) laid the groundwork for subsequent research in the area. Alejandro Portes and Leif Jensen presented their research on Cubans in the article "The Enclave and Entrants: Patterns of Ethnic Enterprise in Miami Before and After Mariel," *American Sociological Review* 54 (1989): 929-49; Min Zhou and John Logan studied the New York Chinese in "Return on Human Capital in Ethnic Enclaves: New York City's Chinatown," *American Sociological Review* 54 (1989): 809-20.

46. Margolis, *Little Brazil*, 77.

47. Bergad, "Brazilians in the United States 1980-2007," 10-14.

48. For more on the rosy scenarios described by early immigrants, see Roger Daniels, *Coming to America: A History of Immigration and Ethnicity in American Life* (New York: Harper Collins, 2002).

49. Siqueira, "Projeto de Retorno e Investimento dos Imigrantes Valadarenses nos EUA," 19.

50. Aristotle, *The Nichomachean Ethics* (Ithaca, NY: Cornell University Library, 2009).

51. "Having Fun the Thai Way: Nighttime Entertainment Options," *Udon Thani Magazine* 13, no. 3 (2010).

52. Nicholas Christakis and James Fowler, authors of *Connected: The Surprising Power of Our Social Networks and How They Shape Our Lives* (New York: Little, Brown and Company, 2009), surveyed more than 3,000 randomly chosen Americans and found they had an average of four "close social contacts" with whom they could discuss important matters or spend free time. But only half of these contacts were solely friends; the rest were a variety of others, including spouses and children.

53. See K. Roger Van Horn and Juracy Cunegatto Marques, "Interpersonal Relationships in Brazilian Adolescents," *International Journal of Behavioral Development* 24 (2000): 199-203.

54. For more on Brazilian emotional connections, see José Honório Rodrigues, *The Brazilians: Their Character and Aspirations* (Austin: University of Texas Press, 1967); or Phyllis A. Harrison, *Behaving Brazilian: A Comparison of Brazilian and North American Social Behavior* (Rowley, MA: Newbury House Publishers, 1983).

55. C. Wright Mills, *White Collar: The American Middle Class* (New York: Oxford University Press, 1959), xvi.

56. Erich Fromm, *To Have or To Be* (New York: Harper and Row, 1976).

57. Christopher Lasch, *The Culture of Narcissism: American Life in an Age of Diminishing Expectations* (New York: W. W. Norton, 1978).

58. Peggy Orenstein, "I Tweet, Therefore I Am," *New York Times*, August 1, 2010, MM11.

59. For more on American superficial friendships, see Daniel Akst, "America: Land of Loners?" *Wilson Quarterly*, Summer 2010, 23–27.

60. Tamotsu Shibutani and Kian Kwan, *Ethnic Stratification* (New York: Macmillan, 1965).

61. Martes, *New Immigrants, New Land*, 23.

62. W. E. B. Du Bois, "Strivings of the Negro People," *Atlantic Monthly*, August 1897.

63. Recife currently has 4,136,506 inhabitants (the city proper has 1,536,934). It's the fifth-largest metropolitan area of Brazil. Crossed by two rivers and many bridges (by one account 50), the metro area alone spreads over 1,068 square miles. Recife city hall, http://www2.recife.pe.gov.br/a-cidade/atlas-metropolitano/, and the Brazilian Census, http://www.censo2010.ibge.gov.br/sinopse/index.php?uf=26&dados=0, both accessed August 25, 2012.

64. Margolis, *Invisible Minority*, 106–7. Margolis argues that at first Brazilian immigrants are torn between their material and emotional needs: "Brazilians, in essence, become transnational migrants, people who sustain familial, cultural, and economic ties that ignore international borders and span the home and the host societies."

Bibliography

Acock, Alan C., Harold D. Clarke, and Marianne C. Stewart. "A New Model for Old Measures: A Covariance Structural Analysis of Political Efficacy." *Journal of Politics* 47 (1985): 1062–84.

"The Act of Supremacy, 1559." In *English History in the Making*, vol. 1, edited by William L. Sachse, 198–99. New York: John Wiley and Sons, 1967.

Akst, Daniel. "America: Land of Loners?" *Wilson Quarterly* 34 (Summer 2010): 23–27.

Alexander, Robert J. *Juscelino Kubitschek and the Development of Brazil.* Athens: Ohio University Press, 1992.

Almeida Filho, Naomar de. "The Psychosocial Costs of Development: Labor, Migration and Stress in Bahia, Brazil." *Latin American Research Review* 17 (1982): 91–118.

American Immigration Lawyers Association. "AILA Backgrounder: Myths and Facts in the Immigration Debate." August 3, 2003. http://www.visalaw.com/03aug3/ailabackgrounder.pdf.

Anbinder, Tyler. *Nativism and Slavery: The Northern Know Nothings and the Politics of the 1850s.* Oxford: Oxford University Press, 1992.

Anderson, Stuart. "Family Immigration: The Long Wait to Immigrate." NFAP Policy Brief, National Foundation of American Policy, Arlington, VA, May 2010. http://www.nfap.com/pdf/0505brief-family-immigration.pdf.

Archdiocese of São Paulo. *Torture in Brazil: A Shocking Report on the Pervasive Use of Torture by Brazilian Military Governments, 1964–1974, Secretly Prepared by the Archdiocese of São Paulo.* Austin: University of Texas Press, 1998.

Aristotle. *The Nichomachean Ethics.* Ithaca, NY: Cornell University Library, 2009.

Bacchus, Wilfred A. *Mission in Mufti: Brazil's Military Regimes, 1964–1985.* Westport, CT: Greenwood Press, 1990.

Bagby, William B. *Brazil and the Brazilians.* Baltimore: Maryland Baptist Missions Room, 1889.

Barman, Roderick J. *Brazil: The Forging of a Nation, 1798–1852*. Stanford, CA: Stanford University Press, 1988.

Barnes, Taylor. "No Place Like Home: Brazilian Immigrants Leave US for Better Job Prospects." *Christian Science Monitor*, September 24, 2009.

Barrionuevo, Alexei. "Chilean President Rides High as Term Ends." *New York Times*, October 28, 2009, A6.

Basler, Roy, ed. *The Collected Works of Abraham Lincoln*. Springfield, IL: Abraham Lincoln Association, 1953.

Baum, Dale. "Know-Nothingism and the Republican Majority in Massachusetts: The Political Realignment of the 1850s." *Journal of American History* 64 (1977–78): 959–86.

Bear, James E. *Mission to Brazil*. Nashville: Board of World Mission, Presbyterian Church U.S., 1961.

Beckerman, Michael B. *New Worlds of Dvořák: Searching in America for the Composer's Inner Life*. New York: W. W. Norton, 2003.

Bell-Villada, Gene H. *Conversations with Gabriel García Márquez*. Jackson: University of Mississippi Press, 2005.

Bellamy, Francis. "The Story of the Pledge of Allegiance to the Flag." *University of Rochester Library Bulletin* 8, no. 2 (1953).

Bello, José M. *A History of Modern Brazil*. Stanford, CA: Stanford University Press, 1966.

Bennett, David Harry. *The Party of Fear: The American Far Right from Nativism to the Militia Movement*. Chapel Hill: University of North Carolina Press, 1988.

Bergad, Laird W. "Brazilians in the United States 1980–2007." Latino Data Project, Report 33, Center for Latin American, Caribbean, and Latino Studies, City University of New York, March 2010. http://web.gc.cuny.edu/lastudies/latinodataprojectreports/Brazilians%20in%20the%20U.S.%201980%20-%202007.pdf.

Bernstein, Nina, and Elizabeth Dwoskin. "Brazilians Giving up Their American Dream." *New York Times*, December 4, 2007.

Beserra, Bernadete. *Brazilian Immigrants in the United States: Cultural Imperialism and Social Class*. New York: LFB Scholarly Publishing, 2003.

Bladek, John David. "'Virginia Is Middle Ground': The Know Nothing Party and the Virginia Gubernatorial Election of 1855." *Virginia Magazine of History and Biography* 106 (1998): 35–70.

Borjas, George J. "Economic Theory and International Migration." *International Migration Review* 23 (1989): 457–85.

———. *Issues in the Economics of Immigration*. Chicago: University of Chicago Press, 2000.

Bourne, Richard. *Getulio Vargas of Brazil, 1883–1954: Sphinx of the Pampas*. London: C. Knight, 1974.

Boianovsky, Mauro. "A View from the Tropics: Celso Furtado and the Theory of Economic Development in the 1950s." *History of Political Economy* 42 (2010): 221–66.

Boyd, Monica. "Family and Personal Networks in International Migration: Recent Developments and New Agendas." *International Migration Review* 23 (1989): 638–70.

Bray, Hiawatha. "The White Collar Migration: As Economy Gains, Outsourcing Surges." *Boston Globe*, November 5, 2003.

Brooke, James. "In Brazil Wild Ways to Counter Wild Inflation." *New York Times*, July 25, 1993.

Brooks, David. "The Organization Kid." *Atlantic*, April 2001.

Bustos, Sergio. "Backlog Keeps Immigrants Waiting Years for Green Cards." *USA Today*, January 26, 2005.

Caldeira, Jorge. *A Nação Mercantilista: Ensaio Sobre o Brasil*. São Paulo: Editora 34, 1999.

Cardoso, Fernando Henrique. *The Accidental President of Brazil: A Memoir*. New York: Public Affairs, 2007.

Cavalcanti, H. B. "Political Cooperation and Religious Repression: Presbyterians under Military Rule in Brazil (1964–1974)." *Review of Religious Research* 34 (1992): 97–116.

———. "Unrealistic Expectations: Contesting the Usefulness of Weber's Protestant Ethic for the Study of Latin American Protestantism." *Journal of Church and State* 37 (1995): 289–308.

Chang, Jack, and Lisa Yulkowski. "Vocal Minority Praises Pinochet at His Funeral." *Bradenton Herald*, December 13, 2006.

Charon, Joel M. *Ten Questions: A Sociological Perspective*. 6th ed. Belmont, CA: Wadsworth, 2007.

Chiquiar, Daniel, and Gordon Hanson. "International Migration, Self-Selection, and the Distribution of Wages: Evidence from Mexico and the US." *Journal of Political Economy* 113 (2005): 239–81.

Clarke, Harold D., and Alan C. Acock. "National Elections and Political Attitudes: The Case of Political Efficacy." *British Journal of Political Science* 19 (1989): 551–62.

Conlin, Michelle. "Retirement: Why Panama Is the New Florida." *Bloomberg/Business Week*, Special Report, July 2, 2009.

The Constitution of the Vermont Republic. 1777. http://vermont-archives.org/govhistory/constitut/con77.htm.

Corbett, John. "Ernest George Ravenstein: The Laws of Migration, 1885." Webpage hosted by Center for Spatially Integrated Social Science, University of California, Santa Barbara, n.d. http://www.csiss.org/classics/content/90.

Costin, W. C., and J. Steven Watson. *The Law and Working of the Constitution: Documents 1660–1914*. Vol. 1. London: A&C Black, 1952.

Cox, Vicki. *Oscar Arias Sanchez: Bringing Peace to Central America*. New York: Chelsea House Publications, 2007.

Christakis, Nicholas, and James Fowler. *Connected: The Surprising Power of Our Social Networks and How They Shape Our Lives*. New York: Little, Brown and Company, 2009.

Croucher, Sheila L. *The Other Side of the Fence: American Migrants in Mexico.* Austin: University of Texas Press, 2009.

Cunha, Diogo. *Estado de Exceção, A Igreja Católica e a Repressão: O Assassinato do Padre Antônio Henrique Pereira da Silva Neto.* Recife: Universidade Federal de Pernambuco, 2007.

Daniels, Roger. *Coming to America: A History of Immigration and Ethnicity in American Life.* 2nd ed. New York: HarperCollins, 2002.

Dawsey, Cyrus B., and James M. Dawsey. *The Confederados: Old South Immigrants in Brazil.* Tuscaloosa: University of Alabama Press, 1998.

"De Deodoro a Dilma." *Estado de São Paulo,* January 3, 2011. http://www.estadao .com.br/especiais/de-deodoro-a-dilma,128452.htm.

DeParle, Jason. "Global Migration: A World Ever More on the Move." *New York Times,* June 27, 2010, WK1.

de Soto, Hernando. *The Mystery of Capital: Why Capitalism Triumphs in the West and Fails Everywhere Else.* New York, Basic Books, 2000.

Doyle, Charles. *The Posse Comitatus Act and Related Matters: The Use of the Military to Execute Civilian Law.* Washington, DC: Congressional Research Service, 2000.

Du Bois, W. E. B. "Strivings of the Negro People." *Atlantic Monthly,* August 1897.

Duc, Nguyen Y. "Vietnamese American: The Best Outcome of Vietnam War." Lecture at Fifth Triennial Vietnam Symposium at the Viet Nam Center, Texas Tech University, Lubbock, TX, March 17–20, 2005. http://www .vietamericanvets.com/Page-Diaspora-BestOutcomeofVNWar.htm.

Dunn, Ballard S. *Brazil, The Home for Southerners.* New Orleans: Bloomfield and Steel, 1866.

Dyson, Lowell K. "The Southern Tenant Farmers Union and Depression Politics." *Political Science Quarterly* 88 (1973): 230–52.

Edmundson, Mark. "Dwelling in Possibilities." *Chronicle of Higher Education,* March 14, 2008, B7.

Escobar Chavarría, Paula. "In Chile, Departing President Michelle Bachelet Proved Women Can Lead." *Washington Post,* March 14, 2010.

Fairlie, Robert W. "Estimating the Contribution of Immigrant Business Owners to the U.S. Economy." Small Business Research Summary no. 334, SBA Office of Advocacy, November 2008. http://www.sba.gov/advo/research/ rs334tot.pdf.

Feinstein, Adam. *Pablo Neruda: A Passion for Life.* New York: Bloomsbury, 2005.

Fernández-Kelly, Patricia. "The Back Pocket Map: Social Class and Cultural Capital as Transferable Assets in the Advancement of Second Generation Immigrants." *Annals of the American Academy of Political and Social Science* 620 (November 2008): 116–37.

Ferris, Timothy. *The Science of Liberty: Democracy, Reason, and the Laws of Nature.* New York: Harper, 2010.

Finkel, Steven E. "The Effects of Participation on Political Efficacy and Political Support: Evidence from a West German Panel." *Journal of Politics* 49 (1987): 441–64.

———. "Reciprocal Effects of Participation and Political Efficacy: A Panel Analysis." *American Journal of Political Science* 29 (1985): 891–913.

Foote, Kenneth E., Wei Li, Janice Monk, and Rebecca Theobald. "Foreign-born Scholars in American Universities: Issues, Concerns and Strategies." *Symposium: Journal of Geography in Higher Education* 32 (2008): 167–78.

"For Many in the US, the Green Card Wait Is Long." WorkPermit.Com, July 25, 2005. http://www.workpermit.com/news/2005_07_25/us/green_card_wait.htm.

Forman, Shepard. "Disunity and Discontent: A Study of Peasant Political Movements in Brazil." *Journal of Latin American Studies* 3 (1971): 3–24.

Fortuny, Karina, Randy Capps, Margaret Simms, and Ajay Chaudry. "Children of Immigrants: National and State Characteristics." Brief 9, The Urban Institute, Washington, DC, August 2009. http://www.urban.org/uploadedpdf/411939_childrenofimmigrants.pdf.

Frase, Ronald G. "The Subversion of Missionary Intentions by Cultural Values: The Brazilian Case." *Review of Religious Research* 23 (1981): 180–194.

Freire, Paulo. *Pedagogy of the Oppressed*. New York: Seabury Press, 1970.

Freyre, Gilberto. *The Masters and the Slaves*. New York: Random House, 1964.

Fromm, Erich. *To Have or To Be*. New York: Harper and Row, 1976.

Fuentes, Carlos. *Buried Mirror: Reflections on Spain and the New World*. New York: Houghton Mifflin Company, 1999.

Fuligni, Andrew J., Gwendelyn J. Rivera, and April Leininger. "Family Identity and the Educational Persistence of Students with Latin American and Asian Backgrounds." In *Contesting Stereotypes and Creating Identities: Social Categories, Social Identities, and Educational Participation*, edited by Andrew J. Fuligni, 239–65. New York: Russell Sage Foundation, 2007.

Gallagher, Cheryl. "Spain Closes the Door." *New Statesman*, May 7, 2009.

Gammon, Samuel R. *The Evangelical Invasion of Brazil*. Richmond, VA: Presbyterian Committee of Publication, 1910.

Garcia, Adriana. "Immigrants Hit Hard by Slowdown, Subprime Crisis." *Reuters*, January 30, 2008.

García Márquez, Gabriel. *Living to Tell the Tale*. New York: Alfred A. Knopf, 2003.

Garcia-Preto, Nydia. "Latino Families: An Overview." In *Ethnicity and Family Therapy*, edited by Monica McGoldrick, Joseph Giordano, and Nydia Garcia-Preto, 153–65. New York: Guilford Press, 2005.

Gibran, Kahlil. *The Prophet*. New York: Alfred A. Knopf, 1923.

Gienapp, William E. "Salmon P. Chase, Nativism, and the Formation of the Republican Party in Ohio." *Ohio History* 93 (1984): 5–39.

Goertzel, Ted G. *Fernando Henrique Cardoso: Reinventing Democracy in Brazil*. Boulder, CO: Lynne Rienner, 1999.

Gomes, Laurentino. *1808: Como Uma Rainha Louca, Um Príncipe Medroso e Uma Côrte Corrupta Enganaram Napoleão e Mudaram a História de Portugal e do Brasil.* São Paulo: Editora Planeta Brasil, 2007.

Goyette, Jared. "Back to Brazil." *Charleston City Paper,* February 20, 2008.

Goza, Franklin. "Brazilian Immigration to North America." *International Migration Review* 28 (1994): 136–52.

Greenberg, Stanley B. *Dispatches from the War Room: In the Trenches with Five Extraordinary Leaders.* New York: Thomas Dunne Books, 2009.

Greenfield, Gerald Michael. "The Great Drought and Elite Discourse in Imperial Brazil." *Hispanic American Historical Review* 72 (1992): 375–400.

Greenfield, Sidney M. "The Patrimonial State and Patron-Client Relations in Iberia and Latin America: Sources of 'The System' in the Fifteenth-Century Writings of the Infante D. Pedro of Portugal." *Ethnohistory* 24 (1977): 163–78.

Grubbs, Donald H. *Cry from the Cotton: The Southern Tenant Farmers' Union and the New Deal.* Chapel Hill: University of North Carolina Press, 1971.

Guest, Iain. *Behind the Disappearances: Argentina Dirty War against Human Rights and the United Nations.* Philadelphia: University of Pennsylvania Press, 1990.

Gurak, Douglas T., and Fe Caces. "Migration Networks and the Shaping of Migration Systems." In *International Migration Systems: A Global Approach,* edited by Mary Kritz, Lin Lean Lim, and Hania Zlotnik, Hania, 150–76. Oxford: Clarendon Press, 1992.

Hall, Ben. "Immigration in the European Union: Problem or Solution?" *OECD Observer,* Summer 2000. http://www.oecdobserver.org/news/fullstory. php/aid/337/.

Hall, Roger Lee. "The True Story of 'Goin' Home': From Bohemia to Boston." n.d. http://www.americanmusicpreservation.com/GoinHome.htm.

Harrison, Phyllis A. *Behaving Brazilian: A Comparison of Brazilian and North American Social Behavior.* Rowley, MA: Newbury House Publishers, 1983.

Harter, Eugene C. *The Lost Colony of the Confederacy.* Jackson: University Press of Mississippi, 1985.

"Having Fun the Thai Way: Nighttime Entertainment Options." *Udon Thani Magazine* 13, no. 3 (2010). http://www.udonmap.com/udonthaniforum/ viewtopic.php?p=219731.

Hawkins, Darren. "Democratization Theory and Nontransitions: Insights from Cuba." *Comparative Politics* 33 (2001): 441–61.

Hawley, Chris. "Seniors Head South to Mexican Nursing Homes." *USA Today,* August 16, 2007.

"The High Cost of Immigration." Editorial. *New York Times,* June 22, 2010, A26.

"Hispanics: A People in Motion." Pew Hispanic Center, Washington, DC, January 2005. http://pewhispanic.org/files/reports/40.pdf.

Honolka, Kurt. *Dvořák: Life and Times.* Translated by Anne Wyburd. London: Haus Publishing, 2004.

Horton, Myles. *The Long Haul: An Autobiography.* New York: Doubleday, 1990.

Howe, Neil, and William Strauss. *Millennials Go to College: Strategies fo[...] Generation on Campus.* Washington, DC: American Association of Coll[...] Registrars and Admissions Offices, 2003.

———. *Millennials Rising: The Next Great Generation.* New York: Vintage Books[...] 2005.

Iyer, Pico. "Nowhere Man: Confessions of a Perpetual Foreigner." *Utne Reader,* May–June 1997, 78–79.

Jaschik, Scott. "Mixed Outlook on Foreign Students." *Inside Higher Ed,* November 16, 2009.

Kaiser, Frank. "A Rich Retirement in Costa Rica." *Tampa Bay Times,* September 27, 2005.

Kalita, S. Mitra. "For Green Card Applicants, Waiting Is the Hardest Part." *Washington Post,* July 23, 2005.

Kao, Grace, and Marta Tienda. "Educational Aspirations of Minority Youth." *American Journal of Education* 106 (1998): 349–84.

Karp, Jeffrey A., and Susan A. Banducci. "Political Efficacy and Participation in Twenty-Seven Democracies: How Electoral Systems Shape Political Behaviour." *British Journal of Political Science* 38 (2008): 311–34.

Kaufman, Marc. "Jefferson Changed 'Subjects' to 'Citizens' in Declaration of Independence." *Washington Post,* Saturday, July 3, 2010.

Kay, Cristóbal. "Celso Furtado: Pioneer of Structuralist Development Theory." *Development and Change* 36 (2005): 1201–7.

Kenny, Mary Lorena. "Drought, Clientalism, Fatalism and Fear in Northeast Brazil." *Ethics, Place and Environment* 5 (2002): 123–34.

Kidder, Daniel P., and James C. Fletcher. *Brazil and the Brazilians: Portrayed in Historical and Descriptive Sketches.* Philadelphia: Childs and Peterson, 1857.

Kim, Chang-Ran. "Update 2—Nissan CEO Pay Was $9.5 million, Below Overseas Peers." *Reuters,* June 23, 2010.

Kivisto, Peter, and Thomas Faist. *Beyond a Border: The Causes and Consequences of Contemporary Immigration.* Los Angeles: Pine Forge Press, 2010.

Kondek, Deborah. "Herbert Demel." In *Reference for Business: Encyclopedia of Business,* 2nd ed., 2005 http://www.referenceforbusiness.com/biography/A-E/Demel-Hebert-1953.html.

Korin, Eliana Catão de, and Sueli S. de Carvalho Petry. "Brazilian Families." In *Ethnicity and Family Therapy,* edited by Monica McGoldrick, Joseph Giordano, and Nydia Garcia-Preto, 166–77. New York: Guilford Press, 2005.

Kornbluh, Peter. "Brazil Marks 40th Anniversary of Military Coup: Declassified Documents Shed Light on U.S. Role" *National Security Archive,* March 31, 2004. http://www.gwu.edu/~nsarchiv/NSAEBB/NSAEBB118/index.htm#docs.

Kottak, Conrad Phillip. *Prime Time Society: An Anthropological Analysis of Television and Culture.* Belmont, CA: Wadsworth, 1990.

Krass, Peter. *Carnegie.* Hoboken, NJ: John Wiley and Sons, 2002.

vian Democracy under Economic Stress: An Account
, 1963–1968. Princeton, NJ: Princeton University

Narcissism: American Life in an Age of Diminishing
. Norton, 1978.

…dent Leads Lehigh U.'s Globalization Project."
…er *Education*, June 18, 2010, A4.

—, Everett S. "A Theory of Migration." *Demography* 3, no. 1 (1966): 47–57.

Levine, Robert M. *Father of the Poor? Vargas and His Era.* Cambridge: Cambridge University Press, 1998.

Lewis, Paul H. *Guerrillas and Generals: The "Dirty War" in Argentina.* Westport, CT: Greenwood, 2002.

Lipset, Seymour Martin. *The First New Nation: The United States in Historical and Comparative Perspective.* New York: Basic Books, 1963.

"Livro do Governo Culpa Ditadura por Tortura e Mortes." *Folha de São Paulo,* August 25, 2007. http://www1.folha.uol.com.br/folha/brasil/ult96u323017 .shtml.

Loewenstein, Karl. *Brazil under Vargas.* New York: Russell and Russell, 1973.

Mamiseishvili, Ketevan, and Jill M. Hermsen. "Employment Patterns and Job Satisfaction of Foreign-Born Science and Engineering Doctorate Recipients in the United States." *Academic Leadership Live* 7, no. 1 (2009).

Marchak, Patricia. *God's Assassins: State Terrorism in Argentina in the 1970s.* Toronto: McGill-Queen's University Press, 1999.

Margolis, Maxine L. "Brazilians and the 1990 United States Census: Immigrants, Ethnicity, and the Undercount." *Human Organization* 54 (1995): 52–59.

———. *An Invisible Minority: Brazilians in New York City.* Gainesville: University Press of Florida, 2009. ← Maxine L Margolis

———. *Little Brazil: An Ethnography of Brazilian Immigrants in New York City.* Princeton, NJ: University of Princeton Press, 1994. Maxine L Margolis

———. "Transnationalism and Popular Culture: The Case of Brazilian Immigrants in the United States." *Journal of Popular Culture* 29 (1995): 29–41.

———. "With New Eyes: Returned International Immigrants in Rio de Janeiro." In *Raízes e Rumos: Perspectivas Interdisciplinares em Estudos Americanos,* edited by Sonia Torres, 239–44. Rio de Janeiro: Editora 7 Letras, 2001.

Martes, Ana Cristina Braga. *Brasileiros nos Estados Unidos.* São Paulo: Editora Paz e Terra, 2000.

———. *New Immigrants, New Land: A Study of Brazilians in Massachusetts.* Gainesville: University Press of Florida, 2011.

Mascarenhas de Moraes, Marshal J. B. *The Brazilian Expeditionary Force.* Washington, DC: U.S. Government Printing Office, 1966.

Massey, Douglas S., Rafael Alarcón, Jorge Durand, and Humberto González. *Return to Aztlán: The Social Process of International Migration from Western Mexico.* Berkeley: University of California Press, 1987.

Massey, Douglas S., Joaquin Arango, Graeme Hugo, Ali Kouaouci, Adela Pellegrino, and J. Edward Taylor. "Theories of International Migration: A Review and Appraisal." *Population and Development Review* 19 (1993): 431–66.

Matta, Roberto da. *Carnival, Rogues and Heroes: An Interpretation of the Brazilian Dilemma*. Notre Dame, IN: University of Notre Dame Press, 1991.

McAfee Brown, Robert. *The Spirit of Protestantism*. New York: Oxford University Press, 1961.

McClatchy, J. D. *The Vintage Book of Contemporary World Poetry*. New York: Vintage Books, 1996.

Meyer, Mary Edgar. "Walt Whitman's Popularity among Latin-American Poets." *Americas* 9 (1952): 3–15.

Miller, Charlotte I. "The Function of Middle-Class Extended Family Networks in Brazilian Urban Society." In *Brazil: Anthropological Perspectives*, edited by Maxine L. Margolis and William E. Carter, 305–16. New York: Columbia University Press, 1979.

Montaner, Carlos Alberto. *Latin Americans and the West: The Historical and Cultural Roots of Latin America*. Miami: InterAmerican Institute for Democracy, 2009.

Montell, Gabriela. "A Preference for Foreigners?" *Chronicle of Higher Education*, May 11, 2007.

Moreno-Brid, Juan Carlos, and Pablo Ruiz-Nápoles. "Public Research Universities in Latin American and their Relation to Economic Development." Working Papers on Latin America, no. 07/08-1, David Rockefeller Center for Latin American Studies, Harvard University, Cambridge, MA, 2008.

Muñoz, Jorge Luján. *Historia General de Guatemala*. Guatemala: Asociación de Amigos del País, 2005.

Münz, Rainer. "East-West Migration after European Union Enlargement." *Austrian Information*, February 15, 2007.

Neilan, Terence. "World Briefing." *New York Times*, July 17, 1999.

Neruda, Pablo. *Memoirs*. New York: Farrar, Straus and Giroux, 2001.

O'Neill, Tip. *Man of the House: The Life and Political Memoirs of Speaker Tip O'Neill*. New York: Random House, 1987.

Obama, Barack H. "Why I'm Optimistic." *Smithsonian*, July/August 2010, 59.

Olson, James S., and Heather Olson Beal. *The Ethnic Dimension in American History*. Malden, MA: Wiley-Blackwell, 2010.

Open Doors 2009: Report on International Educational Exchange. New York: Institute of International Education, 2009.

Orenstein, Peggy. "I Tweet, Therefore I Am." *New York Times*, August 1, 2010, MM11.

Page, Joseph A. *The Revolution that Never Was: Northeast Brazil, 1955–1964*. New York: Grossman, 1972.

Payne, Leigh A. *Unsettling Accounts: Neither Truth nor Reconciliation in Confessions of State Violence*. Durham, NC: Duke University Press, 2008.

Peluso, Luciana, and Simone Goldberg. "Heróis da Sobrevivência." *Isto É,* December 7, 1995, 124–129.

Pereira, Anthony W. *The End of Peasantry: The Rural Labor Movement in Northeast Brazil, 1961–1988.* Pittsburgh: University of Pittsburgh Press, 1997.

Perreira, Krista M., Kathleen Harris, and Dohoon Lee. "Making It in America: High School Completion by Immigrant and Native Youth." *Demography* 43 (2006): 511–36.

Pierson, Paul E. *A Younger Church in Search of Maturity: Presbyterianism in Brazil from 1910 to 1959.* San Antonio: Trinity University Press, 1974.

Piore, Michael J. *Birds of Passage: Migrant Labor in Industrial Societies.* Cambridge: Cambridge University Press, 1979.

Portes, Alejandro, and Alejandro Rivas. "The Adaptation of Migrant Children." *Future Child* 21 (2011): 219–46.

Portes, Alejandro, and Leif Jensen. "The Enclave and Entrants: Patterns of Ethnic Enterprise in Miami Before and After Mariel." *American Sociological Review* 54 (1989): 929–49.

Portes, Alejandro, and Rubén G. Rumbaut. *Immigrant America: A Portrait.* Berkeley, CA: University of California Press, 1996.

———. *Legacies: The Story of the Immigrant Second Generation.* Berkeley: University of California Press, 2001.

Portes, Alejandro, and Julia Sennsenbrenner. "Embeddedness and Immigration: Notes on Social Determinants of Economic Action." *American Journal of Sociology* 98 (1993): 1320–50.

Poulson, Stephen C. *Social Movements in Twentieth-Century Iran: Culture, Ideology and Mobilizing Frameworks.* Lanham, MD: Lexington Books, 2005.

Preston, Julia. "Surge Brings New Immigration Backlog." *New York Times,* November 23, 2007.

Raab, Josef. "El Gran Viejo: Walt Whitman in Latin America." *CLCWeb* 3, no. 2 (2001).

Rabe, Stephen G. *The Most Dangerous Area in the World: John F. Kennedy Confronts Communist Revolution in Latin America.* Chapel Hill: University of North Carolina Press, 1999.

Ravenstein, E. G. "The Laws of Migration." *Journal of the Royal Statistical Society* 48, pt. 2 (1885): 167–235.

———. "The Laws of Migration." *Journal of the Royal Statistical Society* 52, no. 2 (1889): 241–305.

Reynolds, David S. *Walt Whitman's America: A Cultural Biography.* New York: Vintage Books, 1995.

Rocha, Simone. "Articulações e Confrontos: A Consolidação do Discurso de Esquerda no Movimento Estudantil Pernambucano (1964–1967)." *Saeculum: Revista de História* 13 (2005): 90–104.

Rodrigues, José Honório. *The Brazilians: Their Character and Aspirations.* Austin: University of Texas Press, 1967.

Rodriguez, Nestor P., and Jacqueline S. Hagan. *Investigating Census Coverage among the Undocumented: An Ethnographic Study of Latino Immigrant Tenants in Houston*. Washington, DC: Center for Survey Methods Research, Bureau of the Census, 1991.

Rother, Larry. "Brazilians Streaming into U.S. Through Mexican Border." *New York Times*, June 30, 2005.

Rubin, Emanuel. "Jeannette Meyers Thurber and the National Conservatory of Music." *American Music* 8 (1990): 294–325.

Sales, Teresa. "Second Generation Brazilian Immigrants in the United States." In *The Other Latinos: Central and South Americans in the United States*, edited by José Luis Falconi and José Antonio Mazzotti, 195–211. Cambridge, MA: David Rockefeller Center for Latin American Studies, Harvard University, 2007.

Schneider, Ronald M. *The Political System of Brazil: Emergence of a "Modernizing" Authoritarian Regime, 1964–1970*. New York: Columbia University Press, 1973.

Scheper-Hughes, Nancy. *Death without Weeping: The Violence of Everyday Life in Brazil*. Berkeley: University of California Press, 1993.

Schleef, Debra, and H. B. Cavalcanti. *Latinos in Dixie: Class and Assimilation in Richmond, Virginia*. Albany: SUNY Press, 2009.

Schwartz, Stuart B. *Sugar Plantations in the Formation of Brazilian Society: Bahia, 1550–1835*. Cambridge: Cambridge University Press, 1985.

Scudeler, Christina. "Immigrantes Valadarenses no Mercado de Trabalho dos EUA." In *Cenas do Brasil Migrante*, edited by Rosana Rocha Reis and Teresa Sales, 193–232. São Paulo: Boitempo, 1999.

Shane, Scott, and Charlie Savage. "In Ordinary Lives, U.S. Sees the Work of Russian Agents." *New York Times*, June 29, 2010, A1.

Shaw, Lisa. *The Social History of the Brazilian Samba*. London: Ashgate, 1999.

Shibutani, Tamotsu, and Kian M. Kwan. *Ethnic Stratification*. New York: MacMillan, 1965.

Shusterman, Carl. "Immigration Knowledge Essential to Recruiting IMGs." *New England Journal of Medicine Career Center*, July–August 2000.

Siqueira, Sueli. "Projeto de Retorno e Investimento dos Imigrantes Valadarenses nos EUA." Paper presented at the National Congress on Brazilian Immigration to the United States, David Rockefeller Center for Latin American Studies, Harvard University, Cambridge, MA, March 18–19, 2005.

Skidmore, Thomas E. *The Politics of Military Rule in Brazil, 1964–1985*. New York: Oxford University Press, 1988.

Soga, Toru. "System and Reality: The Camel Trust System of the Gabra." *African Study Monographs* 18 (1997): 157–74.

Somerset Maugham, W. *The Moon and Sixpence*. London: William Heinemann, 1919.

"Snapshot: Global Migration." *New York Times*, June 22, 2007.

Stark, Odek. *The Migration of Labor*. Cambridge: Basil Blackwell, 1991.

Stark, Odek, and David E. Bloom. "The New Economics of Labor Migration." *American Economic Review* 75, no. 2 (May 1985): 173–78.

Stepan, Alfred. *Authoritarian Brazil: Origins, Policies, and Future*. New Haven, CT: Yale University Press, 1973.

———. *The Military in Politics: Changing Patterns in Brazil*. Princeton, NJ: Princeton University Press, 1974.

Streeter, Stephen M. *Managing Counterrevolution: The United States and Guatemala, 1954–1961*. Athens: Ohio University Press, 2001.

Strickon, Arnold, and Sidney M. Greenfield, eds. *Structure and Process in Latin America: Patronage, Clientage and Power Systems*. Albuquerque: University of New Mexico Press, 1972.

Sun, Lena H. "From Curiosity to Eureka." *Washington Post*, September 3, 2011, A1, A6.

Tabuchi, Hiroko. "Japan Pays Foreign Workers to Go Home." *New York Times*, April 23, 2009, B1.

Tajfel, Henri. *Human Groups and Social Categories*. Cambridge: Cambridge University Press, 1981.

Tigay, Alan M. "The Deepest South: Five Thousand Miles below Mason-Dixon Line, a Brazilian Community Celebrates its Ties to Antebellum America." *American Heritage* 49 (1998): 84–95.

Van Horn, K. Roger, and Juracy Cunegatto Marques. "Interpersonal Relationships in Brazilian Adolescents." *International Journal of Behavioral Development* 24 (2000): 199–203.

Vechionne, Michele, and Gian Vittorio Caprara. "Personality Determinants of Political Participation: The Contribution of Traits and Self-Efficacy Beliefs." *Personality and Individual Differences* 46 (2009): 487–92.

Veltman, Calvin J. *Language Shift in the United States*. New York: Mouton, 1983.

Vianna Moog, Clodovir. *Bandeirantes and Pioneers*. New York: George Braziller, 1964.

Vilcek Jan, and Bruce N. Cronstein. "A Prize for the Foreign-Born." *FASEB Journal* 20 (2006): 1281–83.

Viotti da Costa, Emilia. "1870–1889." In *Brazil: Empire and Republic, 1822–1930*, edited by Leslie Bethell, 161–213. Cambridge: Cambridge University Press, 1987.

Weaver, Blanche H. C. "Confederate Immigrants and Evangelical Churches in Brazil." *Journal of Southern History* 18 (1952): 446–68.

Wennersten, John R. *Leaving America: The New Expatriate Generation*. Westport, CT: Greenwood Publishing, 2008.

Weschler, Lawrence. *A Miracle, A Universe: Settling Accounts with Torturers*. Chicago: University of Chicago Press, 1990.

Whitman, Walt. *Leaves of Grass: Comprising all the Poems Written by Walt Whitman Following the Arrangement of the Edition of 1891–1892*. Philadelphia: David McKay, 1891–1892.

Williams, Raymond L. *The Writings of Carlos Fuentes*. Austin: University of Texas Press, 1996.

Wilson, Charles R. *Baptized in Blood: The Religion of the Lost Cause, 1865–1920*. Athens: University of Georgia Press, 1980.

Wilson, Sloan. *The Man in the Gray Flannel Suit*. New York: Pocket Books. 1955.

Wolfe, Alan. *One Nation After All: What Americans Really Think About God, Country, Family, Racism, Welfare, Immigration, Homosexuality, Work, The Right, The Left and Each Other*. New York: Penguin Books, 1998.

Wright Mills, C. *White Collar: The American Middle Class*. New York: Oxford University Press, 1959.

Wulf, William A. "The Importance of Foreign-born Scientists and Engineers to the Security of The United States." Testimony before the Subcommittee on Immigration, Border Security, and Claims of the Committee on the Judiciary, U.S. House of Representatives, the 109th U.S. Congress, September 15, 2005. http://www7.nationalacademies.org/ocga/testimony/Importance_of_Foreign_Scientists_and_Engineers_to_US.asp.

Yemma, John. "The Man Who Would Be Stateless." *Christian Science Monitor*, July 5, 2010, 47.

Zhou, Min, and John Logan. "Return on Human Capital in Ethnic Enclaves: New York City's Chinatown." *American Sociological Review* 54 (1989): 809–20.

Index

Note: Page numbers in italics indicate illustrations.

acculturation, 90–91, 104, 113
activism, 4, 43, 45, 77
Adams, Abigail, 112
Adams, John, 144–45
Aguilera, Jaime Roldós, 38, 160n21
alien/alienated, 4, 14–15, 19–20, 51–53, 55, 66, 68–71, 141–43
allegiance, 16, 69–73, 74, 109
Alliance for Progress, 40; U.S. development aid, 40
Alves, Castro, 26
Amado, Jorge, 12, 26, 160n13
American/British rock and roll, 22, 47n49, 151–52; The Beatles, 22; 48; The Byrds, 48; Carly Simon, 48; Carole King, 48; Cat Stevens, 48; Credence Clearwater Revival, 48; Crosby, Stills, and Nash, 48; James Taylor, 48; Janis Ian, 48; The Mamas and the Papas, 48; The Turtles, 48
American citizenship, 61, 63, 72–74, 91, 107
American folk music, 48–49; Bob Dylan, 48; Joan Baez, 48; Pete Seeger, 48; Peter, Paul, and Mary, 48; Phil Ochs, 48; Ronnie Gilbert, 48; Simon and Garfunkel, 48; The Weavers, 48; Woodie Guthrie, 48
American holidays, 18, 72, 85, 115, 164n3; Christmas, 20, 81, 86, 100; Thanksgiving, 18, 81, 100

American Revolution, 94, 170n1
Ampuero, Roberto, 38
"Apesar de Você," 46, 163n39
Apuleyo Mendoza, Plinio, 38
Árbenz Guzmán, Jacobo, 34, 160n16
Archdiocese of Recife and Olinda, 43
Arendt, Hannah, 61
Argentina, 7, 16, 29, 38, 46, 135, 158n3
Arias Sanchéz, Óscar, 38, 160n20
Arms Fisher, Williams, 121–22
assimilation, xi, 24, 92, 145, 169n23; segmented assimilation, 92, 169n22

baby boomers, 47–48, 79, 99, 150–51
Bachelet, Michelle, 34–36, 160n17
Bandeira, Manuel, 26
Barbosa, Ruy, 26
Barroso, Paurillo, 26
Belaúnde Terry, Fernando, 34, 160n16
Berger, Peter, 61
Berry, Wendell, 12
bicultural, xi, 78, 105, 121, 133
bilingual, xii, 86–87
birthplace, 51–52, 72, 134, 140
Bolaños, Roberto, 38
Bolivia, 31, 38, 127, 128, 130
brain drain, 65
Brazil, xii, 3, 14, 17–18, 21, 29, 39, 41, 43, 52, 56–57, 58–59, 64–66, 73, 84, 86, 91–94, 97, 104, 109, 122, 129–30, 132–33, 135,

193